RELUCTANT JAPS GO

ABOARD SHIP HERE

More Than 500 to Sail for Orient Early Tomorrow

By RAY GARDNER

OCT -1 1946

More than 500 Japanese men, women and childr___
boarded the American transport Marine Falcon here th___
morning to begin th___
them expressed ___
of the adults, b___

NOTICE
MARRIED MEN ARE
WANTED TO WORK
AT 15 MILE CAMP.
REGISTER AT
JAPANESE OFFICE

SPECIAL
NEW YEARS SERVICE
Rev R Tatibana will Officiate
ALL WELCOME

___ THE
___MMISSION

___er Japanese

___se origin re-
___ should ter-
___han the 30th
___ases or rental
___ may be work-
___ must also be
___either to Hast-
___rk camps or to
___nterior Housing
___-four hours no-
___ents whatsoever
___ads may be made
___rs.

晩市内の日本人に告ぐ

廿四時間の豫告で移動出來る用意せよ

晩香坡市内に居住する日本人にして總てのリー
ス父は家屋レントの取極めをしてゐる者は四月
三十日までに之れを解除すべきである。而して
ヘステングス・パーク若しくは勞働キャンプ乃
至は奧地住居計畫地へ二十四時間の豫告のもと
に移動出來る用意をして置くべきである。右の
移動命令はビジネス上で如何なる理由があらう
こも猶豫はしないのである。

ビーシー・セキュリテー・コミション

YEARS
OF SORROW,
YEARS
OF SHAME

Also by Barry Broadfoot

TEN LOST YEARS: 1929-1939
SIX WAR YEARS: 1939-1945
THE PIONEER YEARS: 1895-1914

YEARS OF SORROW, YEARS OF SHAME

The Story of the Japanese Canadians in World War II

BARRY BROADFOOT

1977

Doubleday Canada Limited
Toronto Ontario

Doubleday & Company, Inc.
Garden City New York

ISBN No. 0-385-12550-X
Library of Congress Catalog Card No. 77-76226

Copyright © 1977 by Barry Broadfoot.
All rights reserved.

Design by Robert Garbutt Productions

Printed and bound in Canada by
The Bryant Press Limited

First Edition

 *Preface*

At 7:58 A.M., Hawaii time, on December 7, 1941—a quiet, sunlit Sunday—there flashed from headquarters of the great American naval base of Pearl Harbor this message to Washington:
AIR RAID PEARL HARBOR—THIS IS NO DRILL.
It was true. Dive bombers and fighters from six aircraft carriers commanded by Admiral Yamamoto of the Japanese Navy struck without warning and devastated the huge U.S. Pacific battleship fleet.

From that moment forward and, yes, until even today, that act of war had one extraordinary and terrible effect upon more than 22,000 persons of Japanese ancestry then living in British Columbia, Canada. All that they had achieved in the sixty-four years since the first Japanese had arrived in Canada—all was blasted away and nothing again would be as it had been before. They became "enemy aliens."

Confusion and panic mounted as rumours spread. The Japanese had always been a prime target for racist sentiment; now they were viewed as a threat, a potential fifth column. Secret government plans came out of dusty drawers, orders-in-council were passed, the 1914 War Measures Act was used against them and the entire Japanese population on the West Coast was uprooted in the name of "national security."

Did I say these people were enemy aliens? Well, that's not

true. Oh, there were some Japanese nationals, many of whom had been in Canada as long as fifty years; but most were Canadians, born in Canada of Japanese parents, or Japanese who were naturalized citizens. Yet between Pearl Harbor Day and V-J Day in 1945, they literally became Canada's Forgotten People.

Without being melodramatic about it, this book is the story, told by the people themselves, of how they lived and acted and reacted, how they survived. It is the story of how they endured the shock of leaving their homes, their small farms, their fishboats behind and, with only the possessions they could carry, of being herded into Hastings Park to await relocation in the Interior. It is the story of how they stoically accepted their various fates—in road camps, idling away the war building a few miles of highway; in the beet fields of Alberta and Manitoba, performing backbreaking jobs to save the sugar industry; in ghost towns and hastily built camps in the mountains of B.C., in the country's only Japanese POW camp, at Angler, in northern Ontario; in whatever jobs they could find "East of the Rockies." It is also the story of how most of them re-established themselves after the war, starting from scratch in the face of lingering racial bias, economic hardship, and a government reluctant to recognize them as first-class citizens for many years.

Like my other three books, Ten Lost Years, Six War Years, *and* The Pioneer Years, *this one,* Years of Sorrow, Years of Shame, *is an oral history. In each case I have travelled around Canada with a tape recorder and a notebook collecting stories from persons who participated in some great event in Canadian history. I am putting the people back into history, and as far as I am concerned, the expulsion of the Japanese Canadians from B.C. is an event that deserves this treatment. Their story should be told—not only for historical reasons but also for the lessons it teaches us about the kind of people we Canadians were, and perhaps still are.*

This is the first major book on the Japanese Canadians in peace and war using this oral-history method, but I would be remiss if I did not recommend another work to you. Ken Adachi's book, The Enemy That Never Was, *is a scholarly, marvellously researched, sincere, and dedicated piece of work, sixteen years in the research and writing, which covers the first 100 years of the Japanese in Canada.*

In this book you will hear the voices of many people: the Issei, or first generation; the Nisei, their sons and daughters; and the Sansei, the third generation—the survivors, so to speak. I interviewed them—the old and the young, the embittered and the humble, the rebels and the reconciled, the wealthy, the middle class, and the poor—from Ottawa to Toronto and Chatham in the East across the prairies to many parts of B.C. And of all the people I interviewed, only one man, in Coaldale, Alberta, refused to talk to me and I believe now that he was more suspicious of my tape recorder than reluctant to talk about the events.

I did not want the book to be blatantly pro-Japanese but during the one year of researching and writing, I knew that it would be pro-Japanese. So, for balance, if I can call it that, there are throughout the book interviews with Caucasians— people who knew the Japanese, observed them, administered them, taught them, and often, thank God, helped them. They were good people, most of them. Their one failing? I believe some treated the Japanese as a logistical, housing, feeding, and medical problem, considering them to be no more than a long list of registered identity cards, with a number replacing a name. Perhaps that was the only way it could be done.

I met some wonderful people during my travels, people I admire, respect, and hope one day to meet again. I recorded about 300,000 words, and I only regret that I cannot include more of the stories I was told. But I think that in the 130,000 words in this book you will find a true picture of the Japanese Canadians in their time of travail. We have too long ignored this part of our history. Why? Because, as former Prime Minister Lester Pearson said: "We have no reason to be proud of this episode." And we are a proud people.

The Japanese Canadians have mostly pushed aside the heartbreaking experiences they endured. But they have not forgotten. Nor should we.

Barry Broadfoot
May 31, 1977
Vancouver, B.C.

Contents

YEARS
OF SORROW,
YEARS
OF SHAME

1 B.C.—the Golden Door?

How would you like to live in a society where a newspaper, the Victoria Times, would print this editorial? " . . . a vast, alien colony; exclusive, unassimilative, bound together in a secret and defensive organization with fewer wants and a lower standard of living than their neighbours, maintaining intact their peculiar customs and characteristics, morals and ideals of home and family life, with neither the wish nor the capacity to amalgamate with, or even conform to the civilization upon which they intruded, and gradually, by the pressure of numbers, undermining the very foundations of the white man's well being."

That was a long time ago, 1907, when there were probably no more than 6,000 Japanese in Canada's population of about six million. The problem was that more than 95 percent of them were in B.C. Unfortunately, that view, held by a goodly number of British Columbians, did not change with the passage of time. The economic doldrums of the 1930s served to aggravate the old hostilities and resentment because few Japanese were on relief. These quiet, hard-working people continued to work their fishboats, tend their market gardens, run their small businesses while all around them people were saying, "The Japs are taking precious jobs away from the white man and, damn it all, this is a white man's country."

Coupled with these attitudes, naturally, was the rise of Imperial Japan as a world power, her defeat of China in 1896, her overwhelming victory over Russia in 1904-05, and in the

1

1930s her war against Manchuria and then China and her menacing gestures against the United States and Britain. It all added up.

Because they were different in appearance, because they kept to themselves and worked hard to succeed, the 22,000 Japanese in B.C. were fair game for the rabble rousers seeking an inoffensive target, politicians seeking votes, and newspapers seeking street sales. So, harassment and racist feelings continued to mount as December 7, 1941, approached.

"I Didn't Enjoy That Meal"

One thing I'll remember, I'll never forget how it was to be what I was in those days, a Japanese Canadian. I was able to get a job thinning apples in the Okanagan. In '39. It was at Okanagan Centre. I didn't make any money. Poor Mom. She was supporting the two of us and when I showed her how much I had made, well, it wasn't much. But. . .

But when I went up there I put on my suit. Made by my mom. She'd learned how to make suits from my dad, who had been a master tailor. I got on the boat at Okanagan Landing and I had to make a decision. No steward there to help. He was dressed in white, it was lunchtime, and he was serving already. And there was one long table and it had white linen and the second one didn't. They were dining and the captain was at the head of the first table and some passengers. It was lunchtime and I was hungry and here I am, in my good clothes, eighteen years old, and I am hungry and I have to make a decision. Not worldly enough to assert myself but I know I've got to eat somewhere.

At the long table where the passengers were, there were still about ten empty spaces at the end, so I got enough courage to go into the dining room and I thought it was stupid to sit at the empty table. So I went and sat at the end of the main table.

Everything went quiet. I mean they were talking, the captain was talking, and then there was a hush. And then the steward came up to me and said, "Sir, would you sit over here?" and he was pointing toward the one table that had not been set with linen. He wasn't rude but he made it plain I wasn't to sit at the big table.

So there I was, marooned at this big plain table, all by myself, and this goddamned—don't bother to report that, please—but this stupid captain, this adult—he becomes a captain he's got to have a certain amount of intelligence, common sense—he had a rule on his ship that Japanese could not eat with white passengers. I didn't enjoy that meal but I had to stick it out. I couldn't get up and leave before I'd finished.

I'll never forget. That's probably the cruelest experience in my young days. I could stand being called "Joe" or "Charlie" or anything direct like that where I can see viciousness, but this subtle thing like that where there was not need for it, it is a very depressing thing. That was the state of society. As I say, that was the state of our democracy at that time.

Racism in Canada

Canada has always been a racist country. And B.C. was probably the worst part of the problem before the war. Yes, I'd say that was a quite true statement.

Everything has to have a beginning and racism in Canada started with the first explorers, the French and the English, the Hudson's Bay Company. You see, these people came into Canada and they realized that about all the country had to offer was furs and that the Indians were the most efficient fur-gatherers, so to speak. The best harvesters. And as labour is a major part of the cost of any product, the natural thing for these whites to do was exploit the natives, to get them to work for as little as possible, to gyp them whenever possible, to downgrade them as much as possible. So the Indian unused to European ways was usually at the mercy of the whites and over the generations developed an inferiority complex. Not just an inferiority complex but a massive one, one pervading everything he did, his every action, his thoughts, and his attitudes toward life. And if you look at the native today, apart from a handful of leaders and activists—and there may not be more than 500 in all Canada—the situation is probably little different than it was fifty or seventy-five years ago. The Indian, the native, is still at the mercy of the white man.

But it isn't confined to the native Canadians. You'll find it if you talk to old Jews, to old Polish men and women, to old Ukrainians, to old Italians, Slavs, what have you. They all were exploited by the ruling class. Jews couldn't become doctors or there was a quota at the medical schools. Jews usually started out as a peddler and worked up to a horse and wagon and then to a store. Or got into a dental school or law school. Many worked a killing hourly day for little money in the sweatshops of Montreal. But again, so did so many French Canadians and Italians. On the prairies the Ukrainian or Pole worked up from a quarter-section homestead to what they have today, many quarter sections. And they became prominent in the professions, the arts, and sciences, and as an example, look at the city of Edmonton. And at every turn of the road until probably before the Second World War, there was racism. That curl of the lip when you saw an old babushka on the street. That thought: "Oh, but he's just a Hunkie. He doesn't matter."

And so it was with the Oriental. It was natural they would come to the West Coast. Pacific Rim. Trading. You know all this they talk about now. Well, it had some validity more than 100 years ago, but the Chinese first came to the West Coast for another reason. Work, of course, and then gold. San Francisco. Their gold rush. The Forty-niners. And then Canada or the Colony of British Columbia had its gold rush, or the first of many, on the Fraser River in 1858, and thousands of Americans rushed up to Victoria and then on up the river. And with them came Chinese who had proved that they could be just as good placer miners as the whites. But they stood out. Small, yellow-skinned, black hair, black eyes, slanted, kind of wore their clothes funny, talked in a sing-song hi-kai-chung-kai language, different culture, different religion. They weren't white. So they could be exploited. When the white man had mined the bars of the Fraser River, then the Chinese followed and cleaned up, as they called it, which meant taking up the gold that the whites had left behind. It was exploitation. A pretty good example of it. And of course, the Chinese had to take it. If they put up a protest they might find some ruffian cutting off their pigtail, which is in itself a racist word, or wind up dead. This continued through the Cariboo gold rush and all others, and when they brought labourers over from the Canton district by the thousands to build the C.P. R., God, how those men worked. Under miserable living conditions and for very low wages and they say they died like flies. And the years went by, and they endured and now they are one of Canada's most cohesive and prosperous ethnic groups. I was told by a person who knows these things that next to the Jews and then the Japanese, they are the most prosperous of ethnic groups. It's easy to believe. So much for the Chinese. They're doing okay now, but they still run into racism.

Now, the Japanese. The first Japanese to come to what we would call the Western World in any great numbers landed in Hawaii in 1885—about 1,000 of them to work in the fields. That was the start of the huge Japanese population in Hawaii. But the first known Japanese to arrive in Canada was a fellow named Manzo Nagano, a nineteen-year-old who jumped his ship in New Westminster in May of 1877. He apparently became fairly prosperous working the coast, fishing and other things, a store, but he was the first. Others drifted in, whether they had heard great things about this Canada of ours or whether they just drifted over from Hawaii or from some prefecture in Japan looking for opportunity, for the Japanese are a very industrious and opportunistic people. I think anybody who has known any of them will agree to this, and these factors helped to contribute to their eventual downfall, or putting it another way, their long years in a state of exile.

They are good fishermen. In fact, excellent fishermen and

when Nagano came back to B.C. in 1884 after a visit to Japan he found a group of them fishing out of New Westminster. Figures aren't all that important but as the years passed, more and more Japanese came to B.C. and by 1900 it was estimated that there were about 4,700 Japanese in Canada, and most were living on the West Coast and a great many were in fishing. In fact, it could be said that they dominated the fishing business. About 1,000 came in in 1900 and by this time there were mutterings among the white population. Racism. There was the old business again. The high profile. Little men. Short. Poor where they had lived before but now they were making good money and sending a lot of that money back to Japan. Few spoke much English and most spoke none other than a few words. Their own language, their own religion. Here was another target for the whites, the British, because despite its leanings toward Americanism, B.C. was a very British province. Those jokes about a Little Bit of Olde England in Victoria aren't just jokes. They were true about Vancouver too.

So here was another group to exploit. Except for one thing. This bunch, these Japanese weren't so easy. They weren't as passive as the Chinese. They weren't warlike although Japan has a long history as a war-making nation, but they stood up for what they felt were their rights. And that, of course, rubbed the whites the wrong way. And to top matters off, in 1907 there was a veritable flood of Japanese immigrants, and then came the Oriental Riots in Vancouver. Thousands of whites joined, led on by rabble rousers including one minister, and they sacked Chinatown. But when they got to Japtown, Powell Street, they ran into stiff resistance, and a combination of tough Japanese cookies and the Vancouver police broke up the mob.

Well, the story goes on but you get the picture. The Japanese were not being cowed by any mob. But they were still in a position to be exploited as they were a minority—a few thousand against tens of thousands. And so it went, the Japanese becoming successful, in fishing, in some phases of logging and lumbering, in small shops and larger stores, in commercial enterprises, export and import firms. The heat was off them during the First World War because Japan as an emerging world power was on the side of the Allies. That meant Britain. In fact, Japanese warships patrolled waters off Vancouver Island looking for two German cruisers that were reported in the area.

But after the war the exploitive angle came to the fore again. The Japanese dominated the fishing—not in numbers but in fish caught because they were such successful fishermen, a combination of determination and skill rather than skill alone. And so in the '20s the federal government, after a lot of pressure from many groups in B.C., began to cut back on Japanese licences. There was a saying then: "Not a Jap on the coast by '36." That seemed to be the government's intention.

So they went up the Fraser Valley and into the Okanagan and hacked out farms and grew berries and fruits and vegetables, and by the middle '30s the rabble rousers and the vote-seeking politicians were saying that the Japanese were forcing every-body else out of the industry. It probably is true that they dominated the industry in the Fraser Valley, but it is also true that very few white men would do the work they did, work the hours, the whole family working on that little ten-acre patch.

And they made regulations against them in the logging industry in that no Japanese could work on Crown land, which meant most of the land, and they barred them from civic and municipal, provincial and federal duties such as jury work and council work because they barred them from the provincial vote, along with the Chinese, the East Indians, and the native Indians. The others didn't seem to care much, but the Japanese did because the franchise had been a birthright in Japan and many of them were naturalized Canadians or born in Canada, about 5,000 of them, and they felt they were once again being pushed into the role of second- or maybe even third-class citizens.

And all the while, racism. It was always there. The politicians and the hate mongers used the words "assimiliation" and "peaceful penetration." Always directed against the Japanese. Not the Chinese. Not the Sikhs. The Japanese. Or Japs or Nippons or Nips if you will, as the newspapers used to call them.

Assimilation meant they could be brought in to the Canadian culture. To listen to some it was a process that was supposed to take place overnight, although the whites didn't really want it. Would you want your daughter to marry a Jap? That kind of thing.

But show me one foreign people, Poles, Italians, Greeks, Russians, who ever assimilated in the first generation. It just isn't done. Americans, English, Scots, Germans, Scandinavians, yes. These peoples, I think, maybe can do it. But there are others that can't. Why, there are old Greek and Italian and Chinese women who have been in this country fifty years walking the streets of Vancouver today and they have to take a granddaughter along with them when they go into a store, Woodward's or Eaton's, because they still don't speak English. Are they assimilated? No. And never will be. And it is a fair bet that their children are only partly assimilated. Say 75 percent assimilated. For some peoples, assimilation doesn't come until the third generation. But here were people on the coast, not all, not many, but a pretty vocal bunch, who yelled "assimilation" about the Japanese. And the Japanese continued to go their own way because they knew it could not come about so soon. It would take time. Their own common sense tells them that. Mine would. Yours would. Anybody would if they thought it out.

And peaceful penetration. There's a mouthful. Something dreamed up by William Randolph Hearst, the publisher, down in California along with the Yellow Peril, way back when. Every able-bodied Japanese male was supposed to be a Japanese agent in disguise. The little old Japanese who had a dry-cleaning shop at Broadway and Cambie was supposed to emerge as a Japanese Navy admiral when war began. That sort of claptrap. It was just too much for anybody to swallow. But swallow it, they did.

They were told the Japanese dominated the fishing industry, from the guy in the gillnet off the Fraser to the skipper at the helm of the tug pulling down a barge of canned salmon from a Skeena cannery. It wasn't true, in that sense, but they believed it. They were told the Japanese would dominate the woods industry soon when there probably weren't more than 1,500 in it, all phases, from high rigging to splitting shakes. Same with agriculture. And they got ridiculous when they started on the rooming houses in Vancouver. The rooming-house industry? Hah! Or dry-cleaning. Or little corner groceries. And so it went. They just sat back in their chairs and read the crap in the evening newspapers, some other guy spouting off and being reported, and that was it. So be it.

They didn't question it because they wanted to believe it, because they were, at hearts, in their hearts, racists. They wouldn't be able to put a definition to the word if you asked them, but there it was. They just didn't like Japs. Small. Cunning. Tricky. Money-mad. Greedy. Always trying to do the white man in. Got to watch him. Else he'll get you. Can't be trusted. Still loyal to the emperor. Still loves Japan. Sends his kids to Japanese-language school. Is a Buddhist. The whole bit, from A to Z.

And naturally it all went back to the fur traders and the Indians. Here was a different race, different people, different culture, different language, and they didn't speak English and they lived in funny little houses and they ate funny food and so they were funny people, ignorant, and they should be exploited. Didn't history tell them that lesson? Wasn't that the message that came through in their history books, lessons they learned at school and saw at work in the city and country every day? And so these people should be exploited and what the hell right did they have to fight back, owning fishboats, owning land, businesses, shops? They were different, therefore inferior, and they should be exploited. Hell, wasn't this Canada, a white country?

And so it went on, all through the '30s, getting a little worse every year. And with Japan causing so much trouble in the Pacific, gobbling up Manchuria and China with modern armies and maintaining a great navy and standing up to the United States and Britian, is it any wonder that what happened to the Japanese in B.C. was bound to happen? No. It was bound to happen. And it did. As firmly and neatly as putting the lid back on a can.

The Franchise Was the Main Thing

I was born about 1901. Cloverdale. My mother used to tell me there were only two Japanese women in B.C. at that time, so I am one of the oldest Japanese.

In about 1930 and we were about thirty-years-old then—the next group of second-generation Japanese coming along would be about twenty-five—the community was run by the Canadian Japanese Association, the older generation, and for a little while some of us born in this country joined with them. But still we weren't important parts of the association until about 1931, when there was a movement to have Canadian-born Japanese organized. And so we had a rally in the language school there and oh, there was a good number there and they pick out about twenty of us to form an executive, and myself, I was one, and a schoolteacher and Fred Saiga, who was younger than me. We formed an executive and I was elected president but we didn't know what to do, you know. Not used to the work. So we just invited different persons to come over and talk to us, once a month. Professor Soward came once, I remember. People who could talk to us and tell us about Canada and what it was all about and what was happening to us.

We called ourselves the Japanese Canadian Citizens' Association and for three or four years we just wandered around, doing this and that, having speakers, finding out things for ourselves. They called it Dr. Saita's Organization after myself. So we felt we had to change the name again and so they called it the Japanese Canadian Citizens' League. I retired and let the younger ones take my place.

Our main aim was the fight—to get the franchise. To get the vote. We wanted that. If we wanted to bear ourselves as Canadian citizens that was our main object. We knew we could never be Canadian citizens, really, until we got that franchise and we tried and tried but there always were men, politicians, groups of businessmen, and others who said no, the Japanese, the Canadian Japanese are not ready for the vote. But we kept fighting, going to Ottawa, doing everything we could—the Nisei, you understand—to get the vote.

Then in 1942, sorry, 1941, the war comes along and we have to disband it and go into the Interior, but after a while we form it again and keep fighting for the vote, the franchise.

Then we won. Finally in 1949 we get the vote.

Then the JCCA went on to fight for other things, also to make better relations between the Japanese and others in this country.

But first, when we, the second-born Japanese form this organization it was to get franchise for the Japanese. That is the main thing.

Words from Uncle Seichi

When I was a boy in the '30s I used to deliver things from my dad's small farm near Steveston to people in the district. I had a big iron rack on my bike and I could carry quite a bit of stuff and also more on the back carrier. Then I'd go down to the cannery wharf where my uncle Seichi was mending nets, his own and for other guys, and I'd talk to him about the early days. He was quite an old man then and didn't do any fishing. I think he was too old but I think he didn't have a licence either. He could only speak a little English—it helped if you could speak English but he said he hadn't much chance to learn.

He was or had been a farm boy in the prefecture of Hiroshima in Japan and, like it was then, peasants or farmers had come over to Hawaii to work in the fields, the sugar cane, and then they'd heard about British Columbia and all the money you could make, and it was in letters they'd send back to Japan that they told the people these things. Anyway, my uncle had gone to Hawaii first but he decided to come to British Columbia. He was about eighteen. He had about 40 yen with him when he got off

the boat at Vancouver. This was 1901. Forty yen wasn't bad in
those days because he said 2 yen was a dollar. He'd borrowed
from his father who owned some land. Maybe his father sold a
piece of land to get him the money. So a bit of money here, a bit
of money there and some money for fare to Hawaii and then to
Vancouver but not much because it was cheap. They slept on the
floor of the deck, below, and were fed awful. He said the ship, a
big one from Hawaii, was sure a stinking place.

He knew what he wanted to do. He didn't want to go farming
and I don't think there was too much farming around anyway.
Not his kind of farming. There was a lot of Japanese in fishing
and he wanted to go fishing.

You shouldn't get the idea that my uncle was coming to this
country to be a settler and be a good Canadian. That came later.
What he was doing like most everybody else from Japan in those
days was to come to Canada and make money. I think he said
they called British Columbia "The Golden Door" or "The Land
of Gold." Something like that. What they wanted to do was make
a lot of money, three or four years of making good money, and
then go back to Japan as rich men. You see, Japan was poor at
the time. I mean the peasant farmers were poor. There was
really nobody lower in Japan than a peasant, but if you could go
through that Golden Door and make money you could go back
to Japan with a lot of money and buy land. Rent it to other
peasants and collect the rent money and pay the land taxes and
everything else would be yours and you would be okay.

My uncle and his friends could read and write in Japanese but
they knew nothing in English. Maybe just a few words. There
was a lot of sign language used. So there was the boss system.
The boss was a Japanese who spoke English and he'd meet the
boat from Japan, you see. Go aboard and talk to the new guys
and say, "You want to work? Eh? You want to make good
money?" Well, that was why they had come, so they'd say yes
and he'd take them to the company he worked for, but more
often the company he'd contracted with, and he'd say, "Heh,
look, I got twelve more fellows to work for you. Sign 'em up,

eh?" And they would. The guys from Japan would get a dollar a day and their food and a place to sleep.

The boss could charge them for posting a letter or going to a store, interpreting for them. He could charge them for taking them to sign up with the Japanese consul, because every Japanese had to do that. And when something was wrong with the guys, he could take them to the hospital and get them medicine and he'd charge another 10 or 15 cents for that. He could tell them what to do and what not to do and the companies liked this kind of thing very much. Eh? They weren't talking with twenty-five or thirty workers who didn't understand English but only one, the boss, and if the superindendent felt the gang wasn't working hard enough or good enough he'd tell the Japanese boss, "Hop to it," and he'd pass the word on to his gang and they'd hop to it. That's the way it worked.

My uncle and I would sit on the wharf and he'd tell me these things and I'd ask questions. I remember asking him once if this wasn't one reason why the whites hated us and he patted me on the head and said I was right. You see, if the white man was getting $1.50 and the Japanese would take a dollar, then the company could hire the Japanese. It didn't matter if he didn't speak English. He could do the work. If it was fishing, well, there was another Japanese in the boat mostly and he would tell him. If they went to work in the mills along the Fraser, it was the same. Here is a shovel. There is a pile of sawdust. Shovel it from there into this door. Here is a stack of lumber. Load it on that car. It only takes one person ten minutes to show another person how to load lumber. Dirty jobs, but they got better jobs and still undercut the whites. The Chinese also undercut the whites if they were doing the same job, which they weren't often. My uncle said the Japanese looked down on the Chinese. Some of them called the Chinese *eta*, which was the beggar class that used to be in Japan. The Sikhs never undercut the whites. That's why the white people in those days were never so mad at them as they were against the Japanese.

These people were young. Maybe less than twenty-five. Some

stayed the way they were, just going here, going there, making their dollar a day and spending it drinking and gambling. A lot became drinkers and gamblers. Gambling is big anyway.

But others wanted to get along in the world. If they could become naturalized Canadians that meant they could get a fishing licence, and with a fishing licence they could make more money because they didn't get paid by the day but by the fish. There were a lot of fish in the river in those days. There were a lot of boats too, though. That caused trouble, so many Japanese boats. Japanese were supposed to be in Canada I think it was four years before they could get a licence by being naturalized, but if a company wanted some more fishermen they could arrange it. Even if you were only in British Columbia a few months, my uncle said, you could get a licence. The boss took you to the naturalization place and swore you'd been in for four years and you swore and signed your name—even if you didn't understand English you could become naturalized. I guess there was nothing wrong with it. These guys weren't planning to stay that long anyway. Just make a lot of money fishing and then go back to being rich in Japan.

My uncle said that at one time he knew of only two Japanese women in British Columbia. One, he said, was in Steveston and one up the Fraser Valley. But in 1907, I think it was, they decided to let Japanese women and wives into British Columbia. I think this was a special treaty. So they came. And then the Japanese had women, and kids and more and more thought, "Well, why go back to Japan when I can send my kids to free school here?" So they did that. And then they'd have two or three kids and the kids were doing swell in school and the years went by. Things weren't easy. The Japanese were sure kicked around. No vote. In the rest of Canada, sure, but not here. They couldn't work in the woods on Crown grants. But you've heard all this.

But a lot was our people's fault too. Before the women came in, Steveston was a man's town. That's what it was called in the Japanese language. Powell Street district was called Little

Tokyo. Along the river there, if one Japanese family moves in, along comes another. Then another, then more and you've got fifteen families living there and what is it? Another ghetto. This went on. Steveston was a kind of ghetto with about 2,000 Japanese. Powell Street, Cordova, Alexander, Main Street, Jackson Avenue, solid Japanese. Why, there must have been 8,000 or 10,000 Japanese people there. Hotels. Baths. Stores. Cafés. Toy shops for the kids, schools, newspapers, homes, everything. Another ghetto. The Japanese should have spread out more. Everybody says that.

But then, it was a different matter. How could they work against the boss system? The boss takes you off the ship, takes you to a flophouse to live in before you go to some mine or camp, takes you to the Japanese consul, and you never talk to a white man. Sure, there's a white man standing on that log boom and he's the foreman and he can tell you what to do by waving his arms around or making signs with his stick but you never get a chance to talk to him or go to a night school and learn. You're in the bush, on the track gang. You're on a boat working as long as those fish are coming, longer than morning to night. They never had much of a chance. There are old men today who came to British Columbia in 1910 who can go in a beer parlour and drink beer or order tobacco or a meal of noodles and fish, but they still can't speak English. Never will. They can even work for a white guy, like one old guy I knew, he worked as a gardener for this white fellow for forty years and he couldn't speak English. He was probably the best gardener I ever saw. He didn't go back to Japan after all the war business was over to see who was left. No, he stayed right here in Canada and I asked him why and he said because he was a Canadian. How do you like that?

Other things they didn't do. Unions. Once they joined the big white union with the Yugoslavs and the Indians and the Swedes and everybody, things got better, but when they had their own fishing labour associations they always were fighting with the union. Maybe not fighting in that way, but when the white fishermen were fighting the cannery for higher prices, the Japanese sometimes were for the cannery, and sometimes not. I don't know why.

But they were good people. Good workers and they would work long and hard and do a good job and it didn't matter what kind of a job it was. They were, and still are, good to their families, their kids, and they have the same problems with their kids that whites do now. Before, when a Japanese father said jump the kids jumped. Now it is different. A lot of them don't understand it. It's just the new life and television and all that. Especially the older people. The grandchildren. The grandparents don't understand their grandchildren. But that's another story.

"Stay Out, You Japs!"

I remember when we were kids there were some restaurants we couldn't get into. The White Lunch. You take your girl downtown to a show and go in to the White Lunch for pie and coffee before taking the tram back to Steveston and the first time I did this, the man at the soup pot he waved a big spoon at us and yelled, "Stay out of here, you Japs."

That was just one restaurant. There were others. Some would just say no politely and others would yell at us. This was in 1938, 1939, in around there.

And some of the theatres downtown. They made you sit in the heavens, up in the back gallery, or over to the sides. You could never sit in the middle where the other people sat.

When we were kids we felt that, well, that's the way it was and we took it that way. If the White Lunch and other restaurants say we can't get in there, then why bother? Go someplace else. Why embarrass ourselves over it? Go somewhere else.

We could go dancing, we could go out with other people, we could enjoy ourselves in lots of ways, just like every other Canadian kid living in Vancouver, and if a couple of guys who ran restaurants, a few who ran theatres didn't like us, well, why worry. We didn't care.

I guess we didn't think much about it. That's the way we were brought up. That's the way it was. You grow up with a thing it becomes reality, pretty fast.

Mother Was a Picture-Book Bride

When my mother came to Vancouver she was a picture bride. My father wanted a family, a male heir, a son, and the only way he could get it was with a Japanese woman. It was against the Japanese community's rules for a Japanese man to marry a white girl or a Chinese girl or an Indian girl. I think it happened only rarely—and then that man was run out of the community. He couldn't go to weddings and funerals and festivals and the older men wouldn't lend money to him and nobody would help him. What I'm saying is when a Japanese married someone else he had to join that someone else's community. That made it hard. Of course this was fifty or sixty years ago, I'd say.

There were a lot of girls in Japan though. So the way I understand it, my father sent a picture of himself, all dressed up, to his relatives in his prefecture in Japan, and said he wanted a young woman. My father would be about thirty-five years old at the time and he worked on the Skeena and Fraser in fishing times for the cannery and the rest of the year he lived in Surrey and he was digging a farm.

He wanted a wife but he also wanted a son. Several sons. He wanted people to help him on the farm—that would be his wife and the sons, and any daughters that came along, although not many wanted a daughter. That was me, heh! So he sent his picture and said that he had a boat, ten acres, and some was cleared for berries. The relatives—I think it was his mother—looked around the village and found a girl. The way it worked, his mother looked the girl over and found about her. I don't think there was any money involved and the girl didn't have to be beautiful. My mother was nice but not beautiful. Of course she worked so hard who could ever be beautiful? I think the main thing was, could the girl work hard and could she have sons?

So it was arranged. The girl looked at the man's picture and I'm not so sure whether she had much say in the matter and the man looked at the girl's picture and then documents were signed at the Japanese consul's place in Vancouver. The marriage was registered in Japan and, as far as they were concerned, they were married. There was no wedding. You didn't have to have a wedding to get married. You don't have to even be together. You just have to agree and sign. I'm sure this was the way it was, but there are no official picture brides done this way anymore—although I think there are picture-bride marriages among the Chinese. But anyway you could look it up. It's all been written down. All I know is what my mother told me. My father didn't think it right for his children to know what went on, not even when we were grown up.

My mother came over on a ship to Vancouver and there was a Buddhist ceremony, a wedding of several couples because my mother wasn't alone. You see, when there were quite a few picture brides to come over the Japanese consul in Vancouver would arrange it. I think my father paid her fare. I'm not sure, but I think he did. It wouldn't have been much.

This all took about a year or so and my mother went to a United Church school for several months to learn English and my father knew some. But she said what she knew was so little. Years and years after when she was old and living with us, she really didn't speak English. She could read it, and not too bad. She would read my children's schoolbooks, and giggle. But she couldn't really read English. There was just something about it that she couldn't help but keep twisting up with Japanese, so when she was talking English about half her words were Japanese. You know what I mean. All mixed up. But she was a wonderful woman. She had a sewing machine and she was a marvel. She could sew anything, cook the best I have ever eaten in all my life, even at Japanese banquets.

She came in 1920, I think it was. Life was hard. My father fished in the summer and he worked on his farm. He made her work beside him. She used to say they would go to work when there was still mist coming off the land and that it reminded her of Japan. My father was a hard man. He didn't understand, I don't think, what a woman was. He had been so long from a woman because he came to Canada when he was sixteen or seventeen, and then it is the Japanese way. A woman is to work, to cook and sew and have children and be his servant.

First my mother had my oldest brother. That was good. People from all around came and brought little gifts for my mother because she had had a boy. That was good for my father. Then she had a girl who died and my father didn't care much because girls were no good. That was the way he thought. That's the way the peasants, the small farmers in Japan, thought and he was still a small farmer from Japan. Then there was Ted, another boy, and then Jimmy. These are English names but naturally they had Japanese names too, the way they were registered at the Japanese consul in Vancouver.

Everybody was registered there and later, when people were so much against us, they used to say because all our names were down in a big book in the Tokyo government that we were still Japanese citizens. That was crazy because we were Canadians. My husband was naturalized because he was a fisherman. I wasn't. But Willi and Ted and Jimmy were Canadians. When the boys were born, people came and brought more gifts and my mother said my father gave everybody Scotch whiskey and got drunk himself.

Then I came along and then my two sisters came along and this was about 1930 by this time and even having all these babies, my mother still kept the house clean and warm and worked in the fields. What came in from the fishing, until they took my father's fishing licence away because they said there were too many Japanese fishing, went into clearing land and ditching with bought cedar and planting. My father also bought five more acres and that made fifteen acres, but he only bought that so a white man who was his enemy wouldn't buy it. My mother said he paid too high a price for it. Fifty dollars an acre, I think she said. Bush.

We grew strawberries. Some Japanese people grew tomatoes and other things but we grew strawberries and they are hard. By this time my oldest brother was working on a truck and the next two boys had left school and were in a sawmill at Whonnock. They'd get home for Sundays. They lived in a bunkhouse. They were just kids.

Every morning even though she was sick, before breakfast, my mother would take us out into the field and weed the strawberries, pick them, pack, all the things you do with strawberries and my father—he had a truck—would take them to New Westminster and sell. I think it was to the canneries but some he would sell to stalls at the market there on the river. My mother, sick as she was, would be with us, dressed up in an old shirt and those pants my dad had thrown out and a thing around her hair. She looked very old but I don't think she was more than forty. Then when our plants were finished we'd go over to a neighbour, a white man, and do his raspberries, and when they were finished a truck used to come around and take us to Sardis on days-off-school and holidays and we would pick hops. It was very hard work.

In all those years my father only cleared about ten acres, which was still an awful lot for one family to do, but he had a chicken house—no, two chicken houses—and a lot of small buildings and a well and we had a cow. I don't know why because I'm not sure Japanese drank much milk. We mostly had rice and fish and fresh vegetables. We had eggs from the chickens and ducks.

All the time my mother never complained. I knew about her more than I did before because a relative came from Mission to see her once, a cousin from our village in Japan, and he went up to her and asked where he could find her. He didn't recognize her, she looked so old. My father was very mean to her. She got up at six in the morning and when I'd go to sleep at night I'd see her still up, sewing. Doing vegetables in the Japanese way. Washing. She never had any time to herself. When she wasn't in the house you'd find her in the garden, in the strawberry fields, all stooped over. She never had any nice clothes, but then again none of us did, and my father never took her to the festivals they had although you could easily get there by the truck to Steveston. He never did anything for her. I won't say the Japanese words because you couldn't take them down on that thing, but he never said anything kind. Everything was an order. You know the way Japanese have of snapping out their words. That was him. He always snapped out his words.

He didn't get a bride, he got a work horse. She had no friends because my father had none. At first, she used to say, Japanese people in the district came over but they stopped that. He would fight them. You know, we Japanese have a funny streak. Brother used to come home and he'd have a black eye and once one of them had a broken nose, and he'd say that he'd been in a fight at school because somebody had called him a "damn dirty Jap." But no shake hands and be friends again. Not with the Japanese. If they quarrel, they never forget. Never forget. My father was that all over.

I'm sure she used to sit by the stove at night and think of what her parents had got her into, living on this place cleared out of the bush in Canada. She came from a good family. I think she said her family was better than my father's, small merchants, because in my father's letters he said he was a big fisherman and a berry farmer and that meant pretty good. I guess he also looked pretty good in his new suit that he wore for the photographer. So here she was, in marriage, and I guess the only thing that reminded her of Japan were the mountains we could see from the house. There are an awful lot of mountains in Japan too, you know.

But she loved her children. She fought for them. She loved us, and if my father was mad at me, made me do something too hard for me, something I couldn't do, she'd give me a pickle pretty soon after and kiss me and that would make up for it. She loved all us kids.

Then the war came . . .

A Future Harvest—Trouble

Well, before the war there was the conditions in the berry fields. That was economic, mostly.

A Japanese family would go into the bush, oh, south in Surrey or around Pitt Meadows, Mission, around there, and they'd buy five acres or ten acres, maybe as much as twenty acres, although they could never hope to farm that much. But they'd go to work and the old man and his sons would work dawn to dusk clearing that land. Sometimes they'd borrow or rent a tractor and a stump lifter, but most of the time it was black powder for blasting.

One year they'd clear maybe two acres and put up a shack and a shed and a big garden on one of those acres, and the other they'd plant berries. Still working from dawn to dusk, the women too. And if the old grandpa could still hobble around you'd see him out there doing something, even if it was only carrying a little water and some cold rice and pickles for a mid-afternoon lunch to the guys who were working.

The next year they'd clear another acre and put out more plants and then maybe a few ornamental trees, and I guess by this time there would be a pretty good garden and some chickens, ducks. Maybe a pig.

I've known kids who all they remember of their childhood, the early school years, was going out in the fields until breakfast, going to school, coming home and going to work until dark, having supper and doing homework by lamplight, and going to bed. The thing is, nobody never thought much about it. Today we'd say that was terrible, a father exploiting his own children but in those days, back in the '30s, that wasn't so. That was just the way it was done.

This land often didn't even have roads. The kids would wander off through a trail in the bush, the evergreens, to the main road to go to school, and they took their berries and eggs and other produce out the same way. At the start. And remember, we're kind of talking about the '20s and the '30s and this was close to Vancouver. The country just wasn't built up enough. But this is where the Japs went.

And living the way the Japanese did and with the whole family working it was very difficult for the white farmers to compete. The Japanese had beautiful strawberries and the way they worked so hard, and the people in the cities saying they wanted Jap strawberries and raspberries and the canneries buying Jap berries because they would sell at a lower price to them, the white farmers couldn't keep up with that. This went on and on until the farm organizations and the politicians and people in the government said that the Japanese had a stranglehold on the berry and vegetable industry in British Columbia.

I guess it was so. At least it seemed so in places where there were a lot of Japanese families.

Of course, the Japanese were very good farmers. They loved every little plant, every little shrub, every tree, and they gave them all tender care.

So, jealousy first and then hatred. Economics all the way down the line. Here it was, the Japanese doing the best they could—and all they were doing was planting a future harvest of terrible trouble.

What the Japanese Were Up Against

You do run across interesting things. For instance, a document called "Orientals in British Columbia" which seems to be signed by a man named Pegg or Pigg and underneath his name it identifies him with the Department of Labour. Whether that is B.C. or Canada it is impossible to tell.

But it gives figures on the Japanese and Chinese populations of B.C. and would be pretty heavy ammunition for some of the anti-Japanese groups and individuals, politicians and the like, who were beating the drums against the Japanese. Some of them would throw out a wide net and say they included all Orientals, but it was pretty clear that it was the Japanese they were aiming at.

For instance, this report showed that in 1921 there were 15,006 Japanese in British Columbia, with 9,863 males and 5,143 women. In 1931, according to the census, there were 22,205 Japanese.

The thing that the government report pointed out was that between 1921 and 1931 the number of female Japanese in British Columbia had risen by just over 2,000 and that this was significant.

I'll read the report. It says: "In the consideration of our subject it is obvious that quite apart from the factor of immigration, the number of females of each of these racial populations is of weighy importance." But I should point out that he does not talk about the Chinese, only the Japanese. It continues: "The rapidity with which the Japanese in British Columbia multiply is evidenced by the fact that although admissions to Canada were too few to materially affect the result, the natural rate per 1,000 of the computed population of British Columbia in 1933 was 4.72; the decrease among the Chinese was 2.40 and the increase among the Japanese was 27.82. Further testimony is provided by the British Columbia vital statistics records which show that during the six-year period 1928 to 1933 the natural increase of Japanese was 3,065 males and 3,294 females, a total of 6,359."

Now nobody is going to deny that an annual rate of natural increase of 27.82 percent is phenomenal. In fact, it seems hard to believe. It must have been that every Japanese woman who could possibly bear a child did so. A politician could go before any crowd in any part of the province and shout those statistics and he'd sure have people talking for days after about the Japanese taking over the country.

What the politician did not say and probably wouldn't admit was that at the time there were just less than a million people in B.C. and the Japanese were about 23,000 or so, just a drop in the bucket. There was no way they could take over. Hell, when you really get down to it, most of them were in the category of unskilled labourers in one way or another. Labourers.

The report goes on to say that a lot of dried-out prairie farmers had come to B.C. and found that berry, vegetable, and poultry farms in B.C.—which probably would mean the Fraser Valley and the Okanagan—were dominated by Chinese and Japanese and that there was some resentment about them.

It quotes the White Canada Research Committee of Vancouver—as racist a bunch as you'll find—that the Japanese "are gradually displacing white labour in practically every activity, logging, fishing, transportation, retail trade, farming and many of the small trades and crafts in the cities." Now this was just not so. The government's own statistics proved that very wrong. But nevertheless this report said the White Canada Research report was due the most serious and respectful consideration.

It makes you think, doesn't it?

One thing the government was probably thinking about, this Department of labour chap, was that these hordes of prairie farmers coming to B.C. were all on relief and draining the coffers of the province. He went so far as to suggest, in a very small way, that something could be done about what he called free Japanese labour, which was keeping prices low so the white newcomer couldn't compete. He couldn't compete anyway, but it was a fact, whether it be Japanese, Chinese, or white, that a farmer will use his wife and kids for free labour on his vegetable or berry farm and in that way prices could be kept down. And especially with a world-wide depression raging around, prices were down to the bottom anyway. There is no doubt Japanese worked for lower wages, especially on the farms. But enough of that. It is not that important.

The report quoted the British Columbia Board of Retail Merchants Association of Canada, which must have thrown some weight, and it said: "It is a well-known fact that the Oriental can exist on a fraction of what it costs the white man, because of the class of food consumed and also of the savings affected in establishing a home." I guess they meant Japanese and Chinese live on rice and fish and pickles and tea in hovels. It said, "Families of Orientals in Vancouver are brought up in quarters where a white man could not exist and because in many cases of using the members of their families in the store, without having to pay wages, are in a preferred position to the white merchants who could not exist under such conditions." I guess that is true to a degree. They still do it today. Walk into a Chinese corner grocer anywhere and you're liable to see an eleven-year-old girl waiting on you, black-eyed, cute as a button and smart.

And then the report makes a funny distinction. It points out that although there is an acute problem of unemployment, it is claimed that there is no serious amount of unemployment among the Japanese. It points out that only 2 percent of the Japanese population in B.C. was on relief, forty-four individuals and sixty-five heads of families having 349 dependents. To me that is a pretty good thing, and especially when the report points out that the figure for B.C. as a total was 8 percent. Over 8 percent. Somehow, you get the idea that on the one hand the Department of Labour is saying that low unemployment is a good thing, but on the other hand that the method of the Japanese in living is somehow taking away jobs that could be done by a white man. That's the subtle impression one gets, nevertheless.

Concluding the whole thing, the report said that it " . . . is evident that the problem of Oriental economic infiltration particularly as affecting the Japanese has assumed such proportions as to excite the very serious concern of British Columbia and it is only natural to assume that because of the intense interest aroused some allowance for exaggeration and prejudice would be justified." Okay, so be it. Then the report adds, "Even though some of the testimony may be discounted somewhat on these grounds [of prejudice and exaggeration] there still remains a sufficient body of credible evidence to indicate that the agitation which has arisen is by no means a tempest in a teapot."

Well, anybody who had been out here even for a couple of weeks would know this whole business was no tempest in a teapot. It was very real. It was in the newspapers, in radio speeches, in election speeches, in everyday conversation. I'll go back in the report and quote one sentence I missed which was from a resolution passed by the Vancouver City Council in 1938 and it said: "These people, through low standards of living and unfair competition have gained an ascendency over our people in many lines of business." Okay, I should have said that sooner, I guess. It is a pretty hard sentence. I didn't quite realize that before. That was the Vancouver City Council. How would you like to be a Japanese and read that in your evening paper?

The report doesn't say that there were reasons for this situation. Racism. Discrimination. White domination. The Oriental was always on the outside looking in, but with really no hope of getting in.

There is just one thing that should be pointed out. At the beginning of the report this Pigg or Pegg notes that all the information for the report was provided by a Mr. Hugh Thornley. And do you know who Mr. Hugh Thornley is or was? Well, if you read any reports of the White Canada Research Committee, 3900 Heather Street, Vancouver, B.C., you will see the name of Mr. Hugh Thornley as a director listed at the top of the page. The White Canada Research Committee was dedicated to getting new federal government rules and regulations to further control every aspect of Japanese life in B.C. and, for that matter, Canada. It was directed specifically against the Japanese in B.C. and its main object, in the long run, I guess, was to get the Japanese out of the country. Keep B.C. white, pure white.

The committee probably had some good ideas in controlling aliens in the event of war, but most of the things they were

advocating were before the war. In fact, many of the things that
the White Canada Research Committee advocated did come
about in time of war, such as defence zones, evacuation, and
other things. They were just one of the groups in action at the
time and some of their backers they listed were farmers'
institutes, rural municipalities, fraternal societies, Native Sons
of Canada, Native Sons of British Columbia, retail merchant
associations, the Canadian Legion, and parts of the fishing
industry. So their words were not without some effect. But it is
strange that a government department would appoint a director
of such a committee to do the homework for a report to be
prepared over the signature of the Department of Labour. Oh
well.

One thing about the White Canada Committee is that it was
almost 100 percent composed of Liberals and Conservatives. No
CCF. No Communists.

So, you can see just what the Japanese were up against. The
government was watching them. The R.C.M.P. was keeping a
close eye on them. And reports were actually being issued by
the government saying all the things that the anti-Japanese were
saying through the newspapers and radio.

This was not some power-hungry, vote-mad politician up in a
hall before a bunch of people spouting off his yap. This was a
government report, although how credible it was is another
matter. Another matter altogether. But this is what the Japanese
were having to fight. Rough.

The Pool Down on English Bay

Sure there was discrimination. Everybody knew it. Not just us,
the Japanese kids, but the Orientals too. The Chinese. There
was that covered pool down on English Bay and we weren't

allowed to swim there. Some people didn't care. They'd just say, "Oh, that's the way it is." Not me and my gang. We got to know the old guy in charge and he'd say sure, we could swim but we'd have to come about seven-thirty in the morning and we could swim in the pool until about nine-thirty, but then we'd have to go because the pool would open at ten o'clock for the rest of the people. So we'd swim until nine-thirty and then just before we'd get out some of us, and sometimes all of us, would pee in the pool. You know, when you're a kid, that means something, like you're showing them that they can't get away with anything, everything. If you're going to swim in a city-owned pool and not let some of us swim in it because of the colour of our skin, then you're going to have to swim in some of our pee.

The Ghetto of The Mind

Those Japanese people weren't wealthy. They weren't even affluent. By any measurement of today's standards you would have to call them lower class. I knew quite a few within the range of economic endeavour and apart from several groups— and I would say the few doctors and dentists comprised one faction, those who imported and exported to Japan would be another, those who had good-sized stores would be another, and those who had other businesses as you will find in the lumber industry, these people would be considered affluent—the rest were lower class down to poor.

If you saw a Japanese and his lady getting out of a Packard auto outside a theatre on Granville Street you might think that he was typical of the Japanese. He would be very untypical. If the average Japanese owned an auto it would be a 300-dollar Ford or maybe a motorcycle, and quite often a plain bicycle There were few ways for a Japanese to become wealthy, the reason being, of course, that there only were a few in Vancouver and the Lower Mainland and they traded primarily with each other. Taking in each other's laundry, so to speak, in a literal and nonliteral term. They had to live on each other.

They went to Japanese stores, of course. There they could get all the goods and services they expected in Japan and it was a matter of convenience. I imagine, especially in the latter days before the war, that the Japanese businessmen, the storekeepers, went to considerable trouble to get those Japanese kimonos, food, candy, toys, and other things they used to sell.

Of course, Woodward's always was a warm favourite with the Japanese. They used to have sales once a month and you'd see the aisles swarming with Japanese women and their children. Usually a daughter. Buying. I believe in many cases the daughter acted as the translator. All that ended, or course, shortly after the war came along. I understand the clerks refused to sell to these Japanese women. But that was war, as in any war. If you used modern parlance I think it would be correct to say that the white storekeepers told the Japanese to take their business elsewhere.

Unless you were in a position to get money—is "exploit" the word I'm looking for?—from other Japanese, you could really not make much money. Take the case of the Japanese gardener. You still see them around. I believe they still must do all the gardening in Vancouver, although I can't afford them, but in those days they got about 30 cents an hour. That meant they had to have an old truck and their tools, and early in the morning in Shaughnessy and Kerrisdale and other districts you'd see them toot-tooting through the quiet streets to get an early start so they could make more. But they did an honest and thorough job. No cheating that I ever saw.

The men worked in the sawmills. I believe there was still that law in effect that said one quarter of the mill force would be paid 40 cents an hour and the remainder, who would be unskilled labour, would be paid 25 cents. The three quarters, of course, would be Oriental. Not necessarily Japanese but Chinese too. They protested, of course, but nobody listened. The legislature except for the CCF seemed to be pretty well lined up for anti-Oriental bills in those days.

A lot of the men were fishermen and in the fishing season the women would work in the canneries. There seemed to be quite a few more canneries than there are now, but of course they would only be half as efficient as today. Today, everything is efficient. They always said the men were very good fishermen, would work long hours, and would never raise a fuss about the prices paid them. What the men got I don't know, but the women were paid poorly. Very poorly. I know that. Probably they didn't clear 30 dollars a month for long hours working in all that noise and those slimy fish. Ugh. Yes, ugh! I wouldn't want any daughter of mine doing it.

The point is, these people didn't have any money. Not much money. But they made do, like the storekeeper and the little shops, the dry-cleaning places, rooming houses, fruit stores, novelty stores, and, of course, the grocery stores. I think there were more Japanese grocery stores then than there are Chinese corner stores today. They'd live in the back. The politicians didn't like it; they passed by-laws about it but the Japanese just ignored them. This is the way they had done it before, maybe in Japan, and this was the way they'd do it now.

A lot had little houses, although a lot did live in rooms in bigger houses owned by Japanese landlords. Now there was a tribe that I didn't mention. I'm sure they did all right in the money business. But if they had houses they were usually small. You could often tell if it was a Jap house because it would be so neat, every weed in the garden pulled, the flower boxes painted, red geraniums. They seemed to prefer small houses, even though they had large families. Often four boys and four girls. Something like that. A woman's job then was to keep house, cook, and provide babies. I've heard that Japanese men often lack the sensitivities of white men. In a neighbourhood nobody bothered them and they, of course, wouldn't dream of bothering anybody. Good neighbours.

You'd see them going to church. Most if not all in our district went to a white church and you'd see the family start off and you'd say to yourself: "My, but what a pretty parade." All the girls dressed so beautifully, straw hats with ribbons, white dresses, and patent leather shoes and the boys the same, all dressed up in the English style. It was hard for you to believe that the father worked as a labourer down on False Creek in one of those awful mills. How they did it, how they managed to save, I'll never know. But they did. Of course the women were absolutely marvellous seamstresses. Marvellous. That's another thing. Most women got their clothes made if they could afford it, but it wasn't expensive at a Japanese seamstress. They just seemed to have the knack. I don't know why it was. Maybe because they'd been taught almost from babes in arms.

But you've got me off the point. They weren't rich. They weren't even well-to-do. But I think during the depression they made out better than the white people. They had to. Keeping face was, and I believe still is, something quite important to them.

That was outside. Inside it was a little different. Any girl I hired I would want to see her home. I didn't ask her to come and see me. I went to her place. After all, environment is so important and I wanted to see for myself. Would this girl fit into our home? That was the question I asked myself. Their homes were rather barely furnished. There was always that sewing machine. And a sofa, a couple of chairs, sometimes a little shrine and I'd say Aha! meaning they went to the United or the Anglican Church, but the Buddhism they knew and the new religion of the whites had a way of crossing over. You go to a Japanese funeral today and I think you'll see what I mean. The two religious meld. But the house would always be clean and there would be little rice cakes and tea offered and I'd tell them how much I could pay. Sometimes 15 dollars, sometimes more. It was how I felt. We always had Japanese girls around the house. They'd usually take it. After all, they'd answered my ad or the girl who was leaving had recommended them. It was hard for a Japanese girl then.

It was hard for any person of that race then. Boys would go to high school and then scrimp and save and get to university, and then after passing through they'd have to go and work in a grocery or deliver in a truck or something quite demanding. If they'd wanted to go to Toronto their chances would have been better, far better, but they didn't want to do that. They wanted to stay in B.C. One girl who was with me said her husband-to-be was a university graduate and went to Toronto and he did get a good job but he came back. He said Toronto was a desert. He meant it was flat because there was no mountains. Well, speaking of rich Japanese. Rich Japs—those were the words we used then. There were a few wealthy Japanese, and if Pearl Harbor hadn't upset their apple cart I daresay that those wealthy ones would have become a lot more wealthy. Although I'm doubtful that all the rest, the mill workers, the fishermen, the storekeepers, I doubt very much if they would have become wealthy. How could they? Now I ask you, how could they? If their day-to-day progress was just to keep their head above water and save to send a son or daughter to Japan for a couple of years of schooling, where were they going to get the capital to get ahead, make that big jump out of the pool they were in? Impossible. Utterly impossible.

That was why the evacuation was a good thing. It broke them up, got them away from Vancouver. They went right across Canada. Scattered like sowing grain in biblical times. They didn't run into the discrimination they found here, the job discrimination and the personal discrimination which, in the spread of the net, is essentially the same thing. They had a chance to grow. A chance to go to other schools and meet other people. A chance to go farming or into an industry or work in a store or shop until they could get started on their own or do whatever their little heart desired.

Anyway, they'd had no real hope before the war here. You see, the evacuation not only broke up the ghettoes of living, it broke up the ghetto of the mind. It was hard, it was painful. Some people will never forget. A lot of people put it out of their minds long ago. But it was done and that's all I'll say about that end of it, but it was something that turned out right for all but a few.

Growing Up in Kitsilano

Ah, living in Kitsilano as a boy, a youth? As a Japanese Canadian? Ah, that's a good question. I went to kindergarten, to elementary school, to high school. Kits Junior High. Graduated in grade twelve. I grew up in the 1700-block West First, right across from the Seaforth Armouries, and that was a part of Kitsilano Japanese Community centred around the Japanese school, the Buddhist church, the Christian church, the Japanese stores.

Took part as my family did in the school, took judo, went to the Christian church, so I was a minority within a majority, which was itself a minority. Although the Japanese are not terribly religious there were more people had affiliation with the Buddhist church than the Christian church.

I was a cub and a scout, all part of this Japanese Anglican church which was called the Third Avenue Church of Ascension. I would go to school and then come home and do some chores and trot out with a new set of books at four o'clock to the Japanese school where I would spend an hour and a half. I continued Japanese-language school for many years, but that is not to say that I had a really concentrated Japanese education. It was really one of the things one had to do. I did it well but one didn't take it too seriously. Partly because my mother had been a public school teacher in Japan I got a lot of Japanese taught to me at home.

Always conscious of being a part of a Japanese community and a Japanese minority surrounded by a white community. We had classmates, sometimes friends who were Sikhs wore turbans to school, but we were the dominant minority. I remember that most classes in public school would have up to about a fifth of its enrollment Japanese students like myself. Most of the teachers had a lot of trouble pronouncing our Japanese names. Ah, mine was a tricky one. That was part of it. I always remember two or three of my teachers in public school and high school as . . . I will remember them for the rest of my life for being wonderful influences on me. Who pushed me, led me, encouraged me, and even kicked me in some good directions. There was no Japanese-language school that had any influence on you.

Oh yes, there was fraternization between the other kids and ourselves. But cubs and scouts, that was all Japanese Canadians. But apart from that, yes. School, for instance, it would depend on the Japanese Canadian kid. Some of us—and I was one—would tend to have white friends or even buddies. But there was a cut-off point—guys who I knew very, very well, spent all our time together, but I was never in their homes. And, essentially, neither were they in mine. A kind of a barrier there. One didn't notice it much, one didn't fret about it, one just assumed it was just part of the thing. Only later when you think about it you think that was strange.

Also, I believe—and I believe it more so now after having lived in Ontario for thirty years—that British Columbia was the most British of all places. Despite all you hear about it, I think it made most people monarchists. I know it made me one. I still think that the song "Land of Hope and Glory" is one of the greatest pieces of music ever written. I notice it because I have met so many people of my age who grew up in Eastern Canada—always thought that Eastern Canada was closer to the Mother Country, but British Columbia, partly because of its isolation and partly because of the original people, is so bloody British.

That was the way it was, growing up in Vancouver as a Japanese Canadian. That was the way it was at Pearl Harbor. In July or August when the last ships came back and there was to be no more shipping and no more trade with Japan and on those ships were the Canadian missionaries coming home after years in Japan and the newspaper headlines and the newsreels—and everybody went to the movies in those days—well, what could you expect? You had to expect that something was coming. You didn't know what. How could you? But you knew that whatever it was, it was going to affect you because you were Japanese.

An Occidental View

Yes, oh yes, I lived in Vancouver all through those times, the times you're talking about, but I'm darned if I can recall any of the things that were supposed to have gone on.

In fact, I don't even remember if I could really tell the difference between a Japanese and a Chinese.

I was a bookkeeper at the shipyard down in Coal Harbor. The shipyard didn't pay me full time so I did books for other small companies, so I got around the downtown part of the city a lot—Hastings, Main, Cordova. I used to see Japanese. Flatter faces than the Chinese. I would say. Maybe a bit shorter and stockier. Not so much inclined to fat. I think that's the way I could tell them, if I could.

No, I don't remember about this discrimination bit. Well, for one thing we rented a small house on West Seventh near Balaclava and I don't think the Japs came over that far. I think most of them were in Kitsilano, down near where the armoury was, and on the Fairview slopes. Some in South Vancouver as I recall, where the Hindus are now, and you could take the interurban tram out to Stevenson and see hundreds—every two out of three people you saw was Jap. You could buy fish there. Salmon, cod, sole, just about anything you could find in the fish stores, and it would be fresh. It made a nice outing. Of course there was Jap Town. Down on Powell Street. Main down to, I'd say, Campbell Avenue and across from the water. But nobody ever went down there. Oh, sometimes a few of the boys from the yard would take a bottle and go down to a chop suey house there and have a little party.

As far as I was concerned, the Japs never bothered us and we never bothered them. If you bought vegetables from the man who came to the door, that was about your only dealing with Japs apart from going to one of the little stores up on Broadway. The man who came with the eggs and poultry, he was Chinese. Mr. Leung, I think his name was. But the two races, as far as I can remember, seemed to keep apart. Probably each thought it was better, or the best. Then there was the war in China and while it didn't concern us, or at least we didn't think it did, it probably concerned the Japs and the Chinese people as China seemed to get the worst of it from the beginning.

I can't remember much in the paper. We took *The Province* and I read it pretty thoroughly. I do remember there were two aldermen, Halford Wilson and a man named Graves, who were usually ranting about the Japs in B.C. and how they were going to take over but—well, if everybody was like me they weren't paying attention to these people. I just figured they were politicians and you know what they are. Wouldn't allow one inside my door. There were letters to the editor. It seems to me there were. What they said I can't remember, but there were letters and if *The Province* was printing them they must have been bad against the Japs. Nobody writing to a paper ever says a good word about anyone. It's smear smear, smear. It's getting worse, haven't you noticed?

I can't say I had anything against the Japs. Naturally I didn't like what was going on in China, but again I didn't like what was going on in Europe. Bullies at work. And I can't say that I ever heard the people I worked with or my friends say anything about the Japs. For one thing, you never saw them. Our kids saw them in school, of course, because there were always lots of them around, but at work, in the downtown, you never saw them. They had their own places to go and they did their own things. Some were landscape gardeners. Up in Shaughnessy where people could afford a gardener. We couldn't. None of our friends could. On less than 100 dollars a month? No way. They had little corner stores just like the Chinese have now. In fact, the Chinese had them then too. They were gardeners, as I've said, and they were in dry cleaning. Downtown they had the cheap rooming houses. All torn down now. Around Powell Street. In and around where the post office is now. I never ran into any in my rounds who were in business or were bookkeepers like myself or accountants. They seemed to take all the lower-type jobs. I guess it wasn't a case of seeming to take them. It was that that was all they could get. I imagine being a Jap in Vancouver in those days wasn't all that fun.

Were Japanese Schools a Good Thing?

To this day I just can't make up my mind about the Japanese-language schools. Before the war. About whether— well, were they a good thing or not? Did they help us? Hurt us?

Remember, there was lots of anti-Japanese around. Read the stories and you'll find there always had been, but it was getting worse in the '30s. You never saw many, hardly any Japanese on relief, but look at all the whites on relief. Thousands of them, thousands. That meant Japanese were taking jobs from white men. That's just one example.

Then you take the Japanese-language school over there on Alexander. We went, two hours. Two hours a day after regular school. God, how many? Maybe 800, 900. Japanese kids. Coming out of that big building all at once, 900 Japanese kids learning Japanese and all that, Japanese nationalism, the glory of Japan, beating the Chinese, and all that. The anti-Japs standing around or seeing these kids, us, streaming through the streets. They'd say we're learning all about Japan. Saluting the Japanese flag. Singing the Japanese anthem. Well, we did sometimes. I have to admit that. Sure, I admit it. The emperor's birthday. Big celebration. All these guys on relief, the guys who wrote letters to the *Sun* and *Province,* the guys who handed out leaflets saying "Get Rid of The Japs" and "The Rising Sun Must Set." Those guys. And these hundreds of well-fed Japanese kids, and mind you, listen to this, every damn one of us born a Canadian. A citizen. God, that burned them up. Well, for one thing it wasn't good politics.

So they could point and say that big school on Alexander Street in Vancouver is teaching hundreds of Japanese kids to be good Japanese and well, put it another way, eh? Put it that the school was teaching these kids to be bad Canadians. How do you like those apples, eh?

And there wasn't one school. There were dozens. Between fifty and sixty but Alexander had to be the biggest. Some maybe ran for only two or three days a week. Like out in the valley where they needed the kids for the berries. But Alexander was all week, two hours a day. Ten hours. That's a lot of learning. Another thing. This was that these teachers were Japanese. How would you like, if you were a Buddhist, to have a Jehovah Witness come into your house and start a school? Same thing, same deal. The schoolbooks were Japanese too. Made in Japan. When the book said "we" or "us" it didn't mean B.C. or Ottawa or Canada, it meant Tokyo or Japan. I don't know if Japanese school kids in Japan used the same books, but those books were manufactured in Japan. Give this information to the anti-Japanese and they come back at you in newspapers and speeches. Like bullets. Oh, it was stupid.

You want to know something? It wasn't Nisei who wanted these schools. They didn't think they were dumb, I guess, but they, well, were they necessary? Canada is English-speaking. Right? We were living in Canada. Maybe only a few, most for a few months, were going back to Japan. We had to make our living in Canada, so speak Canadian. Right? I mean English. So why two hours a day reading and writing Japanese and learning all about the samurai and the old wars and the way an emperor is crowned, or whatever does happen to him? See, I learned all this and I can't tell you now. I even speak lousy Japanese. When they wanted to send me to Malaysia to interpret they figured I'd still have to go, yes, go to school to really learn Japanese.

I didn't want to go to Japanese-language school. My parents didn't really care if I did, but the old Issei in our house he said I had to go—and Nisei always listened to Issei in those days—Second generation listened to first generation. I wanted to be over on the school grounds knocking around a ball with my Jew friends, Dago friends, Portuguese, Scotch. Christ, you could find any nationality in that place.

But the Issei who ran things, well . . . that's the way it was. Keep the bonds with the old country. Remember, you are Japanese. You got more culture that it makes the Chinese look like a coolie, the English like a ploughman. Remember, you are Japanese. Two thousand years of tradition. Culture. Even today we still got culture coming out of our ears, but General MacArthur and his troops kind of toned that down. Not everything for the emperor anymore. Enough, but not as much. Canada is our country. Fine, it is okay to go back to Japan, see where the old people come from, those dumps, and see what they got now. It makes you laugh. But the old people then sat in their chairs and read the Japanese papers they'd get and say, "Send the children to school so they can know our ways." That's that, and the Nisei, my parents, never said Boo.

I didn't want to go to language school. It was a joke. Everything was English. Go to school, speak English all day. On way to Japanese school stop and buy candy. Ask for it in English, pay for it with a Canadian nickel. Anyway, then go to the Alexander school for two hours and you goof around. Sneak in and take out the screws in the teacher's chair and when he sits down, crash, down he goes. Everybody screams with laughter. What a goof-off. Oh, some fun like that but the teachers couldn't speak English, or just a little, and we didn't speak that much good Japanese. Some spoke it perfectly, but a lot didn't.

But that's no matter, is it? What is is that all those guys who were so much anti-Japanese, this gave them ammunition against us. One guy even said they trained the older boys in naval tactics in the school. Can you imagine a teacher in a school at Hammond with maybe ten boy students, from seven to fourteen or fifteen, teaching naval tactics? They said the teachers, the men, were Japanese Navy reservists sent over. Paid by the Japanese government. They said the teachers were spies. Tell you something. Those teachers I knew were too dumb even to play I Spy with eight-year-old kids.

There's nothing wrong with keeping some of the old ways. I'd go back to Japan tomorrow to see some of the things I know are there. You'd go where your parents came from. It's just natural. We have our festival in June. You have your haggis, your Burns Night, if you're Scottish. But that is something else. Different. Quite different.

In the days I'm talking about, before Pearl Harbor, like in the '30s, you didn't parade this Japanese business around so much.

Or you shouldn't have. Not when the whole of B.C. was waiting to drill you in the back, no matter how hard you ran or dodged. And there the damned simpletons were, flaunting the whole issue with those hundreds of kids clogging up the streets downtown there after classes at Alexander School. Or at Steveston. Mission. Haney. Everywhere. Like a red flag, you know, to a bull.

Another thing. It wasn't the kids who should have been going to language school of the Japanese. It should have been the older people going to language school in English.

I don't think I learned—no, hell, what does a twelve-year-old kid want to do but play baseball and go swimming. I don't think I learned much in that school. After a day in our own school I guess my brain couldn't take it all in anyway. But it was the Issei who laid down the law. There shall be Japanese schools and, by God, they paid for it in an awful lot of heartbreak and grief and sadness and sorrow. That's what I think. It could have been done differently if it had to be done. It is now. We have Japanese-language schools and nobody says anything. They work fine.

But the schools in the '30s. I guess we made a mistake there. Too many, too many kids. Sticking our heads up above the crowd. We were sitting ducks. Why they hated us I'll never know, but my God, I'm telling you, some of them sure did.

The New Canadian

Basically, *The New Canadian* newspaper came along trying to establish an organ to lead the fight for justice and citizenship for Japanese Canadians. Most social movements seem to have some need for an organ to express ideas, convey information, rally the troops, the cause. *The New Canadian* was very much in that tradition.

It was all Nisei. It was the Nisei newspaper. There were, of course, three other Japanese newspapers being published in Vancouver and they were essentially for the older generation so *The New Canadian* came along at a time, in 1938, when there were enough second-generation Japanese Canadians, early twenties, who more conscious of the difficulties they faced in asserting their rights as citizens. So, *The New Canadian* was timely and, of course, in the late '30s with the international situation deteriorating rapidly, there was a great deal more anti-Japanese feeling on the west coast, and a great deal more expression of it by way of speeches and by way of overt political action—the restriction of licences for fishing, the restriction of the right to operate small businesses, and increasingly it was popular. So when any group find themselves under attack they look around to find some way to respond.

One can say that a little seed had been planted with a couple of experimental pages published by the University Students' Club. Ah, one of the Japanese-language papers offered to publish a kind of a page or so and as it turned out we produced about four pages. I wrote an essay on some economic problem and a number of other people wrote articles. The editor, the spark, was a chap named Higashi who is now with Associated Press in Japan.

When the decision to start *The New Canadian* was made, the second most important person was a man named Ed Ouchi, born in Japan but came here at an early age, fluently bilingual. An insurance salesman.

He was the man who went out and raised the money. This was now in the fall of 1938. I had gone to Woodfibre to work in the pulp mill after looking for a job in Vancouver for several months, and in the Christmas holidays I got an urgent call from Higashi and Ouchi. Would I come back to Vancouver and join the group that was going to start the newspaper? I think I had 300 dollars saved up. When I got back to Vancouver they said they were going to start up in January and if I had any money they'd need that too. So I said, why not, so I gave them my 300 dollars and I think we got the first issue out in February, 1939. Our editorial office was in a back room down on Alexander Street. It was the room overlooking the street of a boardinghouse and on the lower floor was a small print shop that some immigrant had bought with his hard-earned money. We said, "You do the printing and rent us a room for our office," and that is how *The New Canadian* came into being.

I don't think we ran into any actual opposition from the Issei. But I think we ran into a great deal of skepticism, doubt, what's the use, futility. So, but nevertheless, there were enough people who were prepared to subscribe and a number who were willing to contribute, donations. I don't think we missed many issues. I think we were more or less a weekly from the start and then we got enough subscribers within the Powell Street area to get a carrier boy and then we extended that—Kitsilano, Fairview, and then New Westminster, the valley, the island, Prince Rupert, all the little fishing villages up and down the coast. Lumbering centres, Cumberland, Qualicum, Chemainus. Up and down the Okanagan.

And then came Pearl Harbor and that was a very significant break in the whole situation. The other Japanese newspapers, the dailies, were shut down, leaving *The New Canadian*. I don't know what the authorities thought but it was clear there was nothing subversive about this particular newspaper—the whole tone had been in the opposite direction and so we were allowed to stay in business. And immediately we became very much more important because the people had been relying for their news on the Japanese-language dailies and they were cut off and not long after that, as you will recall, radios were also banned and there was no means of communication other than our newspaper and subscriptions just flowed in.

The government saw our newspaper after Pearl Harbor as a means of getting word out to Japanese Canadians wherever they were dispersed. That was a bizarre twist. Once the government decided they were going to go ahead with the evacuation they found they had no way to communicate the news, so we were it. People scattered over a hundred different communities. The first thing that happened was that the B.C. Security Commission came to us and said they wanted us to print this advertisement—and this ad must have been the one with respect to the evacuation of aliens, able-bodied Japanese-born men, up to the camps in the Yellowhead area. We told them we did not have the facilities to handle ads like that as we were using the *News-Herald* typesetting facilities and we were in quite heavy debt to them. So the Security Commission said they would pay the ad and other extra costs, so we made a deal with the leading Japanese-language daily that had been shut down and we borrowed their type so we ran this little ad and then they came along with further ads.

I said that these ads told the people what they were expected to do, but they didn't give any real explanation of what was going on. I said I thought it would make much more sense and be much more effective if we ran a little explanatory news story too. They said, well, okay. So we went on that way and then I told the commission that this was costing us additional money and they said okay, and they gave us a grant to handle this extra cost. Something in the order of 50 dollars a month or 100 dollars a month. Something like that. And that just opened the door to writing more of the more general stories, and the commission agreed that after the general evacuation was ordered it was somehow necessary to communicate with all Japanese Canadians. So it was particularly important to the people who felt more isolated.

Then when the general evacuation was finished, then we moved out of Vancouver ourselves. They didn't ask us, of course. They ordered us. If we were going to stay in business and continue this communication with all Japanese Canadians, we'd have to find someplace to publish. So I went up into the Interior and found that Kaslo was the only location where there was any printing press, any newspaper, and they had an old linotype machine. So we made a deal with the chap who ran the business, a very kindly old fellow who wasn't occupied full time really and he was glad to have the revenue and company and somebody to run his press for him.

I was still around when we moved to Winnipeg. It was clear that most of the camps were going to be closed. This was in early '45. It was clear the war in Europe was going to end and neither did anyone have much doubt, frankly—I didn't—about how the war was going to end in the Pacific. I said look, more people are moving East and we had been encouraging that move all along in our columns and it was really time for us to make the move too. It was only a question of where would be the best location and Winnipeg seemed very central. It was uncertain how the eventual distribution of Japanese Canadians across the country would be, but Winnipeg looked like a logical move.

So I went to Winnipeg and fortunately I encountered the Israelite Press there and I met the old man and he was very sympathetic. Sure, he said. He quoted a dirt-cheap price which we needed and we packed everything up and went to Winnipeg, bought a house in Elmwood, with the type, the Japanese type in the basement, and the living room became the office and we all crowded into the house.

I think it was in Kaslo when we began to print more of the paper in Japanese because a great many of our readers read only Japanese and they were the ones who would write in the most sad little stories about the troubles they were having and they would write in poetry and so we began publishing in Japanese too and eventually I guess it was half and half.

Censorship. Oh, yeah. There was no problem on the English side. We had to submit all the copy beforehand to the censor in Vancouver and he could run through it in half an hour, but when it came to the Japanese side, they had to find someone fluent in Japanese. And when we went to Kaslo we had to send page proofs to Vancouver and then we'd get a wire back saying "Okay" or we were to delete such and such an item or sentence. Yes. There was very little censorship that actually occurred.

There was only one real awkward incident. On the front page, at the top, there were two small boxes that are called "ears." Well, there was nothing to put in one of them this one time and there was a mayor of Vancouver called Jack Cornett at that time, and he had made a particularly violent speech about how all Japanese should be deported to Japan immediately. And somebody wrote in the ear: "Cornet Blows Nazi Tune." This got by the censor and it was brought to the mayor's attention and the Mounties arrived a couple of days later and there was quite a flap about that. It looked as if we were going to be shut down. Just for that. Yeah. Just because it was in the ear and that little piece of copy never got to Vancouver, the bureaucracy got upset because the mayor was upset and he, of course, accused them of not doing their job effectively and that had repercussions all the way back.

I was the editorial board. I formulated policy. It wasn't hard to get mad. It was hard not to get mad.

We had a good bunch of correspondents. I give them every credit. The oddest people would turn up, people who would want to express themselves and would turn up in the darndest places and, of course, there was the group who actually put out the paper. We had Christmas supplements when people would write in of their hopes and dreams and their frustrations and their new lives, and there would be social notes and a lot of sports. A lot of sports. An awful lot of the frustration of the young people of those days was taken out in sports.

After the newspaper moved to Winnipeg, and I had done the preliminary work in setting it up, I joined the army and so I had nothing to do with it after that. Later it moved to Toronto and it is there now.

Two Government Documents

The Canadian government had their eye on Canada's Japanese before the war. Long before. There is no use denying that the government planned to take restrictive methods against the Japanese Canadians because it is right there in the records.

I won't quote the records exactly as they are, but the two I have are marked SECRET and come from the Department of National Defence in Ottawa and are addressed to an F. C. Blair,

Director of Immigration, Jackson Building, Ottawa. The first memo is dated 2nd June, 1938, and the next one which follows up is dated 15th June, 1938. Both are marked SECRET and are signed by L. R. LaFleche, Deputy Minister of the Department of National Defence.

The first says that the paragraphs represent the Department of National Defence's views on national defence with respect to the Japanese in British Columbia, "because of the problem they represent with respect to internal security and the protection of vulnerable points in time of war." That's putting it pretty bluntly.

The next paragraph says that the census of 1931 showed there were 24,000 persons of Japanese origin in B.C. and that 5,000 were men of military age "owing allegiance to Japan." The report said that accurate intelligence as to the whereabouts of many of these men is lacking and that the Japanese may have increased since 1931. We know now that the figure actually decreased by about 2,000.

The report goes on to say that "In any event, the above figures are, in themselves, sufficient to make it expedient to draw up somewhat elaborate plans for the internal security of British Columbia in time of war."

It said that in the First World War all enemy aliens who appeared to be subversive were interned but most of them, in fact all of them, were later released on their word of honour to obey the law and go about their work peacefully.

However, this document says: "While the question has yet to be inquired into by the Committee on the Treatment of Aliens and Alien Property, it would appear doubtful if such a course of action could be safely followed with respect to Japanese nationals in British Columbia."

Further: "Indeed, there seems to be little reason for an assurance as to the peaceful behaviour of even Canadian nationals of Japanese origin."

And the next statement is important: "It is therefore quite possible that action will be required (it seems possible that public sentiment will so demand) to restrain the activities, consequently, the liberties of such Canadian nationals of Japanese origin whose sympathies may be deemed hostile to this country."

Fair enough, I guess. If a Canadian citizen of Japanese ancestry is going to be disloyal and cause trouble, then take care of him. Probably every other country of the world would too.

The document then goes on to say that it would not be the army to arrest and collect these people but some other authority. It talks about setting up camps to quarter the internees and to make "provision for their administraion and safe custody."

The next sentence is revealing though as it says: "It follows then that the Department of National Defence may some day find itself required to provide facilities for the detention of upwards of 10,000 persons in British Columbia alone." Do you see what this means? They're talking about Japanese nationals, those born in Japan and not naturalized, and also Canadian-born Japanese, and they've earlier said there probably are about 24,000 Japanese in B.C. so somewhere between 40 and 50 percent of these people could be disloyal, subversive, a threat to national security in time of war. That takes in old men and women, wives, children, everybody. In other words, what they are in effect saying is that they pretty well consider the whole of the Japanese Canadian population of B.C. in 1938 as troublemakers.

The document said that experience has shown that it takes one soldier to guard and care for five internees, so the department would have to hold in readiness a force of about 2,000 troops for this duty.

The next part is okay, I guess. It says that the security of defence establishments must be maintained, bases where the air force and navy send out their patrols, and that the "presence of enemy aliens near these points is obviously undesirable. "But what the Department of National Defence seemed to be advocating was that the government would give the authorities a blank check to move these undesirables out of these areas, like Esquimalt, Yorke Island, Prince Rupert, and other places. But one thing sticks out. Earlier in the report, it stated that while there were 5,000 men who might be, or as the report says could owe allegiance to the Emperor of Japan, it says the authorities really don't know where these men are located. So, any Japanese near Esquimalt or Prince Rupert, which is their northern fishing headquarters, could just be considered as an undesirable. It is kind of tricky but it makes a point.

The last paragraph said the department hoped that there would be a "diminution in the number of Orientals, especially Japanese, in British Columbia, or at least to ensure that the present number is not allowed to increase." What are they talking about? Immigration laws, which they already had? Or stop the Japanese men from making babies?

That was the June 2 secret memo and shows that while nothing really had been done about the situation, there appeared to have been some considerable thinking into the matter. It was obvious, anyway, that the Canadian government through the Department of National Defence expected Japan to be entering the war and trouble with the Japanese in B.C.

The second report of 15th June is a little puzzling. It leads off with the statement that "While representations are from time to time made by private persons as to the danger of espionage by the Japanese in British Columbia, few, if any, specific cases of illegal activity have actually come to the Department of National Defence." It did say, however, that the Japanese "appear to be most inquisitive and it is current knowledge that, in the course of their fishing activities they have acquired a profound knowledge of Canadian territorial waters off the British Columbia coast." No one is denying this, but the same can be said for a Norwegian fisherman or an Indian fisherman or any fisherman at all. Then it adds: "As has been previously noted, however, there are but small grounds for suspecting that in this they have acted illegally."

The rest of the document merely points out that Canada's military force and stations were so small that they have never attracted any known espionage work by other nations and that Canada itself has never felt it necessary to set up a counter-espionage organization. In fact, it said that any work that had to be done in this regard would be done by the

R.C.M.P., as it would fall more into the category of police work than espionage work.

What the two documents mean, I can't really say. What I mean is, at the time how important were they regarded or was it just a form of bureaucratic playing of games?

But one thing is certain. The reports don't refer to the Chinese as any threat or the East Indians or any other group. It refers specifically to the Japanese, with figures and intentions, and there was a plan in mind although each line and figure had not been drawn out. What the documents do show is that the plan for the evacuation of the Japanese was not entirely the result of the blowing off of the politicians and labour unions and service clubs and other outfits and individuals, but was part of the planning of the government. The politicians and others may have forced the government's hand in relocating all of B.C.'s coastal Japanese, all of them, and not just those considered a risk or a possible risk, but there was a plan there. In a way there is nothing all that surprising, I suppose. I'm sure the U.S. had a similar plan and I'm sure the two governments would get together on these matters from time to time. After all, British Columbia was the northern flank of the U.S. and no general can afford to let his flanks be unprotected.

Anyway, there was a plan to move up to 10,000 possible troublemakers into camps under armed guard. Now, as you wouldn't expect old people and children and housewives to be engaged in terrorism and espionage, that would mean that the 10,000 possible involved would be the able-bodied men of the Japanese in British Columbia. So, it worked out almost as it was planned, except the old people and the children and the housewives went along too. Someone had to look after them and it was best, I guess, to keep them together.

Anyway, it makes interesting reading. I just wonder if the politicians and the labour leaders and the Jap-haters knew if such a plan was in existence and how it would have affected their campaign against the Japanese. The funny thing is, they seemed to have their anti-Japanese campaign won and didn't even know it.

Before the War, Suspicion

I don't think many people remember or have even heard of the Board of Review, which was set up by the federal government in 1938.

The board was set up because of the speeches and complaints of B.C. politicians in the House of Commons as well as a lot of private citizens and unions, associations and clubs, et cetera, that a great many Japanese were coming into Canada illegally, many of them through the Queen Charlotte Islands, and were moving into the fishing and logging and agriculture industries in B.C.

Well, there was some basis for this feeling in the fact that in 1931 a Japanese interpreter who worked for the Department of Immigration had been behind a scheme to provide forged papers for Japanese nationals, and he was charged and convicted on a number of charges. One was breach of trust and another was taking gifts. The report said that at least 1,500 Japanese had come into B.C. that way and in the next six years the R.C.M.P. tracked down 213 of these illegals and 161 were deported and forty-seven allowed to remain in Canada on compassionate grounds. The R.C.M.P. also estimated that about 2,300 Japanese had left Canada voluntarily on the fear they might be arrested, so it would appear that the figure of 1,500 Japanese was a low estimate. Maybe 3,000 illegals would be closer.

The board, which was chaired by Hugh L. Keenleyside of Vancouver, figured the best way to handle it would be for everyone to have his say. So, it was decided the board would travel around to cities and towns on the coast and in the Interior and everybody who had any suspicions, any facts about illegal immigrants, could tell it to the board in secrecy. The whole thing was very well publicized, of course. Stories and advertisements were put in every paper that counted.

But nothing happened. As the report said, it soon became apparent that results were going to be very meagre, if relying on information from the people of B.C. was concerned. In its report it said that many of the people who had been making the strongest claims did not appear before the board, and not one positive name turned up or one item which would lead to an arrest. Everything was based on rumour and second-hand information, all this coming from the people who had been most active in the campaign against illegal entry—which was, in effect, directed against the Japanese. Oh, they did pick up some evidence but it came from fellow nationals of the suspects or those with grudges against other persons or private citizens who happened to have some specfic information. In this phase of the inquiry the board came up with an even hundred suspects and only nineteen were Japanese. As a matter of fact, fifty-three were East Indian and the rest were Americans and Europeans. Some were deported, some allowed to stay.

So the board decided to try another tack after projecting figures that the number of Japanese illegally in Canada could not be much more than 100! It decided to make what you would call spot checks on a large number of B.C. areas which had Japanese populations.

They called it sampling Japanese communities. These were all over B.C. and the board set up what they called patrols and they would move in on a community on a given day and nobody in that community would know when or even if such a sample was to be taken. Just in, sample, and out.

In the patrols that followed, up the Fraser Valley, Vancouver Island, along the coast, in fishing, logging, and agriculture areas they checked out 1,862 Japanese and they found only eight who were in Canada illegally. One went out of the country voluntarily and the other seven were deported. The report said it was obvious that there was very little positive information behind the publicized assertions regarding the Japanese illegally in Canada. Projecting their figures further, they estimated there was about 120 Japanese in Canada illegally.

But there was still the Queen Charlotte Islands and all the publicity that Japanese were being run across Japan, put ashore on the west coast of the islands, and then they made their way to the mainland. That was a story that had been around a long time. So the police made a very careful investigation of the allegations and finally came to the conclusion that there was no evidence whatsoever to back up the stories. Actually they found that the people living on the islands believed the stories the least because, isolated as they were, every man knows everybody else's business and it would be impossible for an influx of Japanese to pass across the islands and get to the mainland without being seen by many people. As it turned out, the report said, the people who believed these stories the most lived in Vancouver and Victoria.

So much for the great myth, the influx of thousands of Japanese into B.C. to push the white man out of fishing, logging, and agriculture. But even so, despite a months-long investigation by the board, the police, and the immigration department and the throwing of cold water on the whole business of illegal entry, the stories persisted. Even in 1941 and during the war years, politicians and others were still claiming that it had happened and were using it as one of the reasons for justifying the repatriation of all Japanese Canadians back to Japan after the war.

And Then Registration

Well, they said that every Japanese or Canadian of Japanese race had to be registered. Now why didn't that tip off our leaders, or if they knew, why didn't they warn us what was going on? It was because they were gutless or just plain stupid. This was in the spring of '41. Pearl Harbor wasn't to come along for months. In December. December 7.

Why did I, and my wife, why did we have to tell the R.C.M.P. all about us, where we were born, our ages, how many children, who they were, where our farm was, what we did? All these things. Why?

Our leaders said, "Okay, go and be registered. That will show the Canadian authorities that you are loyal." What I should have said, although nobody was thinking right in those days, was that I am a Canadian and no other Canadian is being registered this way, so what is this all about? No, we just went and were registered.

I know why it was. Everybody hated us. They hated us for what our fathers had done. My father told me that in the big sockeye run of 1901, when he'd been in Canada just one year, and there were so many fish that all the fishermen in Canada couldn't catch what was running up the Fraser, even then he got bashed on the head because he was catching white man's fish. They hated my old man forty years before Pearl Harbor. Or when we'd go into Woodward's on Hasting Street there, my wife and me, and there'd be three clerks behind a counter, say at the meat counter, and finally one would come up and serve us and act real snotty as if to say, "Why don't you stay in Japtown?"

They hated us for, well, because we were good fishermen and farmers and we minded our own business and said to let us alone. A fellow came up to me one day when I was in the yard and said, "Why do you paint your house every two years?" and I said I did because I liked it neat and clean and he said, "You goddamned rotten Jap." What can you do with people like that?

So when they registered us, and they didn't register the Germans and the Italians, everybody said it doesn't matter. It is war. Well, you know why they registered us. Because they knew there was war coming with Japan. I'll bet King and Roosevelt knew that. And they wanted to know were we all were and who we were and what we were doing. Then they could jump in with both feet and grab us—and that's just what they did.

You went and you had to produce your Canadian birth certificate or, like my father, his naturalizaiton papers, and they took your picture, your fingerprint, and gave you a serial number. From then on, as it turned out, in relocation, when they dealt with you it was always your name and then your serial number. You were a number to them. They gave you a card and if you didn't carry it, even all the kids under sixteen who were registered by their parents, there could be a fine. I don't know if there ever was. The card was yellow. That must have been old King's joke, eh? Yellow Peril, yellow registration. But pink if you were born in Canada. Just yellow if you were not naturalized. But a joke just the same.

And any time one wanted, a cop could stop you and ask for your registration. I was picked up speeding on my motorcycle once at Hastings and Commercial, and the cop wanted my identification. I gave him my licence and he wanted my registration. I wanted to know why and he told me to button my lip. If I hadn't had that registration I might have been in real trouble and if I had no registration—and I mean none at all—I could have been in the hoosegow.

Why didn't people protest? Because, damn it all, at the time it didn't seem like much. But if you asked yourself, why didn't the Germans get the same business, why didn't the Italians? Why just us? What have we done? Was there one damn thing we did that would make them think we were going to blow up their damned bridges? No, not one thing, and all the investigations they ever had before and since proved that. There was not one thing of sabotage or going to the enemy by one Japanese Canadian or non-Canadian Japanese before that war or during that war. They turned the hose on some stupid guards down at the Immigration Hall once, but that was all. A few yelling sessions at the road camps up in the Rockies because of poor food. Hell, I've had guys who were in the army tell me they had real riots over little things. Half the guys would be in jail.

No, there never was anything about the Japanese that would make them feel we were a menace. Just Reid from New Westminster and that other Member of Parliament from the island, those two yelling off. Boy, they must have laughed their fool heads off.

The only time I can remember anybody protesting was when the Japanese Canadian Citizens' League, the JCCL, sent a telegram to Ottawa, to King, saying registration was discrimination. I'll bet the old bastard never even saw it. Somebody else answered it. Anyway, nothing happened about it. By protest, I mean a big rally on Powell Street or in front of the city hall and people protesting. We had newspapers then. Three of them. I don't remember any of them yelling hard enough. Not so I was hearing anyway.

No, everything was kind of mixed up in those days and when our leaders told us to go get our registration cards we went. Mommas and daddies, the old ones, everybody.

Now I ask you, like you take today, if you were Mexican and all of a sudden the government said every Mexican has to be photographed and fingerprinted and given a serial number, wouldn't you think something was very wrong? Damned right you would. You'd call it discrimination and everybody, the NDP, the churches, the universities, everybody, would be yelling for Trudeau's scalp. But just a lot of those dirty Japs. Huh! Nobody cared. Not even us, far as I could see.

2 *War!*

The bombing of Pearl Harbor on December 7, 1941, was an act that tore apart the lives of 22,000 Japanese Canadians—an act by a government and a country that many of them knew very little about despite the fact that several thousand had been born there many years before or had visited or had heard about from their parents or in the Japanese-language schools they attended after regular school.

Wherever I went, I heard people describe their reactions that day: "I was stunned", or "I couldn't believe it, it couldn't be happening." "We knew something terrible was going to happen to us."

Shock, pure unmitigated shock would be the best description. And yet why? Were the Japanese on the West Coast of B.C. that politically naïve? Yes. Apparently the great majority were. Despite what they read in the newspapers, they did not grasp the situation.

Nor did the Japanese Canadians really visualize what was in store for them. From what I can determine, many thought it would be a short war. Who would win was another matter.

But all of them, from December 7 onward, were in the hands of the government. A government with partial plans, plans written dimly, plans that had to be inked in. By faceless men.

Within Two Hours—Action

Don't think the authorities weren't waiting for us when Pearl Harbor came. Don't ever think that. They were.

This is the way it was when bango! Pearl Harbor came. It was impossible to believe but there it was. War! Japan was loose in the Pacific.

And within two hours things began to happen. Two hours. I was secretary, English-language secretary, of what we called the Upriver Fraser Japanese Fisherman's Association—that would be from Deas Slough all the way upriver—and so I got a call from navy headquarters in Vancouver to report to their headquarters at nine o'clock Monday morning. Here it was two hours after the Japanese bombed Pearl Harbor and I already was connected into the whole situation.

When I got there next morning the commander was very frank. He said, "Mr. Suzuki, we were caught with our pants down." Those were the exact words. He said, "This is what we intend to do," and he said that all fishing vessels on the river and coast would have to be turned over to the authorities, right then. He said, "We expect your full cooperation." That was it.

To this day I don't know what they thought about these fishing boats. They were our living. They were small boats, made of wood. We had no radar, no radio, no echo sounder. No anything. Just tiny vessels with their chuggy little motors and space for the fish we caught.

I'll tell you how dumb it was. We were accused of having a sounding line. You know what that was—a rope marked out in fathoms so we would know where we were in the river, where the shoals, the bars were. Dammit all, we had to have a sounding line! That's the dangerous equipment· they said we had. A long piece of rope with markers in it so we'd know the depth of the water, where it was dangerous.

And they said that we were charting the coast and waterways. All these boats out with their sounding lines charting the coast. Why, we could go into Vancouver any time and buy British

Admiralty charts of every single mile of the coast. The best charts that could be made. And we could buy them for 50 cents a piece. We all had them. Hell, we had to have them. Sure.

But try and convince these people that we were not spies, we were not spying. That we were not making charts. That we were just ordinary fishing. But oh no, no way.

As far back as the late 1890's they had determined that one day they would kick the damn Japs off the river. And all through that period right up to the war there was one common statement you could hear along the river and that was: "There's only one damn good Jap and that's a dead Jap."

We knew this. We heard this. No newspapers to back us up, that we were just fishermen, just good Canadians. Nobody to go on the radio and say what we were like.

They Just Couldn't Believe It

When the Pearl Harbor business came along I know most Japanese Canadians were hurt. They just couldn't believe it. And I know some that wanted Japan to win the war. Maybe there were more than I realize. I know that. Everybody knows that. Just as there were German Canadians who wanted Germany to beat the English. You can't blame the older people. They were still tied to Japan. That was their homeland. Their ancestors. Emotionally, culturally, spiritually, even if they came to this country as Christians, as many did, spiritually they were still tied to the old ways.

I'm not saying they would take guns in defence of Japan or signal to a Japanese sub off the coast if they had fishing boats, but in their hearts of course there were some who wanted Japan to win. Or maybe I should put it this way: there were some who didn't want Japan to lose. An honourable peace. That's what you hear some of the old men talk about. Maybe they knew the war was lost before we did—say, in 1943, early 1944—but they wanted an honourable peace. Not for their sake. For Japan's sake. Maybe everybodywould have felt the same way, if they were in that position. I think maybe they would.

The Writing on the Wall

I was living in Marpole when it happened. I grew up in Marpole. I was born in Vancouver, in Marpole. I had a dry-cleaning shop. It was a hard struggle, the depression days and getting married, but I would be working away and idly thinking that I would be able to send my boy to university. You couldn't get rich, you couldn't make any money, but you could still make a living and there would be enough over for his education. Then this thing started.

I knew what it was like in Vancouver. It had been building up for years, the tensions, the agitation, and I knew what was going to happen to us after Pearl Harbor. You didn't have to be a professor to see that. So I went to the barber next door and I said to him, "Cut off my hair because if they're treating us like Japs, then I'm going to look like one," and I've been wearing my hair brush cut ever since.

First, they gathered up all the intellectuals in the Japanese community, the people that they think have connections with the intelligence operation of Japan. In fact, my father's good friend, the man who converted my father to Anglicanism, a schoolteacher in Haney, he was seized and put into the Immigration Building. A very highly educated man and his colleagues were, well, navy men who had been back and forth to Japan. This schoolteacher later went back to Japan and wrote a book and revealed that my father had offered himself up as a prisoner in place of this schoolteacher because the schoolteacher would be very much needed to help the Canadian Japanese in the days to come. He was a very intelligent man, this schoolteacher, but unfortunately people like that are suspect.

I don't know how many were picked up that way. Forty?

Then they started to bring in all the people from the outlying islands, places, and their boats were all tied up at Annasis Island and then there were fools writing in the newspapers about the Japs being financed by the Japanese government to own good cars which could be used by the Japanese troops if they landed on our coast. Anyway, with all these things I saw the handwriting on the wall. I sold my car because I knew they were going to confiscate all our cars. I got a little for it, but I got cash.

Watching the pages of the newspapers you could practically tell what was coming. The Vancouver *Sun* was against us. Oh yes. Some of our people refused to buy the paper, but you had to buy it to see what they were saying about us.

When I was in Marpole I had my own house. It was a frame house. In those days they were all built by ourselves. My father bought it for me. There were six boys and my father wanted property all round him so we could all stay close together. Then I bought the house from my father.

They seized the house but not the dry-cleaning shop on Hudson Street. They took everything I had. I've still got a receipt around here somewhere for that. I got 700 dollars for the house. At that time it was worth 2,000 dollars. My wife was still home when I was away and she sold the dry-cleaning shop on Hudson Street to an Edmonton couple for 150 dollars, the machines, cabinets, and everything. That's the only price she could get. What can you do? That's not the value of it. That's what they offered. The whole thing. So I figure my wife did pretty good.

Of course, I didn't say about the furniture. That was just left in the house. We didn't get anything for that. That was just left.

But the important things I had, my father put into a shed behind his house and locked up. Like Festival Dolls. March 3 for the girls and May 5 for the boys. Old, old Japanese customs and very important to us, used during our festivals. So you see, white people that broke into the Japanese houses and sheds they don't realize the value of those things to us and they just robbed us, gave the stuff away.

I asked my father years later, I asked was he bitter. He said, "No, property and money you can get again. I didn't lose any of my sons. In a war you lose sons. I didn't." He was a man of property, an official, and he could have been bitter but he wasn't.

A Japanese Godfather?

Well. Let's talk about the first step after Pearl Harbor.

The night of Pearl Harbor. There were a group of businessmen from Vancouver and the Lower Mainland, they were all suddenly scooped up by the police, the middle of the night, early in the morning, and taken to the police station. All these prominent Japanese. About forty-five, I think.

Nobody knew what happened to them for about three weeks or so, not their families or anybody, and suddenly they found they were being held in the Immigration Building. Later they were sent to Alberta, to a POW camp, and they were held there. Later on they were transferred to Petawawa and then to Angler, which is in northern Ontario.

Japanese businessmen? Yes, but not exactly community leaders. The funny part of it is that. The R.C.M.P. had close connections with certain elements within the Japanese community, but they took most of their advice from this one man and on his advice they more or less picked up people at random. These people who were arrested seemed to have no connection with anything like subversion or anything at all like that. That is what the Japanese community thought.

I myself have a strong suspicion that this one man whom the

R.C.M.P. listened to so much was putting the finger on people, Japanese, who were in opposition to him alone. He was a powerful man in the community and this was a way of getting ahead of his enemies or people who were in opposition to his ideas. It has happened before in other situations and this is what we think.

Another thing, this man was the head of a group who wanted to go along with everything the government and the authorities wanted to do to us. Just do what they say, do what the police say, jump and jump high when they tell you to jump. And if people protested he would come out and say, "Well, I'm telling you, do what you're told or else!"

He was in with the police. The police used him and he used the police. A lot of men spent years in prisoner-of-war camp because they displeased him. These men were not subversive.

He was an enforcer . . . well, it would be too strong to call him a Mafia, but he had Mafia strength, the Godfather strength with the Japanese community. In this area.

This is what happens when you do not have full rights of citizenship. Someone assumes leadership and this man did have quite an influence. And he was a bad man.

"They've Gone and Done It"

You ask, what were my thoughts on Pearl Harbor Day and did I suspect it was coming? I didn't suspect it. I've often thought of the clear prophetic insight that Professor Angus of the University of British Columbia had had in August of 1940 in a lecture to the Vancouver Institute when he said that Japan's entry to the war was certain and would probably take the form of a surprise attack on Pearl Harbor or some other American installation. Guam or someplace like that. He said the only thing that surprised him was it hadn't happened already.

But on that day . . . I was sitting in my office trying to write
the editorial for the newspaper and a very good friend of mine
who worked with me through a long period—his name was
Shimuzi and he had a room on Powell Street—he just came in
the door and said, "Did you hear the news? The Japanese have
bombed Pearl Harbor." I said, "Oh my God, so they've gone and
done it."

And what did I think then? Obviously, what do we do now? I
guess a little later we found the R.C.M.P. had visited all the
Japanese newspapers and shut them down, but we got no visit. I
did not receive any kind of a show visit from the R.C.M.P., but
when I got home the R.C.M.P. sergeant came around with his
Japanese-speaking assistant and told me a certain number of
people had been arrested as of that date and that we would be
allowed to publish.

Yes, I would say they had a contingency plan, that if Japan
enters the war this is what we will do. They knew, I'm sure, that
Japanese entry into the war was largely a matter of time and
planning and it would probably be directed against the
Americans. So . . .

There was great mystification then on how they decided who
they would arrest. Even to this day there is great mystification. I
knew some of these men who were arrested right after Pearl
Harbor. They had no subversive activities that I knew of.
Indeed, there were a couple who had been rather staunch
supporters of *The New Canadian* newspaper and what it stood
for, financially and morally. We were just astonished that they
had been picked out, when there were a great many others
about whom I would have had sufficient reason to be worried
and apprehensive that I would have plucked up. It was that
which gave rise to this great suspicion and great division in the
community about the liaison between Mr. Morii and the
R.C.M.P.

I never ran into anything—and I say this as complete
honesty—that suggested any kind of—that would give rise to or
give concern about any kind of subversive action. Never at any
time. There was no doubt there was a good deal of sympathy for

Japan and that was sympathy that went back, you know, right to the Manchurian adventure, sympathy and a feeling that if any country needed Lebensraum Japan was one. In this case I think one could have made a political case, a political rationalization, during the '30's when the main instrument of economic policy was to raise the tariff and shut out everything. How does a nation like Japan survive under those circumstances?

There was actual sympathy and once in a while there were campaigns to raise money to send to the injured, wounded soldiers in China before Pearl Harbor, but I never ran into any evidence of subversive activity in Canada.

"They Wouldn't Give Me My Money"

Pearl Harbor was on a Sunday. I knew what was going to happen to the Japanese in British Columbia, so Monday morning I went right down to the bank and withdrew my money. Even then, next day, they wouldn't let me draw it out. Bank of Montreal. Right after Pearl Harbor, you see. They hadn't been given any order that I know of to stop the payments, but because I was Japanese they wouldn't give me my money.

My brother-in-law worked for the Bank of Montreal at another branch. I didn't put my money in his branch because I didn't want him to know what little money I got in the bank, so I told them to phone my brother-in-law. These bank people all know each other. I said I needed the money for business. He gave them satisfaction, I guess, because then they let me withdraw my money. I took it out. About 800 dollars. That's not too bad for the depression years.

And then I went and cancelled out all my insurance policies. All my children's too. You know, we paid by the week in those days. Prudential of America. You know what they did? By God, they made out the papers and let me think that they were going to give me the money in a lump sum of cash surrender and then you know what they did? They gave it to the B.C. Security Commission and that money was doled out. Oh boy, they were dirty, that Prudential of America. That was my money, cash surrender on the policies. At least they could have told me they were going to have to turn it over to the commission.

The News Was Such a Blow

I still remember the time we heard the news, that it was such a blow to everybody and oh, we were stunned when the news came over and a neighbour came in and nobody could say anything . . . I don't know, I just can't describe it and I know that I felt that I could never go outside, outdoors again. I don't know . . . I just can't explain . . .

There was two families beside us. We were living on Cordova at that time. The neighbour on one side had just bought this house, just a few months, and they were remodelling it and the father was a friend of my father, and I still remember that he refused to believe that he had to leave Vancouver. He said, "Oh, no, they wouldn't do that to us," and kept on fixing his home until the day before he had to leave. Finally I guess he realized he would have to go and he left everything and his family went to one of the Interior ghost towns.

And the family on the other side, they went to a ghost town, too, and they had quite a few heirlooms that they had brought with them from Japan and they had been in the family for a long, long time, for generations. We understood that we were able to come back to our own places after the war, and so he thought he would be coming back to his own home and I remember him telling us he had put them away somewhere, a place in his home, where they would be safe while he was gone . . .

No, we did not get any compensation. Any money, no. Not a cent. My father was fishing at that time. Up at Skeena. He came back at the end of October and this Pearl Harbor thing happened in December, so he had just been back one month and he lost his fishing equipment and his boat and everything. He always left it up at the cannery in the winter and went back in the spring, and he had just repainted his ship and he had had the engine overhauled and my daughter was only a year old at the time so he said he named his ship, his boat, *Nancy*, for her. And he was so happy. They just took it and he never got anything for it. I don't know what happened.

Just Made-up Stories

I don't know. I am just a dumb fisherman. After Pearl Harbor I think there are people they want Japanese boats. I don't know. They say Japanese on west coast of Vancouver Island they have a big mine there, an old mine, all hollowed out, that's where they said the Japanese fishermen store oil for the Japanese submarines.

People just want to make trouble for us. They make up stories. I fish out of Ucluelet. I don't know anything about this. I hear nothing. To me it is just a made-up stories people make up who want to cause trouble.

Before the war I . . . we hear these stories. Finnish people, Norwegians, Indians, they talk about them. They ask us. I say I don't know. People just make up these stories. They say Japanese got these places on Vancouver Island to hide things. I don't know that. Me, I just fish. I don't listen to these stories.

Why do people say things, like lots of Japanese fishermen are Japanese officers and all that kind of thing? I know all Japanese on coast. None of them are navy officers. They are just fishermen working awfully hard on the salmon. So that's the way it is, you know. A lot of prejudice that way.

The government knew we didn't have any kind of plan like that. We just fished quietly, talked among ourselves, came home to our families. We didn't have anything to do like that.

When war starts, government makes big investigation, a big hunt. They don't find anything. Nothing. Nothing at all. People just make up stories like that to get Japanese fishermen in trouble. Politics. Politics and big shots want our boats, our licences. They want to take living away from us. Why would people make up stories like that? I just don't know. Just don't know.

You Could See Trouble Coming

Even when I was young you could see that something was going to come to blows. Hatred in the Pacific. It was coming. The Japanese in Canada could see it. We could feel it.

And the funny part of it, in the first World War Japan was an ally with Britain and the United States and in those twenty years since you could just see it building up the point where they were going to be enemies. In a very small way in Vancouver. In a very large way in the headlines.

And so in a way Pearl Harbor was a shock and in a way it wasn't. If Japan had just declared war without Pearl Harbor nobody would have been surprised, but I guess Japan had to think of getting in that first blow. First punch. That was good military thinking. Nobody disputes that. It was a stroke of genius. But I think Japan knew herself that unless she got that first blow in she didn't have a dog's chance.

Like my father, to tell you the truth, he felt that if Japan at the

Manzo Nagano and his family. He was the first Japanese known to arrive and settle in Canada, in 1877. (*Japanese Canadian Cultural Centre*)

British Columbia attracted many Japanese immigrants as the years went by. (*JCCC*)

The Shinto Shrine in North Vancouver (above) and the Tea Garden in Victoria (below) were part of the culture that the Japanese brought to their new country. *(JCCC)*

Sumo, part of their heritage (above), and baseball, a Western sport. *(JCCC)*

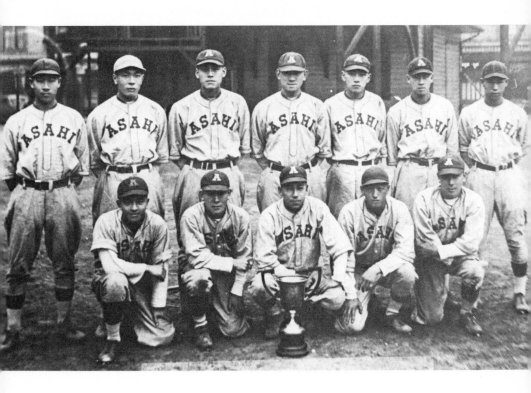

The Japanese Language School on Alexander was one of many that Japanese students attended after regular school. (*JCCC*)

Powell Street, Vancouver, in the late '30s, where some 7000 Japanese shopped, carried on the businesses, and socialized. (*JCCC*)

Dramatic view of the scores of Japanese fishboats that were turned over to
the authorities as soon as war with Japan was declared.
(Public Archives of Canada)

Hundreds of Japanese-owned cars, vans, and trucks were confiscated and
held at the Hastings Park race track for sale after Japan's attack on Pearl
Harbor in December, 1941. *(Vancouver Public Library)*

What does a man do, where does he go,
when he loses his home, his livelihood?
(Public Archives of Canada)

Steveston, a big fishing community near Vancouver, became a ghost town
when the Japanese were ordered to leave the 100-mile Protected Zone on the
coast. *(Vancouver Public Library)*

The Japanese were allowed to take with them only what they could carry when they were ordered out of their homes. Here in the B.C. Security Commission Clearing Station, Vancouver, their baggage was being held. *(Public Archives of Canada)*

Thousands of Japanese passed through these huge dormitories at the Exhibition Buildings in Hastings Park on their way to road camps, ghost towns, and internment camps in the B.C. Interior. *(Vancouver Public Library)*

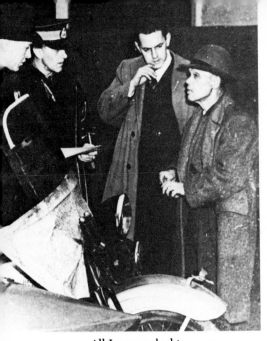

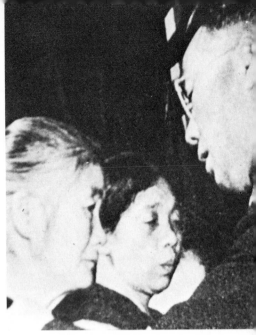

All Japanese had to carry identification cards in case they were stopped and interrogated. *(Vancouver Public Library)*

A sad and bewildered farewell as a man leaves for a work camp. *(UBC Special Collection)*

Dressed in their Sunday best, men wave to families and friends as a train pulls out of Vancouver en route to road camps in the Interior. *(Vancouver Public Library)*

start couldn't finish it off in six months she had no chance at all. He used to tell me that over and over again.

My father at least knew that much. But he kept saying one other thing after Pearl Harbor and I'm starting to believe today, that even if Japan lost the war and knew she was going to lose the war, starting the war was the thing she had to do. Even though she knew she was going to lose.

He could see the hatred building up everywhere and that the boil, the war, had to come and it had to be drained. The pus had to be drained. The pus was the hatred. It had to be gotten rid of.

He thought that and so Japan started the war, got knocked about, picked up the pieces, and started all over again with a new relationship and it has worked out that way. I think my father was a wise man.

Rumours Were Everywhere

When Pearl Harbor came along I was really surprised and I think in those days I was pretty well the average fellow in Vancouver. Too old for the army, which I wouldn't have gone in anyway. The navy or nothing. Too many kids too. But then all this stuff came out in the papers. Not at first. Not the first few weeks or so but gradually it got more and more, and finally I guess you could say the whole goldarn roof fell in on those people.

I used to say to my wife that the Japanese families we'd see walking around Stanley Park on a Sunday afternoon, mother, father, four or five kids, these people couldn't be traitors. I knew enough to know that most of them had been born in Canada. But then at work you'd hear stories. Somebody had told somebody who had told somebody that up the coast the Japs had houses and in the upstairs window the police had found this lighting arrangement. Two lights on top of one below and when you pushed a switch you could send out signals and these signals were to be picked up by the Japanese Navy or saboteurs. Now did you ever hear such rot? I mean, you can tell me some things I will believe, but I'm not going to believe such rot. But people did believe these things. That was the point. I guess anybody could start a rumour in those days. That a bunch of fishermen were actually officers in the Japanese Navy. That submarines were landing off the Queen Charlotte Islands and putting men ashore. I mean, come on, we're grown-up adults and yet these stories were going around. And people were telling them and passing them on, not stopping them dead in their tracks, which they should have done. I'll say this though. As I remember, none of these stories showed up in the newspapers. I guess the editors had more sense, but you could hear a new one every day down at the shipyards. Boats coming in from everywhere to get repairs, new equipment. Things were picking up. And every boat brought a rumour. I must say this, that I never passed on one of these stories even when we were having a few glasses of beer on pay night.

I can say this, too, that I never had anything against the Japanese. From what I knew of them I thought them to be fine people, hard working and probably low paid. Ha! Just like the rest of us. But probably paid even lower. When they did to them what they did to them, taking them away and all that, I was sorry. I thought it was wrong.

A Souvenir of Those Days

Because I had worked with the authorities before the war and the Japanese people trusted me, I was given liaison work with the people in Vancouver from the time of Pearl Harbor until the last had been moved out of the Protected Area. That would be until about early October of 1942.

One of the first things the army did was slap on a curfew for all Japanese. It worked for Greater Vancouver and you had to be in your house by dusk and not out before dawn. Dawn to dusk. That was a hardship on a lot of people because it meant stores had to be shut down, restaurants, baths, everything, no late ball games, no sports. It meant no visiting, or put it another way, it meant no social life at night. The Japanese are sociable people, as you must know, and this was a real hardship on them, believe me.

But I could go around. I worked out of a store right across from the police station. I'd taken over a Japanese newspaper office. They closed down the three Japanese-language newspapers when Pearl Harbor came and I worked out of there. They gave me a curfew pass and every once in a while they'd stop you, the police, the military police, as they were making the rounds at night. If they saw you in a taxi they'd stop it and check you—even though they knew me.

That was when the Chinese all around there had badges made that said I AM CHINESE—because some people have trouble telling us apart. Chinese stores also had cards in the windows saying it was a Chinese store. The cards usually had a light hanging over them so you could see them good.

Some people would break the curfew. One fellow got six months for being out during curfew and it was in the paper; Magistrate Mackenzie said he was giving him a jail sentence to teach others a lesson. But later on they picked up a bunch, about twelve or so in Little Tokyo. I think it had something to do with a gambling game and they came up in court and the magistrate just scolded them. I don't think he even fined them.

I've still got my curfew permit. I keep it as a souvenir. When I came back after the war and when I moved onto this place the Mounties came around one day and said they want the pass back. I don't know why. They just wanted it back. I said I didn't have it, lost it or something and now I've got it for a souvenir of those bleak days for us people.

The Little White Spies

One day our teacher dismissed the Japanese kids in our class, told them to go out for recess early, and then when there were just the white and English kids left she told us that Japan was at war with Canada and that a lot of Canadian soldiers were prisoners of the Japanese. She said that it was well known and everybody knew that when the Japanese soldiers attacked, the Japanese people in the town or country would come out and help them. I think we'd heard about this before. Everybody was talking about the Japanese then.

She said that if we were going to do a job for Canada we should keep a close watch on Japanese that we knew. Of course she meant the Japs in our class, the kids she'd dismissed for recess. Age? Oh, I guess we were about thirteen or so. Just about the right age for this kind of stuff. If I'm not wrong I think there even was a comic book around which showed how you could spy on Germans, although in this case the Germans would be spies themselves.

This teacher shoved us these wild ideas and I remember I had two or three friends who were Japanese. One was Midori but we called her Mildred. She was crazy for music, Benny Goodman, Artie Shaw, "One O'Clock Jump," always jitterbugging, even by herself, and she had stacks of records. She had a sister Kiyoka and everybody called her Cheerio-o. Well, I'd go to their house on Saturday and I remember looking around and picking up this book and that book and when they weren't looking I'd look in closets and all this sort of thing. That next day I'd write up a report for this teacher on what I'd seen at Mildred's house and what her father had said to me, but it was all dumb stuff.

Other kids did this too. I think the Japanese kids knew what we were doing or that something was up. After all, they weren't so dumb. In fact they were usually the smartest kids at school, science, maths, literature. I never found out anything on Mildred's parents. No, I can't think of the last name. It was something like Saito or Sasaki. Began with an S anyway. But I guess I always thought I'd find a Japanese war sword or a machine gun in the cupboard. It was dumb stuff, as we know now, but think of the impression it had on kids in those days. The blackouts, the soldiers in the streets and those guns by the park. Posters showing ugly, grinning little men. Japs. Why, Mildred's brother Arnold was a tall big guy and the best-looking boy in the whole school, the best athlete and the best everything. All the girls were crazy about them. About him, I mean.

Anyway, it all came to nothing. School ended and some of the families were shipped out of Kitsilano to the camps. One day they were there and then they were gone and the house would be empty and there would be some guy putting up a TO LET sign on the house. We'd sneak around after he'd gone and blacken in an I between the TO and the LET and it would come out as TOILET. Big stuff.

But there we were. Sneaking around their houses and looking in their basements—bombs, guns, Japanese flags, anything we could find. No, I don't think anything about it. Not one way or another. We were just kids. Kids act that way. Anything big gets them all stirred up. What I do think was silly was the government letting this silly business go on, letting people think that every Japanese gardener was a Japanese general or was trained to blow up the Burrard Street Bridge. I don't think that was the way it was at all. Not at all. Mildred and Cheerio-o and Arnold and their parents were just ordinary people. Japanese but ordinary people.

Those Hysterical Days

The hysteria! You had to live like we did to understand it. It was several things. They all came together at one time. December, 1941.

First it was because of the radio and the newspaper. They just heard of Pearl Harbor and the rumours they heard, like the Japanese fleet was 150 miles off San Francisco and heading north and all the talk. Anybody could start a rumour in Vancouver and it would be on the radio, it would be in the newspapers. People didn't think. Oh, thousands and thousands did think, but so many more didn't. Right off the bat, invasion. You know. That sort of stuff.

And then there was one thing not many people nowadays think about, I think. That was the weather itself. You know, first there was the blackouts and that made everybody conscious, vividly conscious, that there was a state of war. It was a bad winter. Murky. Fog. Mean, dull, black out there and there were lots of people who thought the Japanese Imperial Navy could steam up the Strait of Juan de Fuca and into the Strait of Georgia and then English Bay, and the weather, well, it would protect them. It was as if the weather itself was on the side of the enemy. Right, right.

But it was also something that had built up over the years too, this feeling of Japan in the Pacific and her strength. Japan didn't help the situation in Canada at all by claiming her navy was stronger than the naval strength of United States and Britain combined and her air force was superior or as good as anything the United States had. And her rape of Manchuria and the hate she had brought about by her actions, every bit of it seemed to come drifting across the Pacific and stick to us, the Japanese.

The Canadians just couldn't seem to differentiate at that time between those of us who were born here and the Japanese over there who were doing these things.

So it was several things. There was the hate in the newspapers and the radio. Anything for a good story about the Japanese menace and we were here to get both barrels of it. Then the winter, the weather, the gloom and the murk, as if everything was going wrong, and there was a terrible enemy lurking out there in the dark—and then with it all was what Japanese admirals and generals and politicians were doing, boasting of Japan's military might and everybody knew that the Pacific coast was without any protection, just a few small guns. Nothing to save the coast at all and I guess it was pretty terrifying at that.

It was pretty terrifying for us too.

Hush Money was Futile

When Pearl Harbor came and we lost our boats I remember that Japanese all over the coast were having meetings. This was at the beginning of the whole thing.

We still had our nets and gear in our net lofts, so a lot of Japanese fishermen thought that it was just a temporary thing and when it was straightened out they'd get the boats back and we'd be fishing by spring. After all, they still had their nets.

The stupid nuts, that is among the top executives of the Japanese Benevolent Association, they had hired some whites to go and represent them in Ottawa, to speak on their behalf and all this, and they were collecting money to send this man or that man to Ottawa because there was some hush money needed from time to time. Those white politicians and lawyers really shook down the Japanese community at a time when we didn't have much money, but these men told the elders that this money was needed to be given out in Ottawa and soon we'd get our boats back.

I protested this. I knew it was wrong. After years of agitation against us, taking away our licences, making life miserable and then the war, who was going to think a bit of hush money in Ottawa was going to make everything different? This war was going to get worse, things were going to get worse, and I told the young people of the community that this was wrong and that they must protest giving this money to the white men.

I remember one meeting of the fishermen in Steveston and somebody got up and said that so-and-so said we'd be getting our boats back soon and be out fishing. I stood up—I was speaking in a northern Japanese accent to a predominantly southern group—and I yelled at them, "You're not going to go back fishing anymore. This is the end of the line for us." They wouldn't listen to me.

I said, "If you have any nets and gear, sell it now. Sell it to the Americans who are coming up here from Bellingham to buy. Get what you can for it, when you can."

One old guy got up and said to me: "Listen here, you punk. You still got eggshell stuck to your posterior. What the hell do you know about anything?"

But you couldn't get mad at the guy. He was so completely out of touch with Canadian society that he had absolute faith in those that represented districts where the Japanese lived, these politicians that were shaking us down, when anybody with a grain of sense could see that we were finished.

He couldn't even learn from history, like in the years before Pearl Harbor during elections the campaign managers used to go to the Japanese settlements and demand money, saying their candidate when he got elected would see to it that things were made less harsh for the Japanese. Not that these bad things would be eliminated, just that the federal or provincial government would be less harsh on us. They'd cut your throat but they won't cut it as deeply if you give them money.

You'd think these old guys on the association would have learned from that.

So my work all came to nothing. I couldn't make them believe that they were just being shaken down for nothing. Japanese social structure is such that a junior voice doesn't have anywhere the prestige of a senior voice. Age is equated with wisdom.

We Didn't Stick Together

When the war did come and we knew, or we figured we knew, what was in store for us, we decided we'd have to fight. Not fight in the physical sense but fight for our rights. After all, a lot of us and especially all the children and young people were born in Canada and a lot were naturalized. I think of 23,000 Japanese-origin people in British Columbia, more than 60 percent were Canadian citizens. Born in Canada.

We didn't know about deportation yet. Expulsion. These were things we feared, things we'd talked about, things we'd heard mentioned. There were politicians who were saying, "Kick out the Japs; kick them back to Japan." We worried about these kinds of men but we thought mostly they were just trying for votes. And so they were.

We decided we had to make some protest and organize. Now we did have organizations, the Japanese Canadian Citizens' League and the association of the younger people, and we decided we'd have to continue as a corps and expand and be better organized and stick together. The wise old men, the advisors, came in with us and a lot of the others who had been born in Japan, the elders, and we decided that we'd have to stick together. That's the only way we could survive.

But like all incidents that happen we differed in what would be the best approach to the whole situation that was facing us, and I am sorry to say our community split three ways.

One group went along with the authorities completely, holus bolus, no questions asked.

Another one was our group. We wanted to go and sit down and talk with the authorities and make it easy as possible for us. Like if movement was inevitable we would go along with them, but please make it as easy as possible. Help us keep what we have because at that time, early in the war, we all thought we would be able to hang onto our property and everything. We wanted them to protect our property. We wanted them to look after our elderly people, the sick, and everybody else and the children and to do everything in an orderly manner. But they felt the war was so urgent that they wouldn't listen.

Then, the third! They said they wouldn't bloody well move until the authorities comply with what they wanted. If you're going to move, they'd have to move them as a family—or else!

And it split three ways.

The second one was the best. That's the one I belonged to. But everything was in a turmoil, there was so much panic, everybody was running around, that the authorities couldn't see it. They said the laws were going to be made and we'd have to obey them, right away, now! Well, that's what we planned, wanted to do, but in an orderly manner. Not seizing everything, breaking up families and shooting them off here and there and causing so much emotional hardship that some have never recovered from it. Not even today.

But I'm sorry to say, we couldn't agree among ourselves. When the great and important decision was to be made, we just couldn't decide. I guess we still couldn't understand whatever went on in a white man's mind.

3 *Where the Horses Were, That's Where They Put Us*

First it was decided that males, nationals, between eighteen and forty-five, those who could give aid and direction to any Japanese invasion, would be shipped out to the mountains or the wilds of northern Ontario to build roads. Then, by order-in-council, virtually every person of Japanese origin was ordered out of a 100-mile Protective Zone from the West Coast and the islands. It was not an original idea. Anti-Japanese elements in the community had advocated some sort of measure for years.

The wiser and more sophisticated began to liquidate, to sell, to cash in. About a thousand were given the opportunity to move to nonstrategic areas in B.C., on their own, as self-supporting families. As the weeks went by, others sold their homes, businesses, bulky possossions, for what they could get. But thousands just sat and waited for the knife. And it fell. People were scooped up, in one day, two, three days, and shipped to Vancouver and that peculiar form of captivity that about 20,000 of them underwent. First they were herded into Hastings Park, the exhibition grounds with large buildings in the eastern end of the city, where they were segregated, men from families, and guarded by troops.

It was "terrible." It was "unbelievable." One woman said, "They kept us in the stalls where they put the cattle and horses." One man said laconically, "It wasn't the Hotel Vancouver but it was okay. Good poker games every night." Another person, a child at the time, said, "The store always seemed to run out of

Orange Crush." So it all depended. It was, essentially, a holding pen. For people.

To carry out the plethora of orders dealing with 22,000 people in a situation absolutely unique to the Canadian experience, the federal government set up the B.C. Security Commission, headed by a Vancouver financier named Austin C. Taylor. He and his two sub-commissionners and an advisory board had absolute authority over all Japanese. The commission did what was necessary to provide housing, transportation, medical care, and employment. After studying its "constitution" and its methods and results, I would have to say that it probably worked considerably better than most people expected. But to put it mildly, it flew by the seat of its pants. The success of the huge project probably rests with the dedicated people recruited and with the cooperation of the Japanese evacuees.

So, while administrators turned 22,000 people into numbers on pieces of paper, the Japanese sat in Hastings Park and waited to be shipped out, living from day to day because any future they might have had had disappeared.

A Strange Argument

One argument I heard which I find very doubtful was that the reason the Nisei, the second generation, born in Canada who considered themselves Canadian, and were in fact, in word and deed Canadians, were sent away from the coast was for their own protection.

Supposing a Japanese army had landed on the coast and the Nisei, being Canadian citizens, had refused to help the Japanese invaders, then they would have been considered traitors to Japan and would have been shot. So they were sent away. For their own protection.

In wartime you get many strange stories. I think this is one of them.

The Tables Were Still Set

We were training in infantry tactics out of our base, camp at Nanaimo and one day they took us in trucks further north for a scheme in house-clearing tactics. Well, by George, this was a Japanese fishing village where they took us, not much of a place but a bunch of houses on the water and not a bad little place at all.

Here we were, a bunch of army guys, and doing this house clearing exercise and do you know, in those houses the tables were still set and there was rice in the bowls at the table and vegetables on dishes right there. All mouldering, of course, but you could see what it had been. It was an army location now, so nobody could get in—no civilians is what I mean—and here were these Japanese houses filled with furniture, kitchen, dishes, pots, pans, beds, dining room tables, and the whole business and none of it touched.

You know, I've often thought that those people must have been moved out of there in an awful hurry to get up from their meal and leave it untouched. They must have told them to get out in an hour or so. I was just a kid at the time and too dumb to ask an officer what had happened, and to this day I still don't know. In fact, I can't tell you exactly where it was. Just north of Nanaimo there. But it was a funny feeling going into somebody's house and seeing food on the table, just left there.

The War Measures Act

Before you get far into this, you've got to understand how it all came about, how they were able to do this to the Japanese and treat them so and do it with clear consciences. It was all done under the War Measures Act, which I think was first passed in

1914. So you could be a man from the moon and not know what a Japanese looked like, not have any prejudice against him and working with the B.C. Security Commission, which was set up under the War Measures Act, and you could do anything and know—not only know but feel that you were doing your duty.

It would be no more different than evicting a poverty-stricken widow with her six kids out into the street on a winter's night. You had the law behind you and you were doing your duty. That's why these administrators could do what they did. As you will see, it was all laid out for them.

Let me read you part two of the act, which says: "The issue of a proclamation, or under the authority of the Governor in Council shall be conclusive evidence that war, invasion or insurrection, real or apprehended, exists and has existed for any period of time therein stated, and of its continuance, until by the issue of a further proclamation it is declared that the war, invasion or insurrection no longer exists."

Well, there it is. The phrase "conclusive evidence" and the other wording "real or apprehended" and the government has all it needs.

The next paragraph reads, and listen to this carefully: "The Governor in Council may do and authorize such acts and things and make from time to time such orders and regulations, as he may by reason of the existence of real or apprehended war, invasion or insurrection, deem necessary or advisable for the security, defence, peace, order and welfare of Canada; and for greater certainty, but not so as to restrict the generality of the foregoing terms, it is hereby declared that the powers of the Governor in Council shall extend to all matters coming within the classes of subjects hereinafter enumerated, that is to say;

"Censorship and the control and suppression of publications, writings, maps, plans, photographs, communications and means of communications;

"Arrest, detention, exclusion and deportation;

"Control of the harbours, ports and territorial waters of Canada and the movements of vessels;

Transportation by land, air or water and the control of the transport of persons and things;

"Trading, exportation, importation, production and manufacture;

"Appropriation, control, forfeiture and disposition of property and the use thereof."

That is what they had in this country in 1939. I guess most other countries have something the same, no matter what they call it. But, and the act goes on and on, just try and lift your little finger against the state and wham, they've got you. Got you good! In short, there is absolutely nothing any individual citizen can do, anybody can do. That War Measurers Act is like a vise and the more you squirm, the tighter they can put the pressure on. That is what the Japanese were faced with, what they had to live under all those years, and any lawyer or group of citizens which decided to take up the fight on behalf of the Japanese—and remember most of them were Canadian citizens—this is what they were up against.

There was another tricky bit of goods in the act and I'll read it to you: "No person who is held for deportation under this Act or under any regulation made thereunder, or is under arrest or detention as an alien enemy, or upon suspicion that he is an alien enemy, or to prevent his departure from Canada shall be released upon bail or otherwise discharged without the consent of the Minister of Justice."

Now, just apply that to the case of the Japanese and see where that put them. It put them mighty close to the jailhouse door, even though they were allowed to move about the country, as long as it wasn't in B.C. In fact, every avenue the Japanese had, or hoped they had, was blocked.

I think the ironic thing of the whole business is that this act was drawn up in 1914 when there was a great hysteria, especially on the prairies, especially Saskatchewan, about German settlers on homesteads and in the cities. But in 1941, when the Allies and Canada had been fighting Germany and Hitler for more than two years, this act was used against the Japanese—and the Germans, be they naturalized or enemy aliens, they were barely touched at all. The pertinent parts of the War Measures Act were used mainly against the Japanese, and the Japanese often wondered why the Germans and the Italians were not touched.

They could only come to the conclusion, as they had to, that it was race that counted. That it was a racial thing. But that is too simple. The whole business in the end result was economic. There were people in B.C., people in politics, in government, in business, in industry, who didn't want the Japanese in B.C. because the Japanese were successful and the war, well, what better excuse to get rid of the lot? And what better way to do it? Use the War Measures Act, which was in effect anyway.

I am not saying the War Measures Act is not a good thing. I am not saying it is a bad thing. I think it is a necessary thing if, like Canada was, you are conducting total war. But to use it as a club, and to use it as a club long after the war and especially against one group of people, about 22,000 of them, that seems to me to be going too far. Put it this way. They could have used the act to grab off the few Japanese who they thought, the police thought, the government thought, were subversive. There must have been some. Let's face it. A few, although you'll not get any Japanese to admit it today, but there must have been some. So grab them and stick them away, just as they did some Germans and Italians. But not the whole 22,000, grandmothers, grandfathers, Nisei who got it in the neck mostly, and their children. Let them stay. Fish for salmon and cod. Okay, under supervision if necessary, if that's the way they wanted it. Let them continue their farming instead of buying up all those farms and letting them go to seed. Keep their business in Vancouver. Let them stay, those that could would have been contributing to the war effort, food, fish, labour which soon got in pretty short supply, and so on. But no, the business interests, the loud-mouths in the community, those who had grudges, and others, they wanted those Japanese out and they put pressure on the government in Ottawa—and the government, the ministers, and the Cabinet who probably couldn't tell a Japanese from a Chinese from an Eskimo from a Korean bowed to that pressure, even though they had reports from their own investigators that the Japanese were no problem.

But they bowed, and they had that War Measures Act which says in its preamble: "An Act to confer certain powers upon the

Governor in Council in the event of War, Invasion or Insurrection."

Enough said.

Canadian Citizens—Enemy Aliens

That evacuation came as a shock. Oh yes, big surprise. Steveston was just, well, a fishing village. When the men were bringing in the fish, then everybody they'd come from all over to work in the canneries along the river. Hundreds of them. Mostly women. There were hundreds of boats in the river and outside and hundreds of women canning the fish. Nobody thought of anything about war. What was Japan? Somewhere across the sea. Sure, we knew we were Japanese. My father and mother were born there, but they came over here to work and make some money to go back and buy land in Japan. Then they decided Canada was a good place, so they stayed. So I was born a Canadian. I still am. Steveston, nobody was doing any harm, just working and that.

Then they told us after awhile that we were enemy aliens and we had to move 100 miles east of the coast. A Protected Zone, they called it. Well, there is nothing 100 miles east but mountains, so that meant you had to move 200, 300, 400 miles east to where you could find land to live on, to work, you know.

Remember, we were Canadian citizens.

Terrible thing to happen, but then it was an order-in-council. That means it's government decree. You got to do what government says.

Yeah, I thought it was very unfair, unjust, but still it was government saying this, so we got to comply with it. What can we do? Nobody protest, I don't think. They protest a lot among themselves, meetings, but they don't protest anywhere else. You see, it is a government thing.

Life in Hastings Park

I don't know where else they could have put us. I mean Hastings Park. I mean the land and the buildings were there and it was near downtown Vancouver and the train went right by it. Of course, they expropriated it. The B.C. Security Commission just said, "We're taking it," and they did.

This was in wartime, you understand, and by that I mean it was with Japan. With Germany it was different. Germany was thousands of miles away but the Japanese had socked Pearl Harbor and I don't think anyway that anybody knew where the Japanese fleet, like it could have been off Vancouver Island by that time, so all the Japanese, they had to go. A few raised a fuss. The people that raised a fuss later, the newspaper columnists and the United Church and some university professors, I don't remember them raising any fuss then. It was war and the government could do whatever it wanted to do, so it did, and the one big thing it did on the West Coast in that first year was get rid of the Japanese. In fact, I think that was all they did all during the war. The one thing, get rid of the Japanese. Even when they were shown to be very wrong, a year or so later, they still tried to get rid of the Japanese.

First of all, they took all the Japanese from the villages and towns along the coast, from Vancouver Island, and they brought them down to Vancouver. They just had what they could carry, clothing. In bags and suitcases. The police I don't think had real orders other than that the Japanese had to go, so they'd come in their boats or their cars at any time, family by family, and say you've got to go. Some people didn't have time for anything. Just to grab up what they needed, bedding, clothes. They didn't know what was happening. Then they were put on boats, Union Steamship, C.P.R. and brought to Vancouver.

These were the first people and it was pretty rough on them. I wasn't there but I was told. The men in one place, along with the older boys. The women and children in another building. The army and carpenters were making it a place to live in, but what can you do with cattle barns? This was March and April when it was pretty cold still, although not as cold as in October, when some people had to live in army tents at Slocan. But it wasn't nice and people had trouble with their bowels and with people not knowing what was happening to them, a lot of women were pretty upset. Some of them were women whose husbands had been sent away to the road camps and they didn't know what was happening to them.

I'll say this though. The government tried to make the best of what they had, although it wasn't much. Cattle barns, big buildings with no heating, and they brought in bunk beds and mothers put up blankets to make little rooms where she and her family could live, but it was no life.

When I got there it was better, so they told me. People were getting to know each other, like their neighbours in the barn, and people were helping each other and everybody who could worked. I can't remember if we got paid but somehow I don't think so. People did things that they had never done before. Like I worked in the kitchen where they had the food for the thousands of people in there. I think there were about 3,000 people or more and they all had to be fed. The food was good, as good as you can expect, but it wasn't Japanese food and a lot of people, they thought that was wrong. They'd always eaten Japanese food because you could buy it anywhere and make it. Then all of a sudden they're eating, we're eating potatoes and stew and . . . well, I guess bread and butter is fine, but potatoes and stew. Mind you, from what I could see, it was all good food. If I had to say it, I would say that it was what the army got, but when you're cooking in those huge pots you can't get your arms around and it cooks for hours, everything goes out of it.

They had a store, candy, soft drinks, Coca-Cola, orange, grape, Kik, chocolate marshmallows, and a lot of people would buy that instead of eating the food. They'd eat breakfast, but maybe lunch or dinner it would be chocolate bars and Kik. Another thing that used to make people not like the food was that it was cafeteria style, a long line, and one man would give you stew and another potatoes and another bread. There was milk and tea and coffee on the tables and it was usually cold by the time you got there. So some people ate at the store. Then in the summer when I was there a man, the ice cream man, would ride his bicycle along the fence and you threw over a nickel and he'd throw back an ice cream bar. Nobody stopped him from doing it.

The people in charge tried to organize things. There was an infant room, as it was called, and mothers could pick up warm bottles of milk for their babies. They got a few shoemakers together and put them in a shop and they repaired boots and shoes. A sewing room. A big bake shop, just as big as any in Vancouver, all new equipment, and they turned out an awful lot of bread and buns and, of course, there were washrooms, for men and women. At first they didn't have covers around the toilets and I was told some women wouldn't use them. What they did, I just don't know. At three o'clock in the morning, I guess. Playroom for little children and a gymnasium. That was for everybody. I mean boys' classes and girls' classes. Physical fitness: Basketball games. There was also a school. I didn't go to it and I can't remember why, but I remember it and it was made up of funny little desks, all cramped up and the teachers were Japanese people. I don't think they knew much about teaching. Maybe that was why my mother said no. No use to go to a bad school. But there was a school.

This was in the summer, you know, by this time and people were always leaving. Fifty or 100 or 150 would go and you never really knew where to write to anybody because you didn't know where they were going. Sandon, Kaslo, New Denver, Roseberry later, but these were just names to us, they could have been at the end of the world. You know, of course, that the Vancouver [Japanese] people weren't in the Exhibition grounds. They stayed in their homes or the rich ones went on their own to places, and people were talking about how they were traitors for selling their houses and buying a truck and putting all their stuff into it, buying clothes and food to last a long time, and then going to live in Lillooet or someplace like that. I just heard the women talking about it but everybody seemed to be upset about it. Most of the people in the camp around us didn't have much money because all they really had was a fishboat, which was gone, and a house they'd have to leave, and the Indians and the whites just walked in and took what was left. The government didn't try and stop it. So a lot was stolen and so the people in Hastings Camp were pretty poor. If they wanted something they had to buy it from the money they had because I don't think then, I mean then, they could get their money out of a bank. They could later, I know, but not right then and that was bad for them.

Some people could get out of the Hastings Park place. Like if you had a disease you could get a pass because the hospital there was not the kind that treated serious cases. If you wanted to see your lawyer or something like that, visit a relative, there were passes. And people could come in through the main gate. I mean Japanese people, but others came in too. Some church people. I remember some people of the United Church who came in one day and asked people how they were doing, how things were going. Because what could they do? The people they talked to one day, they might be on their way to Tashme the next day. It only took twenty-four hours, you know. You were told quickly and there wasn't much to be done because everything you had was right there with you. It was just packing things up and saying goodbye to friends you had made. You might meet a lady from Port Alice and another from Prince Rupert and get to be friends and then the next day, gone. So the church people would come in and I don't think the police and soldiers liked it, but they let them in because they were preachers. But we have a word in Japanese which is *shikata-ga-nai* and it means that it can't be helped and that's what the people said. They knew there was a war on.

One man asked for a pass and said he wanted just to walk around Stanley Park and they let him go. People said, "Well, that's the last we'll see of him," but he was back on the streetcar that night. So that's the way it was. I think there was trouble at the Immigration Hall one day but I don't know much about it, and I think the only trouble at Hastings Park was when a lot of men threw meal on the floor saying they couldn't eat it, and then they had to clean up the mess.

We didn't see the men. They were in another part of Hastings Park, but my mother could get permission to go and see my father. But we were kept apart.

I think I stayed with my parents about two or three months in Hastings Park and then we went into the Interior. We could have gone to Alberta but what did we know about farming? So my father, who was not well anyway and was always going to the hospital, figured it would be best to go to the Interior where we would be looked after. So that is how it worked out for us.

"They Put Us in Horse Stalls"

It was awful. Where the horses were, that's where they put us. Single boys and those that didn't have friends or parents in Vancouver, when we come down from the island, that's where they put us.

Whole families in horse stalls. They put up army blankets as partitions but what good were they? People used to come and visit us and they would say, "Say, how can you live like this? You're living where the animals were." I'd tell them to go talk to the soldiers about that, but they wouldn't because everybody was afraid.

These people who would visit us, they'd make some rice balls and bring pickles and then they'd get a pass and could get in. We'd sit on the floor and on those army beds and have a little party, rice balls, pickles, anything else they brought, and we'd talk about what was going to happen to us. It was like a prison. You know, it was smelly. From all those animals. It was awful.

Some people really sick. They had a hospital, same place, where the animals were but they had it all fixed up, divided, so it was different. Women's and men's quarters. The hospital part,

I guess, was okay. The floor was laid down, so that was good. Yeah, a wooden floor. If a person was really sick, like intensive care, then she would be in a different part of the hospital. Not taken to a Vancouver hospital. Surgery? Oh yeah, then they went to a Vancouver hospital. All English nurses and English doctors in that place. Sure, there were Japanese doctors but they wouldn't let them work in that place. All English.

A Stupid, Vicious Policy

Hastings Park was not bad, not bad when you consider what it was being used for.

It wasn't nice, the fact that you just had row after row of these camp cots, army cots, hundreds of them, and the only privacy they had was to string ropes or wire across and hang blankets or their clothes on the wire in between the beds, between families. In that way it was bad, very bad.

But the conditions were good. It was sanitary. They were supplied all that they needed in the way of food and they did their own cooking, their own type of cooking. Everything that was required in the way of medical equipment and supplies was there.

Except it was a damn, stupid, vicious policy.

The B.C. Security Commission handled it well. Austin Taylor was a fair man. Mead of the R.C.M.P., I remember him as a very fair man.

But there was hysteria, yes. They were being torn out of their homes and being sent they didn't know where and they lost everything they had. All their belongings jammed into a suitcase and a pillowcase, all they had out of their happy homes. So there was hysteria and a great deal of emotion. Naturally.

Although I hated the damn place it was comparatively well handled as far as I was concerned. But it was a brutal policy.

The orders for it came from Ottawa but it was fostered provincially. All the appointments were made from Ottawa. But it was a policy that would have happened, regardless of the agitation of the Liberals, the Tory Party, the Canadian Legion, a lot of other groups that could be named. Yes, this policy of relocation would have happened. I'm convinced of that.

A very shameful episode.

I can point the finger at the powers-that-be, but I can also point the finger at the average common Canadian.

I was in it from the beginning to the end and after the war too, when I saw them building up their farms, the best damn farms in every district, or starting their trades in inland towns and cities, and I kept in touch with them and they kept in touch with me.

Our support, the CCF government's support, for their rights, the right to vote, the protest against the evacuation—I'm certain it all cost me the government twice. Cost me the premiership twice. Everyone who is legally a Canadian is entitled to the vote, and no discrimination—those were two of our planks. For Japanese, Chinese, East Indians, and for that matter the native Indian too. No first-, second- or third-class Canadians.

Headlines in the Vancouver *Province* and the Vancouver *Sun*, big headlines, quoting Captain Ian Mackenzie: "A Vote for the NDP Is a Vote for the Chink, the Jap." God, yes. That scared off the voters.

"*Fluid Drive*"

The Livestock Building at the P.N.E. was the worst place I have ever been in. I never want to be in a place like that again. It was where they had the cattle and horses and oh, it was awful. Just blankets hung up and then a family would live between those blankets. All sorts of strange people. People . . . well, one night a man, a woman's husband, came in from the men's building and he had got some whiskey and he was drunk and he caused a lot of trouble beating up his wife. That was when he found her. He spent a lot of time tearing off these blankets and looking into all these little rooms for her. The guards finally came and took him away.

It was at the time that there was dysentery. Oh, that was terrible too. Everybody had it and they'd give you stuff at the little hospital they had fixed up, but it didn't do no good. Dysentery is terrible. Well, I shouldn't say this but you know where the animals go when they had to go. They just did it out the back end of the stalls and that was that. Our people did the same thing. They were too weak or it was too dark to go to the toilets . . . yes, they had toilets in the building. I'm sure of that. Quite sure. But people would just go in the back of the stall, where the horses did it, and they would come along and clean it up next morning. The smell was awful. You couldn't stand it but you had to. Somebody called the place where they did it "Fluid Drive" and I think that was the only laugh we got in the three weeks we were in the building.

Nothing to Do—Just Wait

There was nothing to do in that place. Hastings Park was a place for nothing to do. Just waiting.

Of course, you could go outside, inside but there was guards along the fences. You could walk around though.

It was hard on the men and women. The women and children, see, they were all in one building but the men, all the men, were in a different building. So they split up the families. When a woman wants to go see her husband, well, you know, she could walk across to the men's building but there's a guard there, so the lady would ask this guard to please bring out her husband and the guard will tell the man. You see, that's how it worked.

Then they come out and they talk, you know, and they sit on the park benches and talk and when the time comes they each have to go to their different . . .

The guards were army—army age. Khaki, dressed like soldiers and they got their guns. You can't do nothing, just what they tell you to do. They're not mean, really. They're told what to do too, I guess. But guns, rifles.

I cried. I don't think I ever cried so much in my life as I see how we're all stacked in there, living and sleeping in the barns, and how they've got soldiers and top brass R.C.M.P. around all the time, those guns, and we're Canadian citizens. I was born in the 700-block East Hastings and I'm a good Canadian. Oh, how I cried.

The Feeling of Hopelessness

In December of 1941 I was at home. I was a high school graduate but that meant nothing because very often you couldn't find any work. Because you were Japanese.

So, eventually, I went into Hastings Park. If anything, the Hastings Park experience stands out for me because it was in there, cooped up with all those terrified women and children, and men too, that we began to understand what was happening to us.

My first night in there was the only time in my life where I thought, "Jesus, this is a good time to commit suicide." The miserable conditions that were in there. It was just a big assembly hall kind of thing. Double-decker beds. Just in shambles. Dust flying all over the place. No place to hang your clothes. No place to put your suitcase. The crappy meals we had to eat.

Of course it is all understandable. Masses of people in there. Certainly they hadn't as yet prepared that place for accommodating so many people.

But the thing you realize that was happening to you was that almost every night they called out a lot of numbers. You see, we had—each had a registration number. And if your number was called you were expected to report next morning for a medical, which was a very cursory sort of an examination, and then they would stamp on your sheet FIT FOR WORK and within three days you would be shipped to a road camp, out in the Interior, up near Jasper and through there down toward Kamloops, and be building roads.

Most of these people had families—mothers, wives, and children, and they were just tearing the families apart. The men going to road camp with all the other men, under guard of the R.C.M.P. and soldiers, and the women with their children, young women, grandmothers, people who maybe didn't speak English or not well going to the camps in the ghost towns. A woman with her children might be in a camp where she didn't know anybody else. Most of the other people might be from the Fraser Valley or from Prince Rupert. People say, "Oh, they're all Japs." As though every Japanese in B.C. knew every other one. This was not so. Not so. So it was a terrifying experience.

If a man said, "No, I won't go. I need to be with my family. They can't do without me"—maybe he was the only support of his old mother or his wife was sick—if he refused to go to road camp, then he was sent to prison camp and that was in Ontario. What was worse?

Every night or every other night they'd call out these numbers. From that I could imagine what these concentration camps in Germany were like, where they called out the numbers of Jews and when they herded them up those Jews were never seen again. Of course, of course, Germany was a lot worse than Canada.

Perhaps we lived in a better situation but the feeling that you had, the uncertainty, the feeling of hopelessness. . . . Once you got used to it—it took a little time—but once you got used to it you were able to accept it, I suppose, but it was frightening.

There were guards, of course. Veterans and that sort of guard. Some looked after stores and things like that and if you wanted more than two blankets, then you had to pay the guard some money. That was his little deal. These kind of things were going on.

There was a lot of gambling going on too. It was illegal, of course, but it went on just the same. Very little drinking. No place to drink it anyway. You were in one big hall or room and there was just no place. Everybody could see what everybody else was doing.

There was a food riot. One morning we were told not to touch the food because the food was terrible—and perhaps this was a way to demonstrate our objections to what we were being fed—so this morning we didn't touch our food. Then one man got up and said, "Well, if we're not going to eat here, let's go downtown and eat," so we sort of rushed the gates, but it was a very half-hearted attempt and nothing came of it. I remember that eventually that man, the Mounties grabbed him and shipped him off to the road camp. The so-called committee members of us who were in there they tried to appease everyone, saying it was no use fighting and doing this, so nothing happened.

But I think the worst experience of all for everybody was an outbreak of diarrhea. That was bad. It occurred at least twice. They talked about how it must have been the stew. It could have been worse. Nobody died. There was also an outbreak of measles. Some of these women, confined to a very small area, some with four or five small kids. It must have been awful for them.

Police, Pretty Fair All Round

I can remember when the first batch of Japanese were being moved out of the coast here and the police had riding crops, and I remember going down to the train at Hastings Park to see them off at the siding. And by golly they had all the Japanese young men lined up and some of the Mounties were yelling, "Come on there, get in line there," and they were whacking the boys on the leg. Not hard, but the fellows resented that.

I remember saying to myself that one of our young fellows was going to grab that riding crop and take it away from him and he was quite capable of doing it too.

I remember going down and telling the R.C.M.P. corporal in charge. I said, "You know, Corporal Davidson, they're not scared of your men. They haven't got a damn thing to lose. A lot of these fellows of ours have judo and they can throw your men just as far as they want to, in any direction. You keep that up and you're going to run into trouble. They're going to pick your men up and give them one hell of a time."

You know, next day I went over there and there wasn't one Mountie with a riding crop. The authorities were really quick to rectify any situation which might cause any friction.

No, the police were pretty good. Pretty fair all round.

The Injustice of It All

What did the Japanese expulsion mean to me? Personally. Well, it made me aware how weak we Canadians could be in protecting our self-interests.

Imagine, when Mackenzie King ordered the Japanese Canadians out, they didn't have one case of sabotage, of suspected sabotage, but the prejudice in B.C. was something awful.

The Chinese disliked the Japanese. The whites disliked the Japanese. It had to do with economics more than anything else because the Japanese were successful.

And I remember hearing described how the Japanese would go out fishing, fishermen, and they would stay out five, six, seven, eight days until they got their full load of fish. You'd hear guys say, "We, we, we Canadians wouldn't miss Saturday night with the missus but those guys, they stay out there until they got this fish load." So there was this tremendous envy and distrust of the hard-working Japanese, out there to bring back money, to give up the social life the others wanted. It distressed me that these Canadians on the West Coast should be so misled in thinking in terms of colour and race. You know.

Then meeting these people, the Japanese, the gentleness, the politeness, the culture, the courtesy, and these people should have rebelled and fought and screamed about what was happening to them. They didn't. Authority in a uniform. That's what got them. That obedience to authority going back many generations. You did what the man said.

Every person is a creature of his background. You have to realize that I came from a Jewish home, from a socialist home, from parents who ran away from Russia because of oppression in Russia, a literate home where we knew what was going on and we were sophisticated enough not to accept things as they are, appear to be, but to be suspicious of any motivation of government, power. With that kind of background it wasn't a shock for me to know that Canadians could be treated this way. I was very distressed, I know, but it wasn't a shock. Also by the time I learned what was happening to Japanese Canadians in 1942 I already knew what was happening to the Jews in Germany.

But the terrible thing was in realizing that in what we thought was a democracy, where we had equal rights in Canada, my country of birth, that it could happen. And though I knew very well that the German Jews never thought that a guy like Hitler could be of any consequence because they thought that the German people would reject him. I'm not comparing the two. It would be a terrible thing to do, what the Germans did to the Jews and what happened in Canada. No, believe me, not at all.

But the injustice, the loss of political and physical freedom that we imposed on the Japanese, came while I way in the army. It came at a time when I was in Vancouver, at that time there were mass meetings staged by my party, the CCF, protesting the treatment of the Japanese. I remember men like Black and Turner, and I didn't know these people, and they would have corner meetings like we used to have in Winnipeg during the depression. Get a vacant lot and hold a protest meeting.

I remember attending these meetings in Vancouver and they were violent because the speakers were being hooted, always being attacked, very little support because the mood against the Japanese was just vicious.

Now by this time they were already gone. Into the Interior, the camps, to the prairies, but you could see their fruit stores, still some evidence of signs that they had been there, but the Japanese were all gone. These stores had been taken over by other people.

But all these people in that city were so bitter and antagonistic toward the Japanese. Even though they had gone. There were no more Japanese left.

The bitterness I could accept intellectually because of my background and so it wasn't a surprise. But it still made me wonder. I would always wonder and try and figure out these people who attended those meetings in Vancouver—and their hatred.

4. *We Lost Everything*

On March 27, 1942, an order-in-council was issued giving the Custodian of Enemy Alien Property the power "to liquidate, sell or otherwise dispose of such property." Japanese property.

There seems to be considerable dispute over whether the Japanese themselves were ever fully informed of this move, but the Custodian gradually went ahead under the terms of the order.

Several Japanese told me they never heard of it, and several said they understood their possessions were in the hands of the Custodian until war's end for safekeeping. "Safekeeping" to these people meant one thing: their homes, businesses, farms, possessions, everything, would be kept safe. Yet looting, theft, and the auction block stripped them of everything they left behind. This misunderstanding was a source of great bitterness among many Japanese, men and women whose labour of years went for nothing.

The ringing cry of "Sold!" and the slap of the gavel on the auctioneer's block. Another lot gone. But I never found a single person who was satisfied with the money that he, she, or their parents received from these enforced sales, whether it was a boat at New Westminister or a box of family heirlooms at Prince Rupert. The complaints against the Custodian were endless. And yet I have been told by people I trust and have seen files that indicate to me that the Office of the Custodian of Enemy

Alien Property tried to deal with these people fairly and as effectively as possible.

But how could you be fair when you put an end to twenty years of a family's hard work, when you denied them the means to make a living the only way they knew how, and deprived them of the opportunity to ever start up again because they were penniless?

"Safekeeping" Meant Nothing

When we left we had to turn over our property to the Custodian of Enemy Property for safekeeping. That's what it said in the order—for safekeeping. Now that meant to us, as it still means to me, that when the war business was over we'd get our property back.

Some people didn't go along with this. They sold their houses for what they could, if they owned houses, which most Japanese didn't anyway. They couldn't do anything about their fishboats because they had been seized. They rented their farms if they could. They stored their stuff in storage firms if they had the money, and while there were some Japanese who were pretty rich and some who were well fixed, as they say, most of the Japanese were poor, so they couldn't put them in storage. Some sold stuff, as I said. At low prices—whatever they could get. Some just put everything in a bedroom and put a lock on the door and locked it and thought it would be safe. Some just left the stuff and people could walk in and take what they wanted. That happened. Oh yes, often.

But we still had this safekeeping business in our minds. It was a terrible shock when we learned that meant nothing. It was a terrible shock to learn that so much, like all of our stuff, had been sold at auction. I don't know the full details. I don't think we were ever told. Some people didn't care, like if they'd only left a table and chairs and a bed or two in the house. But if they left good things, wouldn't you say those people would care? I'm sure they would. I know they did. And in many cases these people didn't know their goods had been confiscated. I mean, yes, sure, I guess it was in the papers. It must have been in *The New Canadian*. Every Japanese got that free, as I remember. But they might not have thought it applied to them. Today, there are people who were never told that they lost all their goods by confiscation because the Custodian just couldn't bother looking after it all, all that time. There were others who would get a cheque or a credit saying so much was due them, and I guess they got their money when they asked for it. I'm sure they would. But there were some people who got no money at all. Now that wasn't right.

Things were stolen. Paintings, statues, carvings. You don't take things like that to a prison camp when you're only allowed 150 pounds. You take clothes and dishes and bedding. In other words, you take what you were told to take and they said take dishes and bedding and clothing and maybe some food for the first few days.

That safekeeping thing caused a lot of bitterness. People would say, "That's all we had and now we've got nothing." They used to talk about it in the bathhouse, where everybody gossips and talks and all the business is done, and it made a lot of people pretty mad. First they take us from our homes and stick us in this dump, and now this. That's what they were saying.

I'm not saying the government was 100 percent in the wrong because a lot of this stuff was being stolen or probably rotting and some of it was junk, but they should never have said for safekeeping. Get around it somehow. Say they would do their best to keep it. Then if they couldn't, well, there would be some people who would understand. But no. I guess the government was trying to do the right thing, doing it, ah yes, doing it, that gets you in a very bad position with a lot of people.

Might as Well Sell to Him

When we are in Vancouver we don't have to go into Hastings Camp to wait to be evacuated but we can stay in our homes and then go straight to where we are going. It is funny, you know, these Jewish people come around to our place, you know, to buy things.

We have to sell. Any amount he asks for we got to sell. What can we do? Everybody knows we are going to the ghost towns. It is in the paper. Everyday there is something in the paper. Pictures in the paper.

He comes, says, "What have you got to sell?" I say, "How do you know where we are?" He doesn't say. Of course he knows where we are because he just looks up Japanese names in the phone book, and then he comes around with his horse and wagon and his boy or in his old truck and he says, "What have you got?"

Might as well sell to him. He's got the truck and if we want to take things downtown to a second-hand store, what's the difference? That fellow is Jewish too. They say, "I'll give you 200 dollars for your house, everything in it." We say it has stove, fridge, tables, chairs, beds, books, sofas, all these things and he says, "Then 200 dollars is too much. I thought you had big house. I give you 100 dollars." What do you do? He takes it for 100 dollars and sells it to another Jewish fellow for 200 dollars. Maybe his brother-in-law.

That part of it, giving away all those good things for a few dollars, that was an experience my wife never forgot. Not ever. All those things she liked so much, her new stove, things like that, all gone. What could you do? You could do nothing. They just looked up the telephone book and say "Ah, here is a Japanese on East Hastings. We'll go see him tomorrow, get his stuff." It worked like that. Every time.

Bureaucracy at Work

There were eight in our family. My father wanted us to grow up in a Canadian neighbourhood so we would lose the, ah . . . the ghetto mentality, so we lived in South Vancouver. On what was once an orchard. And when the war came, well, we thought it would be best if we moved East and my parents had all this furniture. What were we to do?

We had so many things, you see. We thought one year, one and a half years, two years, that was the size of our thinking. Then we would come back, so we wouldn't sell our furniture cheaply , like a lot of Japanese were doing, to the men who would look you up in the phone book and then come around and offer you hardly nothing. We had lots of friends, Canadian friends, so we asked them if they would take some furniture. Would you store this for us? Of course they said they would and we split up our furniture and belongings in about four or five places. We didn't ask one Canadian family to take it all. There was one family, a friend of my brother in Kerrisdale. They had just built this big house but they hadn't finished the second floor, so they took the piano and the big record player and a bedroom suite. Others took other things.

Then we went down to Ontario I said to my mother and father that they didn't want to go back to B.C. They liked B.C. very much but there was a lot of opportunity in Ontario, and besides there was no anti-Oriental discrimination. They were doing fine and they thought they would sell some things in Vancouver. So my father wrote the family in Kerrisdale and they sold the piano and everything else and sent him the money. He got good prices too because, you see, people didn't think it was Japanese property, goods, and would offer good prices. So they got what the things were worth.

But we had registered everything with the Custodian of Enemy Alien Property and when they decided to sell everything off they went around to this house and found that it had already been sold. Oh, were they mad. Did we ever get a scathing letter from them!

But they got the things, the goods from the other places, and they sold them at auction. I think we got about 5 percent of what they were worth. Oh, it was ridiculous. Terrible.

A Basement Full of Furniture

When I came out to train at Chilliwack, the military camp at Sardis, I didn't know anybody in Vancouver except my father had given me a letter of introduction to a man he knew in Vancouver. He'd gone to college with him and they'd kept up a correspondence over the years.

So on my first forty-eight-hour pass I went to Vancouver and saw this man. I stood in the hall while he read the letter and then he shook my hand and told me to come in, come in, and I was sure glad. Being in a nice home again after all that barrack life.

That night he took me down the basement where I was to sleep and there was one cot there with blankets on it. There was a furnace and a bin for sawdust and the rest of the place, that basement, was taken up for furniture. I couldn't see how much except it was an awful lot. There was sewing machines and beds and refrigerators and chesterfields and boxes and boxes and more boxes and just about everything you'd put into a house. I asked him what it was and he said it was the possessions of Japanese he knew and he was keeping it for them. Storing it in a warm, safe place.

I didn't know about the Japanese. I had no idea. I came from a small town, Paris, in Ontario and nobody had told me about what had happened to them in B.C. I guess I read the papers as much as anybody else, but I guess it just didn't register or else it just wasn't in the papers at all.

We went upstairs and instead of me going downtown and meeting my buddies like I meant to or planned to, I sat in this Mr. Morris's living room all night and he told me about the Japanese, before the war, when it started, what happened to them and everything. I was certainly surprised. More than surprised. I think that at the first I was in sympathy with the Canadian government. As I recall I was. But when he finished that story—and I had to believe him—I thought what we had done to the Japanese was a terrible thing. Still do.

It Happened All the Time

When we got settled in our little house in Greenwood and the children were going to school and my husband got a job in the woods he wrote to the Custodian's office in Vancouver asking that our stuff be sent to us.

We would pay for it. It was all boxes and big canvas pouches that my husband had made, had ordered from Jones Tent and Awning when we knew we were going to be moved out, and all our stuff was stored in these canvas bags. There was some furniture. Stuff from Japan. Expensive. My husband had brought over this furniture when he visited Japan in 1937. We would pay for it and it would come on the Kettle Valley line which ran from Vancouver and we would pick it all up at the station.

The first letter said they had gotten our letter. Then we wrote again after a time. We wanted to know where our furniture and things were. They wrote and said they were looking for them. This was about 1944, early, about this time. We wrote another letter and they said that all our stuff had been sold. Then I think we wrote another letter . . . of course we did. Where was our money? All we got back about 1945 sometime was a letter saying our lot, meaning our goods, had been disposed and the file was closed. They had closed the file. Just that and somebody's signature that you couldn't make out. It looked like we'd lost everything.

My husband got a pass to go to Grand Forks where there was a lawyer because he wanted to talk to him about it. The lawyer said it was no use. He said it happened all the time. Japanese people had their furniture and clothes and other things sold and that was the end. He told us to forget it. I guess he was saying you couldn't beat the government, even with a lawyer. So that's how it was. No furniture, no money. Somebody got it. That Custodian, I'll bet.

Crooks in the Night

A lot of us went to Greenwood, which wasn't too bad a place but it wasn't all that nice. People were fairly nice to us. We didn't have a nice place to live, but it was wartime and these people at least didn't look at us like we were killers.

My mother got a letter from a friend in Grand Forks saying this lady had died when she was having her baby. Was there somebody at Greenwood who could help?

My mother said she would take the baby, and a police car was making the route and the lady brought the baby with her in the car. The police were mostly nice.

Before this my mother had written to a white family in Steveston who had been sort of neighbours and she asked— well, we'd left the key with this lady in Steveston and my mother asked her to bring out and send all the diapers and little dresses and booties and shawls and blankets and everything that we had stored in our house there. We stored these things because we were sure we would come back.

When the letter came back my mother just sat on the bed in our room and she said, "Gone. All gone. Everything's gone." I took the letter and the woman had written that when she went around to the house the door was broken open. Boxes. Bags. Just junk was left and all the good stuff was gone. Stolen. Taken away by crooks in the night. Thieves. Looting and vandalism. What they didn't want they had kicked around.

There was no baby things. They had all gone. The looters must have wanted them. Oh, we found enough clothes and things for the baby right there in Greenwood, but it was hard to think that this had happened to us.

Everything Went Dirt Cheap

They used to have the auctions of the Japanese stuff. I used to go. Never bought anything. I think it was because my old father felt so badly about what the government had done to the Japanese. But lots of people were buying lots of stuff. It just went dirt cheap. For almost nothing. Sold everything. People stole stuff out of the houses and then they went to the auctions and stole stuff again, legally.

Damn shame too. Those people worked hard for what they had got. I met one old fellow on the street the day before they were to go and he shook my hand and said, "Goodbye, I'll see you again." He didn't seem bitter.

I guess they knew they were for it and all their talk, pleading, wasn't going to get them anywhere. So they just left.

Disposal—or Deterioration?

I don't think the Japanese people got fair prices for their tools and stoves and tables and cars and things like that. The government said they had these things all valued and everything had a value on it, and then the whole system went wrong because it was all at auction. Nothing was supposed to be bought for less than a set price, but I know lots of Japs who got nearly nothing. A 40-dollar washing machine, nearly new, selling for 5 dollars. A cultivator, nearly new, selling for 3 dollars. You can't tell me those are fair prices. You see, people would go to these auction sales and they'd bid. An auction is where the high price wins, but it often happens a highest price is not the fair price.

But after the war when I came back to the coast in 1951 I met one of these guys on the Albion ferry and we went into the hotel there at Fort Langley by the Indian Reserve and we had a couple of beers. I'd known him when we used to have the strawberry farm on Old Yale Road and we get talking. It's eight, ten years since I seen him. His name was Austin. A pretty good guy. I'm working as a stevedore at Westminister getting two, maybe three days a week in. Dirty job. Clean-up man and all that dust. He asks me how it was going and I said I figured the wartime had put me back about twenty-five years, like how was I going to get enough money together after feeding my kids to get some more land in the valley, and anyway I would have to go up around Abbotsford now. I said a good twenty-five years and he said that was tough.

Then I started talking about how we'd been screwed on our goods, our chattels and how everything had been sold, and what hadn't been sold wasn't sold because it had been stolen or was no good. He had had something to do with the Custodian of Alien Property, and he said that they didn't want to sell the Jap property but they had to. There was no other way. He said as soon as we were shipped to Alberta and the camps, people had just started to walk into Jap homes and sheds and taking what they wanted. You'd need a watchman on every farm and house in town if you wanted to protect that stuff, he said. I said yeah, and when we got our money for the sale of our stuff they charged us a watchman's fee, too, so that guy—if there was a guy—hadn't done much good. Austin said, "People would say it's Jap stuff and the Japs are gone for good." That's what the politicians were telling them and I guess they'd been reading the newspapers.

But he said there was something more than people just

walking in and taking things. Maybe not walking in. That's wrong. I know most people put padlocks on their doors or boarded up their windows, but that didn't stop them. But this Austin said I had to realize that if things aren't used they just go to hell in a hurry. It's partly the climate. Like he said all those people up on the coast, on the island, some of them who had to get out in a couple of hours' or a day's notice, or be ready for the next boat down to Vancouver, which might be along in three days. These people just left stuff and the sea air, the wetness—well, it just ruined everything. I know that. You know that. I guess it was the same in Vancouver. If something isn't used, or is in a house that isn't used, things start to go wrong pretty quickly. It deteriorates. Mildewed and then it's no good. Mattresses fall apart. Dust and dirt gets in. Rain leaks, the roof gets a hole in it. Maybe mice. Somebody breaks a couple of windows, kids, and birds get in and shit up the place. You don't use a cultivator for two years and it starts to rust. Another year and it's finished. Got to buy another one. So on.

This Austin said guys from the Custodian's department would go round to these farms, Mission, Haney, Maple Ridge, Surrey, and they'd look around and they'd see what was happening. Neighbourhood kids smashing things. Rot and rust. Same in Vancouver with all those old houses. He said there was no way they they could protect all those things in those houses. I can see that. Nature sneaks in everywhere. It is a tricky thing.

So somebody in the Custodian's office must have said to hell with this, why have all this stuff on our hands, maybe 4,000 families' stuff all around everywhere? Why don't we just sell it? This is what I told Austin—that the guys in charge just didn't want to be bothered anymore.

But he said no, no, no. He said I was wrong. He said the Custodian guys had done a lot of thinking and they had come up with the answer that if things went on, everything would become worthless. He said this applied to everybody except some of those rich Japs who had put their good things in storage in downtown Vancouver and were able to come up with the money for monthly storage. He said there were some of those, a lot who had sold out before the evacuation and gone up to Christina Lake, those places, and sat out the war there. They were the rich Japs and we'd heard a lot about them during the war, one way or another. They were called self-sustaining, and a lot of Japs didn't have too many good words for them. I was one. They snuck out while the going was good. There was a description that fitted them, one that the kids use today. Bananas. Yellow on the outside, white inside.

But anyway, for the rest of us, those who had locked their stuff in a garage or put it in an English neighbour's shed or just left it in the house, there wasn't much hope. Th stuff was going to go rotten or finally be all stolen. So they decided to sell. It had to be done, I guess. I accept that now. I got to, because it's been done. But I guess I would have accepted it anyway if I'd seen the stuff in my house and how it was all going to hell.

Bring in Your Cameras, Radios

They said bring in your cameras. Bring in your cameras. Bring is your radios. All your radios. No Jap can have a radio. That's the dumb rules they had for us.

Why, I ask? Because you be spies. Spies, hah! If we want to be spies we could be spies for ten years early, so why then? Crazy, all crazy. Why radios? Why radios, I ask the guy. He says radios can be made into short-wave senders, like you know, and I laugh and the guy says why are you laughing and I said the radio we had, why you had to put your ear down close just to get the station downtown, just a few blocks away. The kids couldn't dance to that radio. They'd go over to Tanabe's place where his kids got a good radio. My radio, hah, good for nothing.

But we got to surrender, so we do. We're going to be good Canadians even if they think we are bad Japs. It was crazy.

Then the time comes when it's printed in *The New Canadian*

that we can get back our radios and cameras. I say to Poppa, we're going to get back our camera. The radio they can keep. No good anyhow. So I write away saying here's the receipt you give us when we surrender the camera, and they said there is no such thing as that kind of camera. Well, that was right on the receipt, that kind of camera. For heaven sakes. We never got it back. We gave it, they took it away. We think they sold it, somebody down there, they sold it. We had the receipt, you see, so we know. They say they got nothing to record it by. That is crazy. Poppa saw them mark it in a big book.

That happened lots of times. We know Japanese who even lost their cars. They got their cars taken away, got a receipt, and when the time came for them to get money, there was no car, no record of it, but they know they surrendered the cars.

Lots of people like that. Lots of people, they just don't even get one penny.

"Take It or Leave It"

The Kudos had a car. A good car. It would be worth at least 400 dollars in anybody's money in those days. The police told them to take it down to Hastings Park, in the race track there, and it was lined up with all the others. Then it was sold. Auctioned off, I believe. Some company in town here did the work. When the government took off commission and storage fees and insurance and all that, the Kudos got a check for 11 dollars. They complained and the Custodian said, "That's all there is. Take it or leave it."

They Confiscated His Truck

My father had this friend—his wife and the kids looked after the berry part of it—and he had two trucks and he'd haul berries from the berry growers' association in Mission to the wholesalers in Vancouver. Anyway, they confiscated his trucks and stored them at Hastings Park and they made a settlement. They sold the trucks and they deducted the storage and other expenses, and there wasn't enough to pay for the costs. So they sent him a bill. You know, this is one instance where I thought it was unjust, very unjust.

The Fishboat Fiasco

It was utter confusion. Bring in your fishboats, they said. Right away. Steveston, our area, all these other places up and down the coast, over on the island, they got the word. The navy and the police knew where all the boats were. Down at Vancouver, up at Skeena. Bring in your boats.

So the people complied. This was in December, so most of them were all stripped for the winter. No food, no light, no nothing in these boats, and when they got their boats down to the holding depots they were told to stay there. "Now don't you move out of those boats," they were told. And then they were moved in stages, down the coast to the Fraser or up to Rupert. Places like that. Now this was winter and a very cold winter and here they were in their boats, unheated, and having to stay in them while they were towed in batches down the coast by bigger fishing boats. It was a very hard time. Not allowed to go home. Some without blankets or anything. Just the little food they could get. Their wives and kids didn't know where they

were or what they were doing and the fishermen, especially
from up coast, didn't know how their families were making out.

I finally phoned the navy in Vancouver and said, "What do
you want us to do; where do you want us to take the boats? We'll
comply but let's end all this confusion." The navy said, "Hold
her for a while. You'll get further instructions." So there we
were, not knowing what to do. But after awhile all the boats on
the south coast did end up in New Westminister.

It was a bad winter. That's right. Ice and stuff. The navy
wasn't prepared to handle those boats. The men that were
handling those boats, the navy men, didn't have the ability.
How can a navy kid come from Flin Flon or Prince Albert and
come down here and look after hundreds of boats?

I could go down to the slough by New Westminister for official
reasons and go over the boats and they were in one awful mess. I
can remember talking to one petty officer from this coast and he
was talking about his men and he said, "Damn these guys. They
think water is only for drinking. And they've never tied up
anything more than a bloody horse. Look at those knots!" They
had to move a bunch of boats in a hurry and the knots had seized
up and the only thing he could do was cut the anchor lines with a
hatchet, cut the mooring lines, and this was the damage that was
going on all the time. They just didn't know how to handle
boats.

And we mostly had gasoline engines in our boats, not diesel,
and you know what happens to a cold damp boat all winter with
gasoline around. These navy kids would go in there out of the
wind and light a cigarette in the cabin, and the Norwegian
people who lived by the slough said they'd often see boats
burning.

The boats would break loose and I've seen them drifting down
the river. Our good boats. A lot of them disappeared.

Or you could go into New Westminister and hear that
compasses were selling for 2 dollars. It used to be a joke. Buy a
Japanese compass cheap. Or a spotlight anywhere, cheap.
Batteries. Hard to get. You could buy them anywhere. These
navy guys were looting our boats of everything they could tear

off and selling it for beer. I guess it is natural. I've seen it happen in other places. But the navy was supposed to be the protectors of our property.

Finally the government did decide that they couldn't keep those several hundred boats tied there. They were just being ruined, and with the Japanese fishermen without their boats and the salmon production going right down, down, they just had to put those boats back into production. Well, they needed the salmon production for food more than they ever needed it before.

They were fixed up where they could and put out on the open market and they were sold quite cheaply. Cheaply. To people who had never fished in their life before and it takes years, years, to become a good fisherman. And then again it wasn't only the boats that were sold cheaply but it was all the hard-to-get fishing gear that was sold.

The funny part of it was that later on, when these stories were told of boats being sold at practically nothing, the accusation was that the Japs had priced their boats and nets too high. Well, I'll tell you one thing. You take nets that were stored in Steveston. Under the Custodian and guards and everything else. The whites would go down there and only the tags on the nets could tell these people whether it was a good net or a bad net, by the price tag. Somebody would just switch tags like people do in a store today. Take a 20-dollar tag and put it on a 120-dollar net and then the 20-dollar net would have a 120-dollar tag and then somebody who would know about nets would come along and say the Japs were trying to cheat the buyers. "Who the hell do the damn Japs think they're fooling?" they'd say.

It was all the whites who profited. There was no way the Japs could profit.

What Is an Auction?

Sure, they sold the fishboats at low prices. It was an auction. That answers the question. What is an auction? It is what you can get for it.

They say those boats were dumped. Given to friends. No, they were auctioned. I was there. They didn't get much money for those Japanese boats but they did it the right way. The authorities. Advertising in the paper. An auctioneer, a gavel, what am I offered, and so on and so forth and the public, Canadians like you and I, greedy and selfish, knew they were going to get bargains out there and they colluded, some of them—you don't bid on that boat and I won't bid on the one you want. I knew that happened because I was there. The boats were auctioned and under the circumstances they got the highest prices they could.

Some of those boats were in good shape and some were not. A lot, about 900 down in the slough by New Westminister, were in rough shape, some of them, because they'd been through a hard winter. Frost and ice. That's not good for a boat. A boat has to be tended, cared for.

The navy said they did the best they could to protect them, but did they? There is always the big question mark in my mind.

Then, with all the Japanese gone—about 15 or so percent of the fishing fleet and some of the best gillnet men in the west coast fleet—the catch next year was going to be down. So they sold those boats to anybody. Show up at the auction with money and you're just as liable as not to wind up with a fishboat. A licence. But can you fish? That's the question.

So a lot of people bought those boats who weren't fishermen.

What Can You Do? Nothing.

Two collection boats. My father one—me one. Off west coast of island, inside, everywhere. Dangerous lots of times. War comes. They take the boats. Grab them—just take them. Wait awhile. I have a house in Vancouver, 700-block Cordova. One police comes, says, "Your keys, please." Locks door and says get out. I wait. Two days. Grab me. Concentration camp. That place north of big lake. Lake Superior. Angler? Yeah, Angler.

Five years we are there. Five hundred Japanese. Germans there first, then just Japanese. Nothing to do. They give us bread and potatoes and meat two, three times a week—we cook. Nothing to do. Cut wood for fires. Nothing else. Five years. Eight months after war they let us go. Coldest place in Canada . . . . always 40 below.

Take me because I am military age. My father and me, know every part of coast. They think Japanese Navy come . . . father and me don't need any compass, chart, we just go by what we know—know every point. They think we might—government think we might do something against government. Crazy.

After war, ask government what about my collection boat? My father's. Nothing. Get nothing. I don't know.

Not bitter. What can you do? Can't be helped. Long time ago. I young man then. Go to Montreal. Open restaurant. Open another. Then another on St. Catherine's Street. Come back three years ago. Not bitter. It is war. Maybe Japan does same thing those days. What can you do? Nothing.

People Just Moved Right In

The houses? Oh well. People just left their homes. It was all they could do when they were moved out. Some houses had signs saying they were protected by the Custodian, the government, but that meant nothing to all the people moving out here from the prairies. War and everything. War factories. They just tore down the signs and moved in and that was that. They were usually people from the prairies who did this, moved right in. Very nice people though. They needed a place to live and there was a good vacant house so why not? Nobody ever said anything. The Japanese never got the land or houses back, of course. It was sold long before because the Japs weren't allowed back to the coast until the War Measures Act was lifted. About 1948, I think.

Sold: 8.1 Acres for 610 dollars

In 1935 I bought 8.1 acres of land near Port Mann in Surrey in the Fraser Valley. There was one acre cleared and the rest was heavy bush, there was an old house and a shed on the one cleared acre. I paid 400 dollars, but I also turned over land in Japan I owned worth 2,500 dollars to get the eight acres.

I built a frame house, twenty-four feet by thirty-two feet, of two stories. That was in 1937. I bought the materials and with my own labour and labour that I hired, I estimated the house was worth 600 dollars. You must remember that this was in from 1935 to 1937, when the depression was on and land prices were very low, and besides it was all bush, heavy trees, and undergrowth and very difficult to clear.

My wife owned the land and everything with me.

When I was on the land I put in 5,000 feet of cedar-covered ditching and this ditching was from three to five feet deep and that is an awful lot of digging and wood. I also put in about twenty mixed fruit trees and built a picker house and a root cellar.

In 1942 I still had the eight acres but there was just one and a quarter acres that were not cleared of the heavy bush and timber. Six acres were in strawberries and three quarters of an acre were in raspberries.

When the wartime appraiser came along, he underestimated the amount of land I had cleared, and he did not even consider the 5,000 feet of deep ditching that I had done and this was excellent ditching. And the buildings were in much better condition than he said they were.

I felt the value at the time was at least 2,500 dollars.

When we were told we would have to get out of the valley I took my family with me to St. Jean, Manitoba, and I rented my farm to a neighbour, Bruce McCurrach, who was to look after it too. When I left there was a good crop of strawberries and raspberries.

The commission told me that I had to sell my farm and I wrote to Mr. McCurrach about what the commission had done, and he said he would buy my farm off me for 1,500 dollars. That was fine because he had been kind to my son when he lived there. I told the commission, by letter, and Mr. McCurrach wrote them and they said he could not buy the farm from me. I wanted to sell to my friend, Mr. McCurrach. My wife did too. She said she would rather sell to Mr. McCurrach than get 2,500 or 3,500 dollars from somebody she didn't know . . . who would not take care of the farm.

I am a naturalized citizen of Canada and I though I had a legal right to sell my land to any person I wanted to, at any price. Then I got a letter in April of 1944 saying the office of the Custodian had now sold my land. They didn't say to who they had sold it. Just that they had. The land was sold on January 1, 1943, but nobody had told me. A year and four months before I was told that Mr. McCurrach could not buy it. All that time I thought I owned the land.

The land was bought by the Veteran's Land Act and I assumed that because I had an offer of 1,500 dollars from Mr. McCurrach, then the price paid by the Veteran's Land Act must have been better.

No, Mr. McCurrach did not make an offer in writing, but he

came out to St. Jean, Manitoba, and saw me and said 1,500 dollars.

The land was sold to the Veteran's Land Act for 610 dollars, and that was based on the appraisal by the Soldiers' Settlement Board appraiser—and this was at the time when I put a value of 2,500 dollars on it.

I took my case to the Co-operative Committee of Japanese Canadians before Mr. Justice Bird, the commissioner of the Japanese Property Claims Commission, and Mr. Bird agreed with what my lawyer said. That 1,500 dollars was established as the fair market price and he awarded me 890 dollars.

That was February 1, of 1950 when I finally got my money after the government had sold my eight acres, cleared, cleaned, planted, drained, for 610 dollars.

Funny Things Went On

I don't know how it worked. Funny things went on. Some people got almost full value for their land. Like if a piece of land was worth 6,000 dollars they might get 5,000. This is the way I heard it. And then there would be another fellow right next door and he'd have this land and the government would write him and say that his land had been sold and he'd finally, sometime, get a check for 250 dollars, that's all. The government said the rest of the money went for commission fees and insurance and taxes and a caretaker and advertising it for sale and all this. All he'd get was 250 or 300 dollars when he might have ten acres and his family, his wife, his kids had worked from dawn to dark for years building it all up. These were the stories you heard.

A lot of rotten things were done. Oh yes, that's for sure. That's for sure. I can't tell you them because they're just what I hear, heard; but something funny seemed to be going on. We don't understand these things. Maybe it's best we don't.

5 Angler—Barbed Wire and Boredom

While the reverberations from Pearl Harbor were still racketting around the globe, forty-two Japanese on the West Coast were rounded up by the mounted police. They were Issei, older men, respected in their communities but of ordinary vocations—union official, barber, school teacher, and so on.

I have met Japanese Canadians who knew these men and they swear they have not the slightest idea why they were picked up and jailed, without warrant, without trial, and, naturally, without appeal. To this day nobody knows their crime, but somewhere in some file in Ottawa must rest the answers.

I was told by one Japanese in Vancouver: "It was a scare tactic. They may have had a little something on these guys. Something one might have said once, but nothing like you might think. They were just showing the rest of us what they could do."

The forty-two finally wound up in Angler, a prisoner-of-war camp east of Thunder Bay. Placed in a bleak region of low hills with cold winters and mosquito-filled summers, it was formerly a German P.O.W. camp and got its reputation, if you can call it such, from the escape of twenty-eight German prisoners and the death of two and the wounding of three by the gunfire of the guards. Little is known of that incident.

But the forty-two weren't the only Japanese in Angler. There were more than 700 men who, while not actually dangerous to the state, were considered troublemakers.

121

The Canadian government eventually realized that all but a handful of these men were harmless and tried to get them to leave the camp and accept work in Ontario—as free men. A couple of hundred did but many refused saying, "Send me back to B.C. or I'll stay here forever." For a few it was a matter of pride, a show of defiance toward a government and a system that could treat them thus.

"Jack's Been Taken Away"

When my brother Jack came down from Vancouver Island they put him in Hastings Park right away. Then one night he got out of Hastings Park to come home to his old house because he's got parents there and he wants to see them, eh?, and my mother is sick, so Jack stays with us that night. It is not a bad thing to do. He is not raising trouble. He just wants to see his parents, eh?

So next day he's still there and the R.C.M.P. come and pick him up and take him to the Immigration Building. You know, down by the CPR dock. It's still there. It is the Japanese jail, with bars and guards and everything.

I'm twenty then, yes, twenty, and I can still see myself going down to the railway track by the waterfront, by Heatley Avenue there, to watch for the train going out with all the people on it, the Japanese, taking them away to the prison camp in Ontario. On the train, eh? Some would be waving at us people standing at the crossing and others wouldn't. They'd just be sitting there.

Then one day a train goes by slowly and I see my brother on it and I wave and wave, but I don't think he sees me because he doesn't wave back. And I remember, I'm running down the track after that train and I'm crying like anything, just crying so I can't see, and then I go home and tell Mom and Dad that Jack's been taken away to prison. Angler.

In a while we get a letter from him saying he's in Ontario.

He says not to worry, everything will work out for all of us some day.

I was only twenty and I remember crying so hard that day, running.

Angler—a Big Sit-down Place

I think it is important to know that of all the men in Angler, and at one time there were more than 700, darn few were in there for any other reason than they were protesting the way the whole thing was handled.

Some were first sent to Petawawa and that was in the beginning and I think a few went to Kananaskis, by the dam west of Calgary, but they all finally wound up in Angler in Ontario, and it was because they wouldn't take the crap.

In that camp I don't think more than a few were against Canada. But a lot came out of it against Canada. They weren't even arrested, as far as I know. They call it "interned." No trial. There wasn't such a thing. And they call this sort of thing we live under British justice. They weren't prisoners like they were sentenced to five years or something, but that's what happened to them. They went in to protest what was happening to the families. The split-up, you know. No arrest, no trial, and they call this Canada.

There is a word, *gangari*. It means somebody who is a rebel. Won't take it lying down. There were some in that camp and they were really bitter. Some, not only had they had their families separated from them but they lost stores and farms and jobs, and they knew whether they got out in 1943 or 1945 or whenever the war was going to be over, they were going to have nothing. The government would say they could get out, go to work at Neys or Port Arthur or work in the fields around London, and they said to hell with it. Some did, some left, maybe a couple of hundred, but the rest stayed in to protest, like to hell with you, Canada, you've ruined my life and now you can look after my family, food, a house, hospital, and you can look after me too and I'm not going to work for you. Anything I do will be for myself, like exercising or drawing things, but I won't do your work in the camp. That's the way a lot of fellows thought. When you put it down that way, they felt betrayed by Canada because they had been loyal to Canada and Canada had let them down. So the fellows just sat there. Doing nothing. They didn't cause any trouble, I think. I mean those young fellows knew how to fight. They could have thrown any one of them guards fifteen feet or broken his neck right where he stood, but they didn't do that. They just sat. Those men weren't disloyal although some were pretty mad about Canada in the end. They blamed some or most of the old people for saying to the others that they should go to the road camps quietly and use a Japanese diesel and—what's a Japanese diesel? That's a wheelbarrow. That's how most of the roads were made through the mountains. Ask any guy who was there. There were a few pieces of heavy machinery, and dynamite of course, but most of the work was done with pick, shovel, and wheelbarrows. Like they built roads in ancient times. But if everybody had refused to go, everybody, it might have been a different story. I don't think there would have been a place like Angler, snow and frost half the year and mosquitoes and bulldog flies the rest of the year.

It just didn't have to be done that way. There were other ways. Why didn't they do something with the Germans and the Italians? They were fighting them too. Oh, it was a confused time. Who were the Japs? They had nothing. Couldn't vote. Lived in little shacks on the beach. No organization and they were always fighting among each other. So when the time came, the government said, "The Japs? What can they do?" So lock them up, ship them out to Jasper. Put them in camps. Get them out of the way. That's the way it happened.

A Matter of Pride

I was born in the small town of Port Moody near Vancouver and had as my friends many Occidental children with whom I went to school and enjoyed sports and lived a happy and smooth life.

I learned in school and in my associations to believe in British fair play and democratic principles. Although we suffered a great deal during the depression with no work for my father or myself and we came to the point of starvation many times in the course of three or four years, we never became public charges. We never broke a single law and took great pride in being law-abiding members of the community. There were only a few families of Japanese ancestry living in Port Moody and eventually the citizens of the community recognized our sincerity. They could point at us as being models and good examples of good citizenship and an asset to the community.

I left school and in due course started working for Thurston-Flavelle Lumber Company whose owners we knew personally and greatly respected. We came to know the mayor and bank manager and others who took a leading part in community life.

Then came the war with Germany and we tried to do our utmost toward Canada's war effort. We bought as much war savings certificates and victory bonds as we could afford, and the records would show that our contribution was amongst the highest in the firm for our wages. Many of my friends joined the armed forces and I followed with keen interest the efforts of Canadians of Japanese origin to enlist in the armed forces and gave it up in disappointment in seeing their efforts fail.

Then a state of war was declared between Canada and Japan and in time we received news of the orders of evacuation out of the restricted area. I travelled into Vancouver to receive further news and became acquainted with fellow Niseis who had already received a personal notice of immediate entrainment to Schreiber and other points out of the restricted area. There was turmoil and apprehension and worry all over the Japanese community and orders, nothing but orders. Orders to turn in our property, stores, houses, business, farms, for most of us a lifetime of sweat, toil, and hope, our radios, cars, boats, and personal belongings. I, too, had a home, a business recently started, and a car—it all went with nothing to show for it. More orders came, orders for all men to leave their wives and children, fathers and mothers, brothers and sisters, the aged and sick, and go by train to different road projects. First we were deprived of all we had and now our families. Where was the so-called democratic principles and British fair play which I was taught to believe?

To find some way of obtaining permission to evacuate en masse in family groups, my colleagues and I started the Mass Evacuation Group. We had petitions and we said we wouldn't be split from our families. We would go to the Interior or wherever, but with our families. After all, considering the fact that we had given all that we had ever had, isn't it only just for the authorities to acquiesce to such a too human request? We interviewed the members of the B.C. Security Commission and we were told that the order for our evacuation from the West Coast was in the hands of the Canadian government.

In one of my interviews with Mr. Austin Taylor, who was head of the Security Commission, and I had presented a feasible plan of evacuation, speaking for the Mass Evacuation Group, he threatened me by saying, "I don't give a damn if you are second generation, tenth generation, or fiftieth generation; as far as I'm concerned you're all Japs and if you don't obey my orders I'll intern you in carload lots."

So we retained Murphy Brothers, lawyers in Vancouver, and Mr. Murphy travelled to Ottawa on our behalf, since the Security Commission had told us the entire policy lay with the Canadian government. Mr. Murphy interviewed many public officials including the Secretary of Labour. He came back to us with the answer that the matter was entirely in the hands of the B.C. Security Commission. Passing the buck, so to say.

We continued our negotiations with personal interviews with

different officials and then after a time I was apprehended and sent to Angler. That happened just two weeks before the order of evacuation was received in Port Moody.

When I was in Angler I was interviewed by Inspector Saul of the Register General of Enemy Aliens and I wanted to know what we, all the men in the camp, what we were guilty of. I asked that if we were under suspicion why weren't we tried in the proper manner. And if we were not guilty, why weren't we not treated accordingly.

He answered that I, meaning me, was not guilty or under suspicion whatsoever. He said I could obtain my release and go to work as a Canadian with the full rights of citizenship.

I said that if we are Canadian citizens and not under suspicion, we should not have been treated as enemy aliens and we should be able to go back to our families in B.C. if we chose.

He said that at present that was against the policy of the Canadian government.

So then I said that the Canadian government does not intend to accord us full rights, and he answered that we must realize that even white Canadians are subject to government orders and are jailed if they are not obeyed during wartime, and some are forced to report regularly as suspicious characters.

He said that it is the purpose of the Canadian government to scatter the Japanese people all over Canada for their own good and for the purpose of assimilation. I said even against our will and our right as Canadian citizens to live together if we chose? He said yes, if it is for your own good.

He said the citizens of B.C. have been long envious of the Japanese in our success in various forms of earning a living such as trade, labour, business, education, and they put pressure on the government against us, the Japanese, and the government naturally had to act accordingly.

I said that, in other words, if the people wish the government to do something even so undemocratic and un-British as they had done to the Japanese, it must do so. He said yes, because a democracy is a government of the people by the vote and such unfortunate incidents as in our case cannot be helped.

So I said we were a victim of unfair democratic oppression of a minority group. He said, "No, a victim of unfortunate circumstances."

He then asked me why I didn't just accept my release and go out as a Canadian and become a credit to some community and then perhaps I could forget all that I had been through and lead a new life in new surroundings. I told him it was a matter of pride.

He said I mentioned pride but didn't I think it would be much better to go out and work and help out my family, buy things for them, and settle myself substantially somewhere and forget my pride for a change?

I asked him what would he think of a person who hadn't the guts or the pride to fight for the unity of his family, getting the families back together, for their protection and safeguard, and who didn't care what happened to the family of his friends? A man who would take the easiest way out to gain materially and financially? I asked him if such a person would be a credit to his country.

I said if I took the easiest way out now as a Canadian, I would lose all respect for myself. What would I say to my future children or my brothers and sisters who consider the sacrifice of a part of my life for a duty toward my family and fellow men as an action of pride and honour? I asked him what he thought of that.

The inspector said again that we were the unfortunate victims of circumstances and that he wished he knew how the Oriental mind worked.

I told him that if the authorities cared to delve into our minds and could understand us, then it would not have made so many great mistakes and caused so much suffering. I said we loved freedom and have a very high standard of honour and pride and loyalty and those should not have been abused but they have been.

He asked me what I would do if the government left me in the prison camp until the war was over. I said that after all that the government has done to me, depriving me of all that I ever had, my freedom, my family, my pride, and forcing me to lead such a life behind barbed wire, and if the government could not recognize that an injustice was done me, then I don't want any part of such a country. I said I would find myself another country that would treat me as a loyal citizen should be treated.

He said that he sympathized with us and such things should not have been allowed to happen, and he attributed them to irresponsible officials in authoritative office. Such things happen, however, he said, in all countries in the world during wartime and cannot be attributed only to Canada.

The interview just about ended when I told him that I thought democratic Canada was better than the other countries in the world, and with such wonderful principles one would not expect it to use tactics or allow action such as has happened in other nations. I said it now seemed to me that Canada is not so different from other countries with unreputable reputations.

The inspector told me that he thought I would find that Canada was a little bit better than others.

An "Escape" from Angler

There was this one guy in our hut in Angler who was okay in the daytime but at night he drove everybody and himself crazy.

We had H-huts. You know, like the army had. You've got one dormitory sort of and then another dormitory, and the crossbar on the "H" was the washroom and the toilets. They treated us like we were in the army, I guess, although it was a prison with high fences around it. It wasn't too bad but this guy Takashi couldn't stand the nights. He worried about his wife and kids and his mother back someplace in B.C.

Night. It never failed. Lights out and he'd start to walk. He'd go up one side of our side of the H-hut and down the other, back and forth. He'd be talking to himself in Japanese and while I didn't understand much I knew he was talking about his wife and kids. Up and down, up and down. This is after lights out. Ten o'clock. Guys want to sleep, you know. Sometimes a couple of guys would wrestle him down and get him to his bed. Others would try to trip him but how do you trip a guy who's slip-slipping along in slippers? He was driving us nuts. We'd report him to the guard, but they couldn't do anything with him. He'd walk himself until he was exhausted and there was maybe sixty-five or seventy guys in that hut who wanted to sleep and here he'd be, walking at two o'clock in the morning. It was weird. It was worse than that—it was terrible.

Finally they had all sorts of conferences, I guess, and they decided to send him back to his family. The rest of us, we could have gotten out by promising to work in some lumber camp in northern Ontario or in the beet fields near Niagara Falls, but this guy, he gets home that way. Of course that is how he got to Angler in the first place, by refusing to go work on the roads when his family was sent to the ghost town, so I guess it worked out okay for him. Maybe he planned it that way. I don't know. How could I know? Maybe he was just smarter, but it didn't seem like that at the time.

Barbed Wire—and Beer

You see, we, the Japanese, have what they call—you see there is no will made out to anyone. The oldest son automatically handles these things. Well, when the evacuation came we had this house. It was a good house. Everybody was going to the camps and we didn't know how long it would be before we would get back and you know what happens when a house stands idle. It just goes to ruin. So as the oldest son, it was my job to sell that house. Then distribute it among the family.

I was nineteen in 1941. The R.C.M.P. came to round us up.

You see. You were given a slip of paper and on it it said when you had to report to the police so they could ship you off to a road camp. My slip of paper said May 11 and the police stated to me I had to leave by that time. Well, I was still there by that time. I didn't report. You see, I was trying to sell this house, get a decent price for it for money for my mother and younger brothers and sisters.

I was running around, keeping out of sight. I'd stay with my English and Scotch friends and they'd let me sleep there. Hiding out while I made negotiations to see if I could get the best price for this property. It was only a house but naturally you're not going to give it away.

Anyway, the R.C.M.P. grabbed me one night and I was only a young punk and a rebel. If I'm right I don't care who you are, I'm gonna fight. They said I was overdue. Once you're past that date there is no going back. You couldn't say you were sorry. They'd just pick you up and send you to the Immigration Hall and then ship you out to Angler in Ontario.

So I told them they weren't taking me in that night. I said if they tried I'd fight them, and even if there were three or four of them, I'd get one of them. I was a rebel then. I said that I would be at my house next day and if they came then I would go with them, but I'd made up my mind they weren't going to take me that night. They thought it over and then they said okay.

So next day they came. Four of them. Down to the Immigration Hall. No trial, no nothing. Just waiting there behind bars until they had enough to ship out to Angler, which was the big concentration camp up in the bush.

By the old, old coaches. You sat up on hard seats all day and at night they pulled this wooden thing down and two slept up there and two on the seats which pulled out. Yeah, Colonist cars. That's what they were called.

There were lots of us on that train. No, no, nobody was what you called subversive. None of us knew anything about that. These were fellows, like myself, young and rebels, or married men who didn't want to go to the road camp. The military police brought us across. There were some in each car. Nonstop. We ate in the cars, slept on them seats, and you couldn't even stand up to go to the washroom unless you raised your hand.

They lied to us. They told us Angler would be just another camp. But it wasn't. When we got there we found it was a prison camp. When we got off there were soldiers, Veterans' Guards with machine guns, just waiting for somebody to make a run for it. They got to be sick. Nobody was going to make any rush for it.

After we got to know the guards they were very good. They got to know that we were just fellows like themselves and that we weren't out to wreck the country or anything like that. We got to know them well. There was one fellow, a big fellow, and he always had cigars in here [pointing to a pocket]. I used to wrestle with him just for fun and he thought it was just for fun, but what he didn't know was every time I wrestled with him I was able to slip a cigar out of his pocket. That was one thing I used to laugh about.

But at first before they got to know us they would say, "You! Come. With me!" and they would gesture and I put them straight pretty soon. I said, "Don't talk to me that way, goddamn it. I am a Canadian just like you and I can talk English just like you, so don't talk to me in that pig Latin way." You see, as one guard told me later, they hadn't been told who we were, that we were from British Columbia. Canadians. They had been told that we were Japanese prisoners of war. Maybe that would account for the machine guns at first.

But it was a prison camp. It had two big layers of barbed wire, one beside the other, and if you stepped in between those two layers of barbed wire that man in the tower, he could shoot you. It was like that.

I wasn't around at the time but they had this riot . . . well, not a riot, I guess, but a pretty strong argument and the guards did fire, so I'm told, and in one particular case if the fellow had been in his bed he would have been dead because the bullets from the tower came right into the hut and hit right into his bed. That's the only thing that happened I know of.

You got a letter a month and a postcard a week and it was all censored, so it was a prisoner-of-war camp in that way too.

So anyway, after awhile the government said to themselves that a lot of these fellows shouldn't be behind barbed wire in a prison camp. Just for not wanting to split up from their families, leaving a wife and little children. But they were also thinking of money. They fed us good and there was the cost of the guards and coal and electricity and there were about seven hundred of us in there, and we heard that the whole thing was costing the government about 25 dollars a day per person.

They came to some of us and they said, "You got to get out. It's costing too much." This was about after nine, ten months in there, behind the wire.

Get out. Where you going to go?

So some of my friends say no, they're not leaving, and they say that if this is the way the government is going to treat its citizens when they haven't done nothing, then they'll just stay in the camp and eat good food and lie around. So a lot of them won't go. Others said they were going to renounce their citizenship and when the war was over they would have to be shipped back to Japan.

When the war did end, most of those kind of fellows who said they would renounce their citizenship, they did. They went back to Japan. One good friend of mine got in with Pepsi-Cola in Japan and now he is a big shot, head of the whole thing. He could take me back to Japan with him and give me any big job if he wanted. Pepsi-Cola in Japan is like Coca-Cola here, real big.

Oh, it wasn't a bad life in the camp, that Angler. The Red Cross was there and they'd do all sorts of things to help you. Give you things and talk to you. The Spanish consul used to come and visit us. I think it was once a month. If we had any beefs we'd tell him. I think he used to do something about them to the authorities.

Funny thing about the Spanish consul. I got myself into the kitchen as a helper and I did that because I was an awful eater. It meant getting up at five in the morning to prepare the breakfast but I didn't mind. In a prison camp time don't matter much. I used to keep the accounts on the rations, and how much bread and meat and fish they'd bring in for us. But when the Spanish consul came and ate with us, that was the day we always got two pork chops. But I say this, it was wartime and things were short and you can't be giving seven hundred people steak all the time anyway. Mostly always stew. We'd make two stews. One with meat in it and one with no meat. That was the stew for the vegetarians. When the Spanish consul did come we'd be asked how the food was and we'd say it was good. We weren't lying. It was good food. Maybe not enough rice because a lot of our people could live on rice, but it was okay. And people who were under a doctor's strict orders on a diet, then we'd prepare that for them too.

Red Cross and Salvation Army was in there so we had skates and sticks and baseballs and the guys used to play and in the big hall some guys were artists and they used to paint big pictures of movie stars, like Deanna Durbin and Marlene Dietrich. They had a piano there and different instruments if you wanted to play, and there was one guy so good on the piano that after he got out he went to the Toronto Conservatory of Music. He must have got five degrees. We used to listen to him play a lot; he could play "Stardust" five different ways. In plain popular style. Boogie woogie. Jazz. So on. You could listen to him for hours.

No, as far as treatment is concerned, I have no complaints at all. There was always somebody coming in and asking if everything was okay. And after awhile they started having beer.

No, there was no escapes among our group, the Japanese. But they said there had been a break by the Germans who were in the camp before us. They tried to tunnel out from the cookhouse. In fact they did but they were waiting for them when they did. One guard told me that near the camp there were some graves that were the German graves of those who were machine-gunned, but I don't know if that is true. That is only what I heard.

I used to do a lot of thinking in that camp. Like there was no need for penning up seven hundred guys up in a prison camp up in the bush in northern Ontario. If it was war and they thought it was that serious that we should be one hundred miles from the coast, why didn't they do it another way? Why not advertise across Canada? Ask, like say a lady has a farm and her husband has gone overseas. Well, she needs somebody to help her with the farm. Well, my own family, me and my brother and my sister. My brother and me we could learn to do the farming and my sister could help around the house and our family could live on that farm and earn money and that would suit our family fine. Then when the war was over or whatever time they felt best for us to go back, then we'd go back. But to send all the men to road camps and the women and children to those old mining towns and young fellows like me to prison, why, that was crazy.

So anyway, they came to us and said you can go. Well, at first I was stubborn, thinking why didn't you figure this all out when we were all in Vancouver? So I was the third, I think, the third bunch to leave. But what the hell, no sense being stubborn about it. Seeing your buddies going out and you're still locked up in jail, so I decided I'd go too. So we went.

The twenty-third of December. They wouldn't even let us go into a town to celebrate Christmas. We had to go into a lumber camp. They were paying our way by train to the camp. Pigeon Timber Company near Neys. I had it in my mind I'd make a break for it. I didn't know where I was going to go, but I didn't plan to spend all the rest of the war cutting trees. Why, the snow was so high you couldn't see each other.

You know, in Vancouver you never wear winter clothing. A spring and fall coat would be your heaviest. So when we went to the prison camp we got prison clothes, you know. Even the big orange circle on the back like the Germans had. We used to call it the target. That's what the guards would shoot at. Except I don't think any guards would have shot at us. They were our buddies. Anyway, just Vancouver spring clothes and low Oxfords and that's what they sent us into the bush with to cut wood. It was ·crazy. So I said it was crazy and I went and got myself a job as a cookee in the cookhouse so I didn't have to do that kind of work. I would have nearly died cutting that wood in the bush.

Of course they wanted to sell us winter clothes that you could work in, but at the prices they asked and the money we made,

25 cents an hour, that was going to tie you down for a year just paying it off. So one day this buddy and me we decide we'll hike it out along the railroad line to Port Arthur. The day we left the snow was coming down and the wind was blowing and we talked to each other all the time, keeping each other going. We finally got there although there was times I didn't think we'd make it. You'd look behind you and see your tracks filling in with snow.

In Port Arthur I went to the government and said I was a sick man, I couldn't work in the bush and I'd been released from the prison camp. They gave me my release and said they had offers for jobs and did I want to work for Canada Packers or a manufacturing company in Toronto? I said yes. I'd seen nothing, never been to Toronto, so they paid my train fare and that's how I got to Toronto. I guess I must have been one of the first Japanese to come out of the bush into Toronto. That's how I got away from Angler, the prison camp, and to Toronto.

Dumb Things Happen in a War

Oh, sure it was much tougher on us than it was on them. Here we were, joining up for King and Country and stuck in a place like Angler guarding a bunch of Japs. They had no freedom and we didn't either. When I joined up, like the old war horse like I was, I guess I did have ideas of going to England with the rest of the boys and some more excitement; but when they formed the Veterans' Guard that was the end of it for us. Some of us—and I think everybody over forty-five or fifty was Veterans' Guard— some did instructing. Others guarded bridges. I had one friend who spent half his war guarding a bridge over the Red River at Winnipeg, just doing sweet bugger all for two or three years. Others like myself, we were stuck out at Angler guarding these Japanese fellows.

Well, if you put it one way, it wasn't a bad life. I mean the guarding part was nothing. You took your turns, like shift work in a factory, is one way of putting it, I never pulled the trigger once. I didn't have to and I can't really think of anybody who did. I mean, there were no escapes. The Germans, yes, they would try escapes because they were soldiers—and troops behind the wire are supposed to escape. At least it is something for them to do, keep them busy planning and digging tunnels and making documents. But these Japs. First there was no place they could go. Hell and gone to the Lakehead or to those towns in the bush to the east, but they had to follow the iron rail. That was the way in and the way out and there was no point in trying to escape during the winter. Freeze your balls off. In the summer, sure, but where could they go? Everybody in the country knew them. Short. Dark. Black hair. Slant-eyed. Wearing denims, and I don't care whether it was winter or summer issue, everyone had a big orange circle on his back. It wasn't the kind of circle stitched on so it could be unstitched. This was woven into the cloth, so it was there.

I got to know a lot of them. They all seemed to have nicknames. 'Knobby' and 'Fatso' and 'Deadeye' and like that. These were the young fellows, of course. There were quite a few older ones, too, who didn't go along with the foolishness of it all. But I got to know a few.

I met one about fifteen years later, one of the ones who had gone down to Thamesville to work when the government was letting them go. We met at Yonge and Front and I took him over to that cafeteria just up from the corner there and we talked a long time. I asked him if he was bitter and he just laughed. He was a great one for laughing. Giggling is a better way of putting it. He giggled and said no, he wasn't bitter. Was anybody? He said maybe a few, the older ones, those who had lost a lot of property but the young guys . . . say under thirty or so, they didn't care all that much. He said, "It was war. Lots of dumb things happen in war."

That's all he said about it. He was doing well for himself. Said he had a car and a house and a variety store. He said, and this is the point, he said, "I guess you guys had it worse than us." Well, we did. We were prisoners in that camp too. Sure we got leaves and furloughs when they came up, but we were in the frigging army and so on.

I was a corporal, so I didn't make that much. I've seen me time and again bumming smokes off the Japs. They all seemed to have money. This fellow 'Knobby' I'm telling you about, he had worked in a sawmill out in B.C. for three or four years and he'd saved up his money, and while he had to put it in the Custodian's possession, he could draw on it whenever he wanted. So much a month. They wouldn't let them have tailor-mades, or maybe cigarettes were just short in them days, but they used to get Player's Fine Cut tobacco in those blue cans. But the administration wouldn't let them have the cans. Why, I don't know. Figured they'd make weapons or digging tools out of them or some foolish thing. So they'd give them the tobacco in the wax paper wrapper it came in and then they'd put orange peel in it to keep it nice and moist. And here I was, so dry, so needing a smoke, and I'm the guard, and I have to bum off the prisoners for cigarettes. I could have taken those smokes, I guess, but that wasn't the way things were done. We liked them. They liked us. We got along fine. And besides, if we'd played rough they'd have reported us. They had their rights in prison, you know.

One fellow said to me once, he said, "You know, I'm not a prisoner of war. To be a prisoner of war, you have to be a Japanese soldier." He said he was a Canadian. Born right downtown in Vancouver. He said, "I'm a conscientious objector." Then he laughed. He and I knew that was baloney. I'd heard how they'd been kicked out of B.C. by the politicians. They even knew the names of the politicians. They even had a little song about them, using their names, and it wasn't a very complimentary song either.

But they were a happy-go-lucky bunch. They had their musical instruments. They could sing real good. Play real good. They'd have concerts. Played volleyball and they were good at it. Baseball. Very good. They were very good at it. They could beat anybody around, I guess. But no women, and I never realized until then just how horny some of those young fellows could be. But they didn't give us no trouble. Just that when they talked, an awful lot of that talk was about girls. Women. Just like us. We talked too but in a different way. They talked pretty down-to-earth. But even if they had of broken out like those twenty-eight Germans did, what good would it have done them? There wasn't a woman for miles and if they set foot on that road they were dead ducks. Although I couldn't see myself cracking one off at a poor little Jap, far from home, running into the bush. Let the mosquitoes and black flies get him. He'd soon be coming out again.

There was a fair amount of drinking. They'd get together a bunch of potatoes and potato peels and rice and barley from the soup, and just about anything you could name, and steam it up and have a still going and they'd have a party. They weren't very good drinkers, as I recall. One mickey of hard stuff would make two or three of them pretty drunk and then they'd sit around in their hut and sort of croon these little Jap songs to themselves. I remember once doing hut inspect, lights out, and there were these four guys sitting there and the mickey bottle was empty and they were tapping it back and forth between each other like you'd tap a football with your toes and they were drunk as skunks. It would take more than a whole quart to make us that drunk.

I sometimes would go to an Italian place in the Lakehead and buy four, five, six mickeys of home brew, or whatever I could afford, and take them back and sell them—and I never had any trouble in getting rid of them. After all, there were hundreds of Japs in that camp, rows of huts, and a lot of them would get the blues and want to sing. I never saw any fights. I saw fights among our own people, the Veterans' Guard, but it was usually a couple of fifty-five-year-old guys flailing away at each other. But not the Japs.

One thing they did know. They knew how the war was going. They must have had a secret radio because they knew. They'd tell us when the Japanese won a victory over the Americans. They'd show some bitterness then. They called the Americans "those goddamned bastards," and things like that, but they never said things like that about the Canadians. Of course we were hardly in that war. But this "Knobby" guy came up to me once on the playing field and he said, "Andy, I hope those Canadians that Japan got at Hong Kong are getting as good a life out of this war as we are." He was sincere. I know he meant it. Of course, they weren't. They were treated like dogshit. Everybody knows that now. And I know one of them and, boy, is he a bitter man today. He even writes anonymous letters to well-known Japanese Canadians and gives them shit. Still. After all these years. He'd phone them up too. He doesn't care.

Funny thing, most of the young fellows couldn't speak Japanese worth a damn. Swear words and that but the old fellows who wanted to talk with them, they couldn't. Unless they talked English. And their English was pretty bad. Some didn't have much. One old guy who didn't talk English, I heard he had a big store in Vancouver and I asked him once how he did business if he didn't speak English—how did he do his books and all that? He told a young Japanese to tell me that he didn't deal with the whites. You see, he could understand English but he couldn't talk it. The young fellow told me the word that the old man had used for "whites" was considered a swear word. I think it was like the word "dog."

I spent two years up there. That was enough. Cold in winter. Mosquitoes in summer. Nothing to do. The Japs had more to do than we did. They were easy to handle. I forget how many guards we had up there but it was always more than enough, and it was a funny kind of prison camp because we got to be buddies with the Japs. Not real friend buddies but buddies. I got to know a bit about what was going on in their families because they'd show me pictures they'd got. All in all, it was a kind of funny life. It was like we were all in the same boat.

But I learned one thing. Those Japanese fellows. First they were Canadians and even in that camp there were some fellows that when they passed the flagstaff with the Union Jack on it, they would salute it. Yes, some did do that. And another thing I'd forgotten. Some of them were pretty well off. They had money and they'd buy Canada War Savings Bonds when the bond drive came around. I remember one fellow bought a 50-dollar bond every time around.

Another thing, some people, I don't know how, but they got to know that these Japs were good neighbours. The Jews especially. Those Jews around Spadina were just crazy to hire the Japs, and by this time they were letting some of them out of the camp. What the hell use is there in keeping a twenty-two-year-old kid in a camp when he hadn't done anything wrong? One kid punched a Mountie in the nose on a train taking them out to some road camp. He told me about it. He was no more a criminal than you are. But there he was. With the big orange circle on his back. He was one of the bitter ones. Can't blame him, could you? Anyway, when they let him out he was happy to go to work for the Jews. He got a job with this Jew making caps, hats you know, and he sent word back and soon a lot of the fellows were getting out and going to work for the Jews. These Japanese fellows knew how to work. A day's work didn't mean eight or nine hours. It meant till that job was finished. So I respected them for their working ways. They could work and how!

I know this sounds like I'm on the side of the Japs. Well, I am not and I am. Some of them must have done things out in British Columbia there that must have made it necessary to throw them in the can and move them away into the camps; but the ones I knew, they got along fine with us and we got along fine with them.

In fact, one way to get out of that camp was to get the Japs on your back. We had this one Veterans' Guard and he was a bastard. We'd go through the huts at night and there was this one kid. Kind of simple. He was singing this song to himself so the guard switched on the light and said, "Okay, who is singing?" Nobody said nothing. Everybody knew. Nobody would say. I knew. I told the guard to forget it. So he said, "Unless that man comes forward this hut goes on charge." That meant rights would be taken away. So I went and pulled one guy out, a guy I knew who didn't give a damn, and I said this was the singer and he said he was, just to protect the rest of the guys in the hut. After all, you don't pick on a simple kid who sings at night because he's lonely and scared. The guy I hauled out, a big guy named Tosh, he got three days in solitary. So what? But the Japs through their camp committee went to see the commandant and they said this guard was brutal and harsh and they shifted that guard to a lousy job.

I'm not saying the Japs had the upper hand. No, of course not. That was never the idea. But the idea was that we were all in this mess together and the more we helped each other out and the quicker the Allies got the war over with, then the quicker we'd all be home again.

I didn't like that camp. Nobody did. But we were in it. So let's relax and enjoy yourself. We could have made it really rough on them and they could have made it rough on us, but we didn't. So it worked out.

6 *Shovels and Pickaxes*

One of the first government edicts, and one bitterly opposed, was the sending of male nationals out of the Protected Zone, mainly to road camps. They were to open up rights-of-way and build and improve Interior roads, which could be used for military traffic. Not an unreasonable project, since B.C.'s road system was in wretched shape and, in places, non-existent.

The first hundred men were to leave Vancouver, in what appeared to be a voluntary way, on February 2, 1942, and they did go—but not until February 23 and not until there had been considerable argument and objection. In all, 1,700 men between seventeen and forty-five were shipped out.

The order-in-council had a devestating effect upon Japanese Canadian families. Several were the stories I heard of wives and mothers and even whole families running along the train platform, calling out and crying, while the coaches carrying away their loved ones gathered speed.

The system of camps never worked as had been hoped, and within a year men were being allowed to join their families in the ghost towns. At war's end it is estimated there were only about 100 men left in road camps.

What did they accomplish? For one thing, the men—nationalists and the husky young Canadian-born Japanese Canadians who later joined them—got all the fresh air they could use in a lifetime. One man told me that all he did was lean on his shovel. Another said a chap he knew used to pedal down

143

the trail on a bike each day to visit a Finnish farmer's
sauna—and nobody, foreman or engineer, complained.

Another said, "At least I didn't have to go to war and get my
head shot off. But it was all such a waste of time. We could have
been doing something constructive for Canada. Not that."

Not a Man Anymore

Then it came time for my father to go to the road camp. He was a
national, born in Japan, and he was being sent to Yellowhead up
near Jasper to work in the road camp. I remember going off to
the station, the CN, on Main Street to see him off, to say
goodbye.

I remember that night, seeing all these men, most of whom
had been big bosses in their own homes, beaten. It was the first
time I saw my father, who had a lot of spirit and was an extrovert
and had a pretty high opinion of himself, saw him whipped.
Beaten. Not a man anymore but a number on a card in a file,
being sent with a bunch of other whipped men to some stretch
of road up in the north to use a shovel and axe. That was part of
my growing up.

Police All the Time Watching Us

I was scared stiff of the R.C.M.P. First they came and got Daddy
and took him off to a road camp, then they came and got Jimmy
Oyama and then we had five boys sleeping at our house,
sleeping on the floor and hiding because they didn't want to go
to the camps. What could they do? So they came to our house

and hid. And somebody told. People were telling on other people. And the R.C.M.P. came and dragged them away. Boys, eighteen-and-over, menfolk, all taken away, shipped out every day. There was no way of getting away from the police.

When my mother and I would see an R.C.M.P. she would nudge me and tell me to say nothing and be calm and do what they told us to do. No, actually they don't harm, but they're there all the time watching us before we go to camp.

You can understand how scared everybody got, how panicky they got.

They took them all away and they were all Canadian boys, every one was a Canadian boy, but away they had to go into the bush. The day after Mori turned eighteen, they came and got him and then they decided they want older men too and they came and took them. Then higher, fifty something. Then they got up to sixty. Then Grandpa. When Grandpa had to go to the bush that's when I really got upset.

So I just cried and cried and when they put him on that train with all those old men I mean I just cried and cried and there was nothing I could do.

I was not scared of the R.C.M.P. anymore. Not after all this. They got no right to push me around. I got my rights too. A lot of our people forgot that during the war. We were Canadians too, just like everybody else.

Life in the B.C. Bush

It was my turn to go on April 7 of 1942. I joined the army three years later on April 7, so April has always been a special month for me. But on April 7, 1942, they sent us to work in a camp on the Sicamous-Revelstoke section, and where we were was at Yard Creek where we first built a camp. It was a pretty place. Yard Creek was a pretty little stream and I would like to see it again. But that's another thing.

When I was told I'd be going, there was two choices. You could go to Ontario, Schreiber or Jackfish, or up in B.C., and my mother begged me to stay in B.C., so that's how I wound up in Yard Creek.

There were four camps in that area. Solsqua, Taft, Yard Creek, and Three Valleys. Okay? A couple had been relief camps during the depression. Yard Creek was new. It was wartime and they wanted a good road for military purposes. This was the road that became the Trans-Canada Highway. Our job was to break bush. We had guys who could operate bulldozers, guys from logging camps and fishing and things like that, as well as city kids like me.

We started out with 104 but then for various reasons some of the guys decided they would go East, and then the married men were told they could go to the ghost towns and join their families. So after these deletions, people going elsewhere, there were about eighty of us. Made up of two groups. Canadian-born Japanese like myself who could be around eighteen and a few years over that, and the Japanese nationals, born in Japan, who were up around fifty or so. What you got—two sets of people, Canadian-educated people and Japan-educated people. These people would have some education, with a handful of high school graduates among them. Others much less, and often from rural backgrounds who spoke a meagre English. Very Japanese.

And so we worked together and we shared a lot of things together but often in our pursuits and even in our games and so forth we were separate. All camps had this problem.

At Yard Creek we were about five or six miles from the nearest habitation, which were some Finnish farms at Cambie. They had their sauna and we paid them twenty-five cents each until we built our own bathhouse.

The food? Adequate. I know a lot about the food because I was the head flunky, bottle-washer, pie-cutter, and potato-peeler. The food was plentiful, plain, done in bush-camp fashion. Like in every situation at that time we had two or three showdowns with the foreman because everybody picked up food poisoning, or we had some bad meat or something, and everybody would decide we'd go on strike and wouldn't go to work. By the way, the chief cook and the main staff was all white. We were a really motley crew, the kitchen gang. We didn't have to go out and work on the bush and rock, but we had to get up early though. To prepare, get the whole bloody mess organized. Clean up afterward. But we had time off in the morning and the afternoon. And so on. The food was okay, essentially.

But it was the morale. It was never good. Not for us or for the Veterans' Guard. These were old World War One vets and they guarded us, what guarding there was to be done. They usually didn't wear their uniforms when they were around the camps, but they did carry their Lee Enfield rifles with them. Used to sort of walk around. From the first they came out with us, and most of us being Canadian-born anyway, we got to be real buddies. What the hell, we were all stuck in this mess together. But after a while as the camp got bigger and more white staff came in and more guards came in, the ones we had been friends with stopped being friends. The word had been put in their ear. You see, they became more disciplined and organized. They had one little sentry box beside Yard Creek where the road was. That was where any sabotage could happen. They sure looked very lonely standing out there by their little sentry box in the Canadian woods. But I can't remember them patrolling the extreme ends of our operation as we scattered for our work jobs. I don't think they did that. They were trying to do soft time just like we were.

The Mounties used to cruise through once in awhile. Just checking up. There were good ones and there were real bastards, but I remember some who used to come through who were really humane people. One time one of our guys went off his nut and assaulted a foreman and the Mounties came and they really tried to get him to say the right things in the situation so that it would go easy for him, so it wouldn't become a charge thing, so he wouldn't be sent to Oakalla Prison. I was the interpreter for that case because it did go to a court case at Revelstoke, but it wasn't as bad as it could have been because of the Mounties.

I was young but I was the camp spokesman and I had to lock horns with white people, and especially the resident engineer at Revelstoke, a lovely character. He used to tell the local people that we were in the camp because we were the enemy, and we'd meet the local people and they'd ask us what we did so bad that we were in a prison camp on the road. We'd say we hadn't done a damn thing, that we were Canadians like them, and so on and so forth.

Also, the powder man was always getting drunk and forgetting where he'd put his caps for the dynamite and our guys were scared because if they pounded down a hole and old Andy had left some caps down it, then there would be serious trouble. Injuries. One afternoon the seven Japanese on the powder gang came and said they were going to quit because of this, and the rest of the camp said they'd back them up until the engineer did something about Andy. They said they were going to get hurt or killed. Bloody speeches made and everything. When the meeting broke up and the engineer went back to Revelstoke and it was all pretty inconclusive what was going to be done about Andy and the dynamite caps, the foreman came up to me and he said "You do one more thing and you'll be sent East." Well, what could be worse, being sent to Ontario? Exile. For a B.C. guy, especially because my family was still in B.C. So that was the kind of thing that went on when you tried to deal with the whites and establish some kind of rights. So I thought, holy shit, I got to cool it.

So I did. I went to the older Japanese who was officially the spokesman, a nice gentleman, and I told him what had happened, so from then on I pretty well kept low. I had no real enmity against those assholes. It was their job and they had to do it. But I figured if we went easy on them, then maybe they'd go easy on us. That was the way you did things in the camps.

"You Build Road to Hope"

Soon they say, "You go to Princeton, camp, work on road in mountain." That's what they say first. All Japanese born in Japan go to mountains.

So I went Princeton. Where road camp used to be. Old camp for during depression time. They tell us, maybe forty-five of us, Japanese nationals, you build road to Hope. That's where they sent us Japanese nationals.

Then two months they change rules so any Japanese, national, naturalized, citizen, all can go to this camp. Princeton.

Highway. Road. Well, they got no tools. No big tools like bulldozer. Just hands you're working. Pick, shovel, axe, like that. All rock, gravel, big, big trees. We not building highway that way. Just widening. I work hard. Some don't work hard at all.

They don't want us in jail in Vancouver, they keep us in jail in camp in mountains. No prison like, but jail all the same. No family, no kids, no money.

So when the boss comes to me, saying, "You were a gardener?" and I say yes, he says I can get out of camp, out of mountains, be with family again. Just I gotta go to Alberta, sugar beets. Work for farmers for sugar beets. Have own house, money. So I say sure, get me out of prison in this camp, I go to Alberta. So I go. No good to widen road then anyway. Camp there by that Princeton just a prison although not in Vancouver, so same thing though. How come I came to Alberta? That was it. The beets but my family too. With my family again.

A Foolish Thing to Do

I volunteered to go to a road camp. This was when they were sending men to the road camp and nobody wanted to go, but there were some young Japanese from our district were running away from the Mounties because they were being rounded up, so I offered to go with these fellows to the road camp. They were kind of wild and young and in trouble and I thought that if I was there, being older, I could have a good effect on the young people in the camp and there would be no trouble. I could see trouble ahead for a lot of these young people being stuck away in the bush working on roads and trails. So I did that.

No, I abandoned my family. I left them behind because I offered to take these fellows to the road camp and play father to them. Keep them out of trouble. I don't know why I did such a foolish thing, leaving my wife and children, but I did. I thought there would be more amnesty shown toward my family, that they would be treated better, because I was offering to help the authorities with these young kids.

There was another reason too. My brother had a boathouse near Annasis Island, across from there, and that was another thing I asked the authorities. Would they give my brother time to clear the stock out of the boathouse, lumber and tools and stuff, before they took him away? They said they would, they'd agreed to the bargain I tried to drive with them; but in the confusion he was given only a certain time to get out and so he lost everything.

So I went to the road camp and worked there and my wife and children were sent to Slocan and finally I got permission to leave the road camp and rejoin my family.

I don't know why I did such a foolish thing. It was the times, I guess. Everything seemed different then, Nothing seemed right.

All Aboard for Schreiber

Well, they picked me up because I had broken the curfew and took me down to the Immigration Building, and took away my money and locked me up, and there didn't seem to be nobody there then but me and a couple of old guys I didn't know. But soon, next day, I look out and two buses are coming down the road and they're full of Japanese and they get out and they're put in too. I don't think I know any of them. Maybe a couple, them I'd played ball with some time or other.

We're all in there and the food's okay, enough of it, but there's nothing to do and everybody just sits around and argues, about this and that and why we're in there, why they're doing this to us, and so on and they elect a committee, to get us out of there, naturally, but you know how good that's going to be. No good at all. Nothing happens.

Then they come around and say that if we volunteer, then we'll be sent out to a road camp to work on the road. They don't say where or what doing but, Jesus, anything to get out of that Immigration place. So I volunteer. I say yes. I'll go. Just show me the way.

The time goes by but soon the time comes when we're leaving. By train. There's about 130 of us, all Japanese from all over. Rupert, Ucluelet, the Island, up the valley, everywhere, and I'd say about all of us were under thirty but mostly twenty-four, twenty-five, twenty-six.

We're on the train, see, and our people come down and see us off. We're volunteers. That's what they call us, but why do they have the Mounties with us? A guy named Tommy Thompson and another with a Mexican, a Spanish name. They're good guys though but whenever we look up, one of them is always looking at us. I wonder when those guys ever find time for sleeping, but they're good guys.

Nobody causes trouble. It is kind of a big adventure for a lot of us anyway. Our boss is Frank Nagano. He's an older guy, been in the First World War and knew a lot. He'd been across the country, seen it, and he told us what was coming, like when we'd see the Rockies and when we'd get to Winnipeg and things like that. When we wanted to know something he was the one we asked and he'd ask the Mounties. Things like that. I don't think any of the rest had been beyond the Fraser Valley and most not even that far. The Japanese didn't do much travelling.

We were part of the regular train, old coaches with stoves in them and we'd cook our meals. Yeah, they gave us food. There seemed enough of it. Rice, too. We asked for rice and they got it for us and we had some guys who could cook all sorts of dishes with rice. The Mounties got their share too and one said he'd never known there were so many dishes with rice.

We knew we were going to a place called Schreiber. It was in northern Ontario, but we didn't know what it was like and this was still winter and we didn't know what to expect. But anyway, the train just kept going on and on and some guys played music, clarinet. No, that other instrument. I forget it. And a piano accordion and saxophone and other instruments and they'd play Benny Goodman and those and there were also gramophones, a few, the wind-up kind, and stacks of records, swing and jazz. And when we weren't listening, we'd be arguing or talking or playing cards. We sure played a lot of cards. We all had money, you see. It hadn't run out yet, like it did later. A lot of guys wrote letters to their wives or girlfriends. Every time we stopped there always were a bunch of guys looking for a letter box.

We stopped a lot because it was a regular train, you see. We'd get off and buy magazines or cheese sandwiches and coffee in the railroad restaurants. People were always looking at us. Most of us, I guess, we were the first Japanese they'd ever seen. Some people talked to us; like they'd come up to us and ask who we were because to see 130 guys like us roaming around a small railway platform, that must have been something. Anyway, none of the people knew what was happening in B.C., that we were being evicted from our homes and sent off into the bush because they said we were a destructive element. Nobody knew that. It just wasn't something that was known in those days and everybody should have known about it. We figured the government wanted to keep the whole thing quiet.

When we got to Winnipeg Frank got hold of a picture of Schreiber, the camp. That made us feel better because they were talking on the train that we'd just be dumped off somewhere and handed a saw and hammer and told to build a camp. What we saw in the picture looked like a good camp. We didn't exactly know any more about it but it wasn't such a bad-looking place.

Then we got to Schreiber and the people knew we were coming and some came down to the station to get their first look. To look at these Japs. But they were friendly. Some talked to us and told us what the weather was like, what to wear. Remember, we were in Vancouver clothes. In fact I had no work clothes. I was dressed up in my Sunday best and so were the rest of the guys, suits, sports jackets, you know. Finery.

Then after a half-hour or so they lined us up and we walked to the camp. About three miles. It was a tough walk, there was some snow on the ground. Some guys stopped and threw snowballs as if it was the first snow we'd ever seen except on the mountains. Well, we got there and there were the buildings but they were empty, so everybody got going setting up the cots. Army beds stacked there. That took awhile and then we had to organize ourselves. Different jobs. Cooking was one. They gave us food, lots of that, and there were toilets and washbasins and all that. It was what you could say the guys in the army were getting too.

They were going to put us to work on the Trans-Canada Highway, and the engineer in charge, a guy from the Department of Highways, a good guy, he said we'd be organized to cut a trail through along where the highway had been surveyed. A tote road. Which could be used for working on the main highway when we started. I don't think anybody had much say on what he would do. I was put in a gang clearing the tote road but I didn't like that, so after a while I got a job in the kitchen, helping the cook.

We did pretty well what we wanted, but being just a bunch of young fellows we pretty well thought of ourselves. We'd walk down into Schreiber and buy things, just like in Vancouver—milk shakes and clothes and magazines and things we wanted. A lot would go to the United Church in Schreiber on Sundays. The people were friendly, not like the people on the coast. Not a bit. They were nice.

There was a man named Mr. Mills from the government who helped a lot. A very nice man. Problems, we'd go to him.

We got paid, of course. Better having us working and getting paid than lying around doing nothing and not getting paid. Some of it we had to send home but there was enough. Besides, then, we still had our own money. Most of us had anyway. I had some and that's how I could go into Schreiber.

Then in the spring an agricultural representative came up to see us and he asked who wanted to volunteer to work in the sugar beet crops in southern Ontario, down around Thamesville—Chatham and Thamesville. I said sure, I'd volunteer. I didn't like the work in the kitchen and I sure didn't like living in the bush and I hated that winter, so I said yes. They said we'd be in a camp and would work in the sugar beets and then maybe on other crops—tomatoes, that was one of them. I think about fifteen of us went down to Chatham, in that part of the country.

I enjoyed it. Some people tried to make it rough for us, but all in all it was okay and better than working in the bush when it was so damned cold.

Where the Girls Were

There were three or four road camps along that stretch of road west of Revelstoke and I'd say there were maybe 300 fellows in the camps and most of them were single guys because by this time the government had let the married fellows go to the ghost towns where their families were.

So what was there to do? Well, there was softball. We'd play the other camps. We were good players. But that was about it. Oh, we made a little park near our camp where we could go and sit in the evenings and listen to the river go by. And once a month, like every camp did it in rotation, you could go into Revelstoke. On a one-day pass. To do things. Get a haircut from a fellow who knew what he was doing. We had a little money to spend. But we could go to a picture show or walk into a restaurant and have a meal. Jesus Christ! Yeah! A meal. Or buy some magazines. Magazines. Have an ice cream soda.

But where we really wanted to go was the ghost towns. New Denver. Slocan. We'd give anything to go and holy smokes, along toward the end of 1943 when the camps started to disintegrate because they weren't working out like the government or the B.C. Security Commission thought they would, some guys got the chance to go. But why we wanted to get to the ghost towns was because that was where the girls were. Remember we were all about nineteen, twenty, twenty-five, in around there and single, and in those days you never thought of a white girl. You thought of a Japanese girl. And they outnumbered the single guys by about three or four to one. Jeez. Just imagine that! Three to one. Holy cow! You can imagine. For me it was great. All those girls. Girls, girls, girls. We hadn't seen any girls except for one time in the spring of '43 when they let us visit our families for two weeks and all of a sudden, there we were going to the ghost towns. It was heaven. We didn't care what kind of work they'd have us doing or where we would be working or when, we were going to the towns and where the girls were. It was quite an experience telling about it, even now. The girls!

Lots of Rice—But No Freedom

The road camp was at Solsqua. That's near Salmon Arm. I was the only one in the camp who could handle a horse, so I did that for a while, but it was all on steep hills where the loggers cut down the trees for the road construction and one day a log fell on me and I was injured.

I couldn't just sit around in the bunkhouse so I'd hobble out and help the boys. You see, they were drilling to blast the rocks, so I turned that drill. We did a lot of rock work along there. You ask the boys who was in those road camps just how tough it was. It was even tougher than they would tell you now. Most of them forgot.

There were 110 men in that camp, sixty-five to a bunkhouse. We slept four together. We'd have a ten-o'clock curfew, lights out. The guards would be around and some of the boys, a couple or a few wouldn't turn out their lights. So the guards would tell the Mounties and the Mounties would come around and talk to me because I was sort of in charge of that bunkhouse. I told the guys that if they didn't behave I was the one that would be moved out and they might get a real tough guy.

The alarm went off at seven in the morning and we'd eat and at eight we'd walk out to the job. Clearing brush. Piling it. No widening of right-of-way. We had a white person as a straw boss and he was just from the area, a local, and he couldn't handle the men and they'd goof off, you know. I told the men that at least they could work enough to work up an appetite. They were paying for their food, I said, so why not do a little work. So then they did better. Then we'd walk back to camp and have lunch, a hot lunch. A white cook. But when the request came for the men to be given more rice, the chief engineer came along and asked if we wanted more rice, the cook said, "Ah, I give these goddamned sons of bitches plenty of rice," and I tell the engineer we get it only once a week. We are used to it every day. And I explain that rice is the cheapest food they can serve us, so then we had rice almost every day. Then back on the job at one and work to five, so we worked regular hours.

We didn't booze. That's something you never heard about.

It's just that we didn't have our freedom. Yes.

For recreation, I fished. There was some of the boys doing gambling, but that is nothing. There were some gamblers in that camp.

One bad thing that happened was somebody was stealing clothes and sneaking into town and selling them. We blamed one fellow who was a gambler and was always goofing off on a bike and not working. He came to me, nearly crying, and asked to be transferred to another camp because the guys thought he was a thief. I said, "Well, you gamble a lot and you're always sneaking off, so maybe people think you are a thief." But he wasn't. It was the fellow who cleaned out the huts. I lost some good clothes. Suit, things like that. And remember, we worked in our own clothes. They didn't issue no jeans or that. As far as I know there was no issue of clothes. And if you needed clothes you had to buy them and that was hard because nobody had any money. Except some who'd brought money with them from the city.

When we'd sit around at night talking, sure we were bitter. My bitterness started at Hastings Park when I was waiting to go to the camp. I was in Hastings Park and my wife and children were in Vancouver. I asked to go out and see my wife before we were shipped out and the authorities said no. That's when my real bitterness began. Not in the camp in the bush but right in Vancouver.

I tried to make things better in the camp for the fellows but some of them didn't want to do anything, didn't want to get up in the morning, didn't want to work, didn't want to do anything.

So after a while, after I would wake them up and try and get them to work and they wouldn't, wouldn't do anything, I just said to hell with them, I'm not my brother's keeper anymore. I'm looking after myself.

Everything Is a Piece of Paper

One morning my mother is looking out the window and she calls to me in Japanese: "Two men opening gate." Well, I knew what that was. Road camps. We knew the bastards were coming. Every day you'd see them driving the streets and stopping, getting out and going into a house. You just had to wait for them and they'd come to you.

I went to the door and one asked me my name and I said yes, that was me, and he handed me this piece of paper. It said *Royal Canadian Mounted Police* at the top. No, before that I had to show him my registration card. Just in case I wasn't me. They weren't taking any chances. This paper said, and I remember it, it was like a death sentence. I guess you'd remember your own death sentence, wouldn't you? Eh? It said by this order-in-council, forget the number, I was to leave the Protected Area because I was classed as an enemy alien. Officially, I mean. In capital letters. An Enemy Alien. Which I was, I guess, if you wanted to do it that way. The government could say you were whatever they wanted you to be. They could call a pig a dog and it would be a dog. That was about February 7 or 8. In 1942. Just when things really started to get rough for the Japanese people.

The paper said I had to report to the R.C.M.P. Deliver myself, is how they put it. On March 14, I think it was. To the police barracks at Thirty-third and Heather and that I would get arrangements there to a work camp.

It said that if I didn't show up, they'd issue an order for my internment. I didn't know what that meant. I know they'd throw you in the Immigration Hall down by the CPR, but what else I didn't know. We heard stories about guys being picked up all the time and when there were enough they'd ship them out. And later we all know they all wound up in Angler. I didn't go there. I was a good little boy. A good Jap.

The cop asked me if I understood the letter and I said I did. He was polite about it but firm. I had nothing against him. I've met a hell of a lot of guys worse than the Mounties I met during the war years, believe me. He left then, he and his pal, and me standing in the door with this paper, this card, this thing in my hand, and what the hell am I going to do now?

So I went down to the Fuji and some of the guys were there, just talking. All anybody seemed to do those days was talk. A couple of guys had got their notices too, and I asked them what they were going to do and they said they didn't know. Japan seemed to be winning the war and that was something. There was one guy named Harold who'd been to Japan for six years when he was a kid, going to school, and he said he wore a military uniform every day at school. He said all Japan was trained for war and that Japan would win. I remember I didn't think too much of that idea.

Anyway, I just fooled around. I remember it was a good spring and we played ball in the baseball park on Powell there and did some gambling, and I figured if I was going to a work camp, that meant work so I quit my job in the cannery and just took it easy. It looked like there was going to be a lot of work ahead for me. I bought new work clothes and another good pair of boots from Pierre Paris and got ready. The night before I left we had a banquet at the house and it was fun. Lots of jokes. I guess they were the kind of jokes people tell when they don't want to cry.

Anyhow, I slept in my own bed that night, the last of my life in that house, so I thought. But when I got to the barracks they put us through the routine and then they sent us home and it wasn't until a couple of weeks later that we finally left. A bunch of us, by the railway, a couple of police to keep an eye on us. But we weren't going anywhere but where we were going, which was Lucerne. It wasn't a bad trip. I'd never seen that country before.

It was all new—mountains, rivers, lakes, and so on. I spent a lot of time looking out the window. I was young, and I guess I didn't care that much. It looked like Powell Street was going to be finished and I thought I guess I'd miss hearing the late streetcars rolling down toward Main and the stores and the Fuji and the girls. I had a few addresses with me. I wrote a few times, but I can't remember ever seeing any of them again. Kind of cute, some of them. I remember one girl who went to New Denver. She was a movie-star type. Hmmmm.

We got there—I think it was two days getting there. More than one, I think. We seemed to stop a lot, but they fed us okay. It was a work camp all right, and all those guys with me, they were in their three-piece suits, the black polished shoes, the topcoats, and the fedoras and they all looked like fashion plates. Well, they were. But what was to happen when they got out on the grade? Shovel and a wheelbarrow. Lots of fun, eh? Well, some tried to get into the messhall, doing anything because they didn't want to be out in the bush.

Myself, I didn't mind the bush. I was used to hard work and we only worked as hard as we wanted to. The bosses were okay. One came from Revelstoke and another from Malakwa or Malkwa and they didn't push us. But those that couldn't get in the mess hall or the couple that helped with the paperwork, they didn't do those fancy clothes much good and they were sure writing home quickly for their wives or parents to buy them rough clothes. Send them clothes that would handle the wear and tear. They got them, of course, but those good clothes didn't look so good after that.

There was nothing to do with ourselves in the camp. Some made a Japanese garden. You know, like the Nitobe. But different, naturally, because they had to use pine, but they made walks with white stones out of the creek and made a little bridge. I had a picture of it once. We played ball. There were card games and chess. I learned chess up there and I got to play it better when I got a book sent by my mother telling all the games. We'd watch the trains going by, to Vancouver or Prince Rupert. Passenger, freight. Some loaded with war supplies. We figured that would be for the Americans because we heard they had taken over the town of Prince Rupert. One trainman I talked to said they even had their own whorehouses.

I didn't mind that camp. If I had to be away from Powell Street the camp was okay. I had no wife so it didn't matter. I liked the bush and I would sometimes go up this creek on a Sunday, way up, and catch trout. I'd take a friend along, a frying pan, butter from the cookhouse and some rice from last night's meal, cold, and these little trout, about eight inches long, we'd catch thirty or forty and eat ourselves silly. It was nice and quiet up there.

There were bears up there. Or maybe we just kept seeing the same family of bears over and over. I got to like them fellows. You know, I've often thought bears are something like humans. I mean in some ways they act the same. I don't know if you've ever noticed it but a bear's track in wet sand is a lot like a human foot. They got to know Tosh and me on those Sundays and would come close. Throw them a fish and they'd catch it and eat it.

The worst thing, of course, was the pay. Did I say pay? I should have used another word. We got two bits an hour and that came out to just about 50 dollars if we worked a full month. Twenty-five days. If it rained we got less. We had to pay board and they took 88 cents off for unemployment insurance. Here we were, for all purposes in a concentration camp. We couldn't go anywhere unless we got permission and they didn't give out much of that. Oh, they'd take us to town on the train or a speeder if we were sick or cut a foot with an axe, like that, but nothing else. Whenever I hear the number 88 I always think of unemployment insurance. In a concentration camp and paying unemployment insurance. The government sure as hell did some funny things. That was one of the funniest. The dumbest.

When I sent 20 dollars to my mother—and I had to do that; they did it for you—when I sent 20 dollars home, I think I had about 5 bucks left. For everything. If the boss went into town and you got him to bring you back some chocolate bars and comic books and maybe a shirt and a pair of socks, there was your 5 bucks gone. That was the bad part of it. But you had to put up with it.

There was that guy looking at you all the time with the rifle on his shoulder and the Mountie just an hour away. Not much you could do. Oh, there were sit-down strikes, but we usually just talked ourselves out of them. They didn't amount to much. The government would get all upset and send a man in, like somebody would come in from Revelstoke or Kamloops to talk to us, but there was nothing they could do. It was all in the hands of Major Taylor down in Vancouver in the long run and he had his own rules. Nobody threw rocks or punched a guard or anything. All talk, meeting in the messhall at night and talking. What could we do? Since then I've often wondered what we would have done, what the rest of the camps along the line would have done, if they had had one of these fellows they call activists. These civil-rights leaders. What's his name, Eldridge Cleaver. One of those. As it was, we had no leader. We had a few smart-alecks but usually they'd just talk to hear themselves talking. It was like that.

When I got the chance to go to Slocan City to look after my mother and my brothers and sisters I grabbed it. I got that piece of paper and I was on my way as soon as I could pack. It was funny about the war. The same now, for that matter. Everything is a piece of paper. A piece of paper handed you by a cop says you've got to go into the bush for a year. Another piece of paper with a few words written on it and signed by somebody you've never seen before and it passes you right through. Everybody who stopped you, they'd look at the paper, look at the writing, look at the signature, and wave you on through. It seems our lives were based on pieces of paper in those days.

7 A Long Way from Powell Street

By 1942, sugar beet growers in southern Alberta and Manitoba were becoming desperate. Their traditional source of transient labour had disappeared into the services or war plants in the cities or had decided the terribly hard work in the beets was no longer for them. The growers appealed to the B.C. Security Commission for help, and as a result the Japanese were offered a deal: Move as a family unit to Alberta or Manitoba. The alternative, a move into the mountains to the ghost towns, often meant splitting up the families as men were sent to the road camps.

Many felt that keeping the family together was the most important thing of all, so by October 31, 1942, there were 2,588 coastal Japanese working in the fields in Alberta and another 1,053 in Manitoba. They saved the vital sugar harvest, as clumsy and ignorant of this new kind of work as they were. By 1945 more than 3,500 Japanese were in Alberta.

They suffered many hardships. Loneliness was one, as farms were usually far apart. Hostility, especially in Lethbridge, was another. They were banned for years from Calgary and Edmonton. But the worst hardship of all was the type of accommodation they were given. In many cases, it was hardly more than a summer-cottage type of house for the transients who previously worked in the fields. These flimsy shacks and granaries could not keep out the severe blasts of the winter, which the Japanese were unprepared for. Yet they managed somehow.

And as the years went by, they found they liked Alberta. They worked hard, kept the peace, and became part of the community and were accepted. As evidence, when the blow of repatriation fell upon them in 1945, only nine Japanese—three nationals, three naturalized, and three Canadian born—signed up to return to Japan.

In Manitoba, only one Japanese national signed to return to Japan. Perhaps it was because of the ethnic diversity and liberalism of Winnipeg, but the Japanese in Manitoba seemed to have an easier time of it. True, there was some racism, some hostility, but the Conservative government of John Bracken treated them better than anywhere else in Canada where they settled in appreciable numbers.

Canada Needed Sugar

We went to Lethbridge because we were told the families could stay together that way. We had never done any farming. We were fishing people; we worked in canneries, in stores; we did a lot of things but not many of us were farm people and, besides, there were no sugar beets in B.C. But, well, it was one way of keeping the families together. Otherwise the father would be in the bush, working on the railroad or on some highway.

I heard later that the managers or owners of the growers' association went to the government and they said, "Look, Canada needs sugar. To get sugar we need people who will work in the sugar beet fields. Give us the Japs. We will look after the Japs and Canada will have sugar. Britain will have sugar too." That is not the way it probably was said but that is the way I am saying it. And that is the way it was said, when you take it in the long run.

I was there. I worked for a Hungarian near Lethbridge. He was a hard man but there was nothing we could do. We worked, the whole family worked, and working the beets is hard work. I know that I worked and my wife and my sons and daughters worked pretty much like slave labour. That Hungarian, I think, was a first-year—I mean first-generation Hungarian. He worked us hard but he worked hard too. If it had been a Japanese, it probably would have been the same. First-generation Japanese, he works very hard too.

I don't think I blame that Hungarian much. With me it would probably be the same. What I do blame, I know, is the sugar beet growers and the federal government. That's who I blame. They are to blame.

That First Winter Was Bad

The family we hired, we're still good friends with them. My mother still writes. But they were the lucky ones. When they came out that year to work in the sugar beets they of course knew nothing about sugar beets. They had been berries, strawberries, raspberries, and things like that. In the Fraser Valley. So they were pretty green.

But they were lucky to get us and, as it turned out, we were lucky to get them. They were a good family. And we'd built a new house the year before, so they moved into our old house, which was still a very good house, big and warm, and it suited them just right.

But some of the others, around Lethbridge, Diamond City, Picture Butte, they had terrible places to live in. You see, before, we always had transients. They'd come in for the beet season with a roll of blankets and a couple of pots and pans, clothing and anyplace was good enough for them because the season wasn't all that long and the weather was pretty good. So it didn't matter exactly where they lived. But when it got cold, when the season was over and all the beets hauled away, they went back to the city. Calgary, a lot of them. A lot were Hungarians for some reason and we'd get some Indians too, although they were not the kind you could rely on.

So some of these Japanese families they had a terrible time. At least for the first winter. A bad winter to start with and whole families living in little shacks, dreadful places. The wind would blow four different ways in a day and they had just no protection. I think a lot of them put in a most miserable year and the farmers, naturally, didn't think of them as humans. At least a lot didn't. They were considered like cattle. Slaves. Somebody they just contracted out for and met at the railroad siding and loaded up and took back. To get as much work out of them as they could. You see, they just measured a family's worth on the number of people who could work on the beets.

These people didn't consider themselves as Japanese. They felt they were Canadians and that is what they were. Canadians. Born in this country, brought up in this country. And yet a lot of farmers kicked them around. I remember one farmer who was mean to the family he had and the family applied to move to another farm. They could do that. This farmer said before he'd let them do that he'd take his rifle and shoot them. He felt he had the life and death over them. I think they moved anyway. They were in a way a pretty independent bunch. I mean they knew the jackpot they were in, but they knew that as Canadian citizens they still had some rights. Not many, maybe, but some. I remember going into town one day and seeing one young fellow and he had had his hair cut in a real, real brush cut. There was hardly any hair left and I asked, "Tommy, what happened to your hair?" And he said, "Well, if they're going to treat me like a Jap I'm going to act and look like a Jap." Oh, he was real mad. Mad about something that had happened.

But a lot of people treated them right. We were used to the Japanese. There had been Japanese around Lethbridge for maybe thirty or forty years and a lot of people knew them and we knew them to be good workers, hard workers. They worked for their dollar.

I had a good house for my family but others, the government

had to step in and they gave the families material to fix up some of the shacks. Tarpaper and felt paper and wood and boards just to make them livable. That was the trouble with some of those farmers. They were so used to treating the migrants as just any old people who came along during the depression to work in the beets that they didn't recognize that here were good, decent families, people with little kids, and that they had to be given good places to stay.

There are a lot of wealthy Japanese farmers around Lethbridge now. Well, maybe not all wealthy but let's say comfortable. But not when they first shipped them out from the Fraser Valley. That first year was a bad one. A lot of people won't forget that time.

A Hard Time in Alberta

My father came back from a meeting and he looked very upset and sad and he said we were going to Lethbridge to work in the sugar beet fields. Poor but together, he said. That's the way it would be. Going to Lethbridge meant that my older brothers wouldn't be sent to the road camps and we could keep together no matter what it was like.

We went by train. One coach on the train to Calgary. We took lunch, food, and slept sitting up. It was very crowded with all the families and everybody was upset. They, we didn't know what was going to happen. I was about fourteen when the Pacific war broke out and I was so young I don't even think I knew why we were being taken from our homes.

We spent the night at Calgary and then went to Lethbridge. We were dispersed at Coaldale. All the farmers were waiting for us with their trucks at the station. They'd put in their names for Japanese labourers, and when the police called out the name of a family they would all go together to where the farmer was waiting and they'd get in the back of the truck and go to his farm. Loaded our belongings in the truck too. So we went to the farm. All shipped in one family.

The farmers didn't want families with children. They wanted families with working people, so we were fine because my mother, my father, and my three older brothers they were all in the working class. Me and my two sisters, we were too young to do much work but my brothers made up for us. No, there were four of us who were younger.

The farmer's name was Johnson. He was a tall man and my father was a short man and when we first got off at Coaldale and they were standing together the police laughed at them and called them "Mutt and Jeff" from the comic strip of those days.

Mrs. Johnson had a pot of stew waiting for us when we got there.

Mr. Johnson was nice to us. We had no complaints about him. He did his utmost. The only thing is that when we got there I remember my mother's face because she was so disappointed because we had a caboose to live in, a railway caboose, not a house. There were nine of us and there was just one area which could be the bedroom, and the rest was open area where they had the stove and table and cupboard. But you know, from a wood stove to a coal stove like in the caboose we had many failures and we had a hard time cooking.

We lived there in the caboose for a year and then Mr. Johnson sold that property and Mr. Swartzkoff bought that property and he built a house near to his house, and we moved into that and the family was still together. That was the most important thing.

About when we moved, that was when we got more settled with ourselves because we knew that the war was going to last longer than we had expected, anticipated. From then on the Japanese people began to get more settled and think about getting married and settling down.

It was hard on me and my sisters because we weren't allowed to go to high school either. No. Your parents had to have seven dollars a month for each child in order to go to high school in Alberta and my parents could not afford to send girls to school, not at the rate of money they were making. It took everything they made just to buy food.

We were paid by the end of the season, in the beets. Paid by tonnage. If the crops were poor you got paid less. The tonnage was fair because the counting was all done by the co-op. Our co-op was Picture Butte.

Our father had very little to support us. We had to buy food and clothing. It was so cold. The government gave us no help.

Some of the people were worse off than we were because, you see, a lot of the farmers had houses that they used for the people who worked in the beet fields just in the summer. They were just summer cottages and not used in the winter. In the winter the beet workers would move to the city, to other jobs. But the Japanese had to stay in these houses all year andit was very cold. It is cold country down there and it was very hard on some people. I remember my mother saying that a caboose was so small and awful but at least it was warm and that was better than really being in a house.

It was a really hard time in Alberta for the Japanese people who were sent there from the coast. Things got better later and I remember my three younger sisters, by some way, were finally allowed to go to high school. But I didn't. The last schooling I had, except for one month in Alberta when they told me I would have to leave and go home, was the school I went to in British Columbia in 1941.

A very hard time for us Japanese people.

Our Home: Three Granaries

Well, I can only tell you from my own experience, but that first two years we had one hell of a time.

Today it takes less than half a day to go from Slocan to this town but then it took more than a day, by train. A coach stuck on the end of a freight train. That's what it was. Then we were met by our landlord and he had a rubber-tired wagon and a horse and we all piled on to that with our things. Baggage.

The place we lived in . . . I don't know if he was prepared to accept us, sponsor us, although he needed the help, but we were a big family—mother, father, five girls, two boys—but us kids were all little. I mean you need bigger people to work in the beet fields. That thinning is hard work and the topping and throwing into windrows, that is darned hard work. That is tough.

But when we got there, there was three granaries side by side. God! We talk about some of the houses that the present Indians live in while working the beets—and there has been a scandal a year or two back about that—but that was nothing, very mild, to what we had to put up with. Three granaries. I don't even think they had tarpaper on the inside. They were not insulated. Just shiplap on the outside. We had one that we used to cook in and eat and two that we slept in. That was our home.

I'm taking a guess here but I think those granaries would be twelve by fourteen feet. Each.

The only means of making a living at that time was working in the beets. There was no welfare program, no unemployment. Whatever we made in the months of September and October, working the beets, pulling them out by hand, we had to stretch out to spring.

I remember it was the fall of 1943 when we moved into Alberta and I was approaching thirteen years and every member of our family—and I had two older sisters and one about eighteen months younger—we had to get out there and pull beets. We saw the sun come up every morning and then we'd come home, and this was physical work, about six o'clock for supper, and then we'd go out there again after supper and pull again. I know almost every night we were out there until eleven or eleven-thirty.

We were told later that the fellow we worked for, deceased now, he'd irrigate about two weeks before harvest time and they'd just grow that extra bit and in that heavy land around

Lethbridge, you really had to pull those beets to get them out of the ground.

God, but that man worked us. In terms of the average beet family I don't know whether we made more or less, but with young boys and girls working those heavy beets, it was backbreaking labour and we were completely and absolutely broke that winter.

That winter we couldn't live in those shacks, so we moved into the town and we rented a house, which was large enough for us. I think it was ten dollars a month. No water. No electricity. I remember having to haul water by the bucketful.

The next year, after talking with Japanese people and found out how they were making out and how they were treated, we were able to make connections with a friend from Steveston and through his connections we were able to move to a farm near Raymond. Three brothers operated it. They were very fair; they were gentlemen. We were put into a new house, not a fancy house, but when you considered it was for beet people it must have been one of the finest of its type in Alberta. These people treated us fairly. They didn't irrigate the beets for at least a month before digging so working conditions, soil conditions, were just a hell of a lot better.

I would say that the vast majority of Japanese beet workers, children, eleven, twelve, thirteen, had to miss school during vital months so that their families could maintain a living. That was even in good times, working for a good family. You see, when the families were young like that, there was very little else you could do. Maybe a bit of stooking, but most of the time it was just the sugar beets. Older boys and men could go to the bush camps but they would have been out of school anyway. But it was hard on families like most of them were that had young children just growing up.

Somehow or another, by saving all our money, making every bit of money count, we somehow got by. Doing everything we possibly could. After seven years, doing everything we could, we were able to rent a farm and get a start.

We didn't think about going back to the coast. There was a

time, 1949, 1950, when some Japanese went back to the coast, but they were mostly fishermen and the companies financed them, brought them out. We couldn't do that. I don't think we would have had enough money to pay our train fare, even after all those years working. But we got a chance to rent this farm on shares and that's the way it worked out for us. But literally we were broke. A crop-share basis. We probably paid for that farm twice on what we paid that farmer during the next seven years.

Finally we were able to make a down payment on this farm, right here.

"Are You Talking to a Japanese?"

In the summer I did a lot of camp work among young people in Alberta and one of the senior camp counsellors I had appointed for that year was this Japanese girl. This was in 1944 and then I went to Vancouver to visit my mother before the camp started in July and there was some things I had neglected to say. So I put the call through to Lethbridge to this Japanese girl. You see, I wanted to give her some more instructions to be done before I got back.

So I put the call through to Lethbridge and in the middle of the conversation a voice broke in on the line and said, "Ma 'am, are you talking to a Japanese?" And without thinking I said yes. I should have said no, a Canadian citizen, born in Canada.

The call was immediately cut off. The B.C. Telephone would not allow a Japanese on its telephone lines. It was a government order.

Warm Surrey, Cold McGrath

Ten people working, some big, some small. Coming from Surrey where it is warm to McGrath in Alberta where it was cold. But we wanted to do it that way because it meant Dad wouldn't have to go to the road camp.

But the work was very hard. We had worked in vegetables in Surrey but nothing was like working in the sugar beets in Alberta. The pay was hardly nothing. All of us working for this family, we could barely make enough money to buy groceries, if you call that living.

The farmer had built a house, one room, about eighteen feet by ten feet, and we were supposed to live in that. Ten of us. But we couldn't. So he let two of the older boys sleep in his house and that helped. Then later he built another little room onto the big room that everybody lived in.

It was impossible to live though. You just couldn't. All of Dad's savings, all the money he had saved all his life for his old age, that all went on winter clothes and boots and things because Alberta was so cold we had to have warm clothing. Surrey was much warmer.

Even when the older kids went out and found jobs, stooking, whatever we could get, our paycheck we had to bring home and give it to Dad so he could buy things for the family. Otherwise we couldn't have existed. It was a very hard time. For a number of years. Stooking. The bush camp at Rocky Mountain House. The sawmills. Piling lumber. We got about seventy dollars a month, which was good, but by the time they took off our board and other deductions we had very little left. It was a hard, hard time.

Then, a Different Attitude

It wasn't until a certain incident occurred that Lethbridge began to think about how cruel their attitudes were toward the Japanese Canadians.

A young girl from Galiano Island who had had little experience in the world had come, been evacuated with her family to McGrath. While she was there a farmer's wife went to have a baby at St. Michaels and they asked this little Japanese girl to come over and keep house for the man, who had four or five kids. He seduced her. She knew that there was something wrong with her, she knew she had done wrong. So she got away from home and worked for a woman in Lethbridge. She didn't show her pregnancy and it was a premature birth and she strangled the baby and hid it in a suitcase, and it wasn't until she was bleeding so badly that the woman discovered what was wrong, called in a doctor.

That was blatted all over the newspapers. Prior to that a nurse had thrown an illegitimate child into a garbage can and her name was never mentioned in the newspaper. This little girl's name was all over. When I asked to see her the superintendent said I couldn't because she was under guard, in the hospital. When I still wanted to go in and see her, the superintendent said, "Why, these people are enemy aliens." I said she was a Canadian-born citizen and what was he talking about? But I couldn't get in.

The case came up and she was put in charge of the Salvation Army, which at that moment, with that little girl's state of mind, was absolutely wrong. She was in the Salvation Army home about a week and one Sunday afternoon she escaped and drowned herself in Henderson Lake.

Now that, I think, jolted Lethbridge more than anything else. And the man who seduced her, his name never appeared in the newspaper. And he was a good Mormon. Public opinion was in favour of Mormonism there, so he was covered up, but the little Japanese girl. her name was blackened forever.

But it was after that I sensed a difference in attitude.

Experiences in Manitoba

Nineteen forty-one. My place was Haney and I was going to tell you we were the first group to move out. From the coast. Our family. My husband wasn't forty yet and one of my girls had her first birthday and the other was nearly three.

My husband had worked in a box factory in Haney. His uncle and three other men owned it. When the war came the factory had to close down. But. The big sugar company in Manitoba needed help to work in the sugar beets, so we think they came up with this thing that if a family wanted to stay together they had to go to the sugar beets. And as we wanted to stay together we went to the sugar beets. It was sort of a trick, do you see?

We went by train direct from our homes. They wouldn't let us take much. I was trying to remember and I think it was about two hundred pounds. This is why we just took our belongings like clothing and bedding and a few dishes. There were twenty-five families who went with us. Two railway cars. Joyce, who was the baby, I couldn't feed her her formula because we didn't have hot water. So we had to wait for the divisional points where the train stopped and my husband would take the thermos and run down to the restaurant and get it filled.

We left April 11, 1942, and it took three days to get there. No bunks, we had to sit up all the time. That was hard.

We arrived on the 14th and spent the night in the Immigration Hall and we left on the 15th. We went directly to a farm because the farmers had applied for us and it was there we went.

Then we went to St. Pierre, across the river from Morris. The owner of the farm was Mr. Turenne. A French Canadian. He had a farm too at Carey, eleven miles from St. Pierre, and there was an older house there like a summer cottage for us. It wasn't much of a house. The B.C. Security Commission provided us with furniture. Bedsprings. No bed. Mattress. I had a crib for the baby. We had our own blanket. I had a clock too. That one there on the mantel. Stove. Pots and pans. That's what they gave us.

If they had let us take our furniture from Haney it would have been better. We had to leave everything, dining room suite, kitchen table and things, beds, all that stuff. We only took clothes and bedding, the crib, that clock. You see, we thought we would be coming back soon . . .

But we're talking about Manitoba. We thought that when we arrived the job would be waiting for us, but it was only April and winter was hardly over. So my husband went to town and got talking to the postmaster who was a nice man, and he said there was a few days' work at the elevator. We didn't have any money, so that helped, but he would only work when the quota came in and they could load some cars.

Then in May the seeding started and he'd leave at seven o'clock and get back about seven-thirty at night, helping with the seeding.

Pay? Not very much. About fifteen cents an hour. He had to feed three other people with that. We didn't find it easy at all. Not at all. So I had to work in the fields too. Then our uncle came to live with us—he was in his sixties. It was very hard, and for him because he'd owned very valuable property and now he had to work in the sugar beets alongside us and he was getting old. After the war he went back to Japan and nothing was given to him. Everything was sold on him and he didn't receive a cent. He lived for a while in Japan.

We had to thin and then hoe. Long hours. Oh yes. We were working on an acreage basis, and to make enough money to live we had to work so many acres and because we didn't know the work it was hard. We worked very, very hard and for very little money. We didn't have much time to think of anything really. We didn't even think that we were missing the Japanese food we were used to.

But the work was too hard. So when the man who came around to see how the Japanese are doing, when he came, I asked him if there was not a farm where the husband and wife could work together, like the wife in the kitchen and with the chickens and the man on the farm. We knew that the shack we were living in, we couldn't live in it during a Manitoba winter. It was just for summer labour, like a place just to sleep and cook, and we knew we would freeze to death that winter. We just knew it. So this man said he'd look into it.

So he looked one up and we signed for it and after the topping was done on the Carey farm, we left for this other farm. It was pure bred livestock and that was very interesting, but the wages were very low. Come to think of it now, such long hours winter and summer, and in the wintertime it was forty dollars a month for both of us. In the summertime it was sixty dollars. We lived together and I looked after the kitchen, cooking, washing, the house, and sometimes helped in the fields. The little girls even though they were tiny could go out and bring in the cattle for their daddy at chore time and that's how we worked it. It was a family affair, more or less.

This man we worked for was very very nice. He was good to us and just acted like a grandfather to Joyce and Violet. His name was Clark. Shorthorn cattle. He was quite famous as a breeder of these cattle. People came from all over Canada to visit his farm and see the cattle, and this was very interesting and we got to know a lot of people that way, people we would never ever have got to know.

We stayed with Mr. Clark for twenty-two years. Then he got too old and sick to handle the farm, so we helped him clean up the farm, sell the cattle and everything. We helped him with all this because by this time we had been running the farm and everything for quite awhile. Then we decided to move back to British Columbia, the coast, and he said he wanted to come with us and live with us. You see, we were his family. He had a brother in Calgary but actually we were his family.

That's what he said, he said, "I've never lived with anybody else but with you." He was a real true friend, he really was.

That's why we stayed such a long time. The farm, by the way, was at Lilyfield. Have you heard of it? Northwest of Winnipeg eighteen miles.

But then his brother came out to check him and so on, you see, and Mr. Clark, who was ill, very ill by this time, in the hospital sometimes, so his brother took him back to Calgary. He died there.

Then we came back to B.C. where the children had been born.

We Accepted Them Into Our World

I grew up in Manitoba and I remember in 1943 some Japanese families came to work in the sugar beet fields. This was around Morris and Letellier and over to the east, by Niverville.

There were Japanese kids our age and we just accepted them into our group, our society, our world. Fishing, swimming, playing baseball together. They were good ball players. They were smaller in stature than us, mostly, and their skin was dark, their eyes were different. They all had black hair. But they were no different than us. We gave them nicknames and went to dances with them and it was okay.

I can't remember any of them saying why they were at Morris, that they'd been kicked out of B.C. because the government thought they were a menace. A threat to national defence. For that matter I don't think we asked them what they were doing there. I guess we just accepted it as being part of something to do with the war.

Well, to make a long story short, in Manitoba we, or at least the people I know did not know what all this business about the Japanese in B.C. was about. It was only years later, after the war, that I was reading *Maclean's* magazine and there was this long story about it all, the injustices of it, the miseries those people went through, all of it.

I remember putting down that magazine and thinking of going to their houses and seeing the families. The fat little Japanese baby cute as a bug's ear. A menace to Canada's security? That old grandfather sitting in the corner. An enemy alien? Mr. Ito who was such a good fellow, who'd do anything for you. Tommy and Nicki, the kids I knew. Dirty Japs. I didn't know whether to laugh or cry then. It seemed so crazy.

We Showed Them We Could Do It

When we went to the beet fields, in Alberta, in Manitoba, in Ontario, people were scared. They knew about the Japanese. They thought that the Japanese were terrible people. Those people there, they wrote to the government and they said they didn't want the Japanese there. They said they would keep them out of their cities. Like Edmonton and Calgary and Lethbridge did. You can come and work in our fields, they said, but you can't come in our cities and when the war is over, you must go home. Maybe they knew and maybe they didn't that 60 percent of the Japanese were born in Canada and 15 more percent were naturalized Canadians. People who were saying these awful things about the Japanese, I think a lot of them weren't even naturalized.

My friends, they would tell me that when they arrived at a station the people would be there and they'd say, "Oh, look, look at the Japanese," as if they expected terrible people. Or they would say, "Are those little people Japanese?"

When they found out we were peaceful and hard workers and didn't want to cause any trouble, a lot of people changed their attitudes. People who weren't before would become kind and when Japanese boys were having a ball game they would ask them home for dinner after the game. Or sometimes they would ask the Japanese to go to church. It seemed to surprise them that Japanese were Anglican and Catholic and United Church. I remember when I went East with about twenty other guys we were met at the station by a newspaperman and the United Church and the R.C.M.P. who looked after all these things and the story in the paper, after the headline read, *Japs Speak Slang, Know Hit Parade*. Well, what did you expect? We'd grown up in Vancouver where the slang and Glenn Miller is the same as slang and Glenn Miller in London, Ontario. Things like that.

When they found out that we weren't there to cause trouble they changed their minds. I don't think they ever thought we were as good as them—no, that would have been too much to ask, too much, just too much. But they found we were good guys, could play ball against them pretty good and beat them when we were going good, and a lot of things changed.

So we just tried to be good Japanese and we were. We did very well. We showed that we could work and save our money and it did most of us good. No bitter feeling. Because we didn't assimilate in B.C. wasn't our fault, but we showed we could work well with the whites if they gave us a chance. Then, with maybe only four or five Japanese families in a big town or city, we had to assimilate and we showed we could do it.

8 *Home Was Never Like This*

By late September, 1942, the movement out of the Protected Zone was ending. About 2,000 men, from seventeen-year-olds up to grandfathers, had been sent to road-building camps in the Interior of B.C. and a few to Ontario. In family units, more than 3,400 were working in the fields of Alberta and Manitoba. About 1,000 persons were supporting themselves in other parts of B.C. and making the best of it in an often hostile atmosphere.

Twelve thousand Japanese were sent to renovated ghost towns—relics of B.C.'s mining booms at the turn of the century—Sandon, and Kaslo, Greenwood, Salmo, and New Denver. Greenwood and Kaslo, both literally hanging on the ropes of economic survival, asked for the Japanese to come as a shot in the arm. There was little animosity. Japanese dollars were the same as anybody else's dollars. Newly built camps like Tashme, only 114 miles from Vancouver, and Popoff Farm and Roseberry in the Slocan Valley accommodated others. As an example, Tashme had 2,6000 residents living in wood and tarpaper shacks.

There were congratulations all round by government authorities. Before the first heavy snowfall of 1942, 12,000 had been housed. Just how well was another matter, because the winter of 1942-43 was the worst in many a year and for many coastal dwellers the suffering was intense. There are Japanese who remember little of their months and years in the camps except for that first winter.

But really, how well did the ghost towns and camps work?
Government reports of those days appear to present too glowing
a picture. By the standards of the authorities the ghost towns
were fulfilling their function: keeping the Japanese out of sight.
But the Japanese Canadians had an entirely different viewpoint.
For the older people, their past labours were down the drain.
For the younger ones, their hopes and dreams for the future had
vanished. And in this interminable present they were,
essentially, prisoners.

"Why Us?"

I'd lie in my bunk and the rest of the family would be sleeping
and I'd lie there and lie there and watch the light of morning
start to come into the room and I'd ask myself the question:
"Why us? Why us? What did we do?"

I could never get an answer because there was no answer for
me. The politicians in British Columbia and the politicians in
Ottawa might have had an answer, or they might have made up
a question and then put their own answers to it, but I couldn't.
We couldn't.

We hadn't done anything wrong. No sabotage. No loving
Japan. No fighting the English. And yet here we were, there we .
were in this awful camp in the mountains with nothing. We
didn't have nothing. For the young people like me that didn't
mean too much because we were just starting out in life anyway
and nobody has nothing. But my parents, everybody's parents,
all they had was taken away. Seized. Sold. Stolen. Just as if they
had never had it before. My father's store. My uncle's job in the
mill, which was all he had. My mother's dining room set. All
gone.

And I used to lie there and say, "Why us? What did we ever
do?"

How the Ghost Towns Began

I got this headache when Mr. Austin Taylor, a friend of mine, was made commissioner for the handling of the Japanese. One day he asked me to have lunch with him and he told me he'd taken on this job and he wanted me to work for him and he knew I was familiar with that upper country. He said they had about 27,000 of these people at Hastings Park and around the Lower Mainland and he knew where they were going to put them all, except about 5,000. He wanted me to go and make a survey of some of these ghost towns and find out what accommodation there was and what it would take to make it all habitable.

So I said yes, I would do it and I figured it would take a couple of weeks. I got hold of a contractor and my secretary came along to make notes and first of all we went to Greenwood. Then we went up to a place caller Lumberton near Kimberley and the manager of this place, the mine at Kimberley, he spotted me and wanted to know what we were doing. I told him we were looking over this Lumberton place and he said that he didn't think the manager of Consolidated Mining and Smelting would like that, having Japs there, I didn't pay any attention to that, but within forty-eight hours I was instructed to lay off Lumberton. Then we went on to the old town of Sandon. That town was lit up all the time. They had a hydro plant and they never turned the lights off. Then we went to New Denver and Slocan City and we made a report and said what we thought we could do and what could be done and at what cost, and I put in my report and forgot about it.

About two weeks later Mr. Taylor called and said the government had accepted the report and they wanted me to implement it. I told him I had a real estate business and he said, "Oh, that's all right. Fred, your partner, can look after that." He said the accommodation was just for the 5,000 and Alberta would take some, Manitoba would, Ontario and Quebec.

So I started off on the first job and the first batch arrived at Greenwood just at Eastertime of 1942 and we had men working there almost immediately—whites until we got the Japanese in there. We had Greenwood in shape in about two weeks to take 2,000 Japanese.

The first problem we had was with the Presbyterian minister. Can't think of his name. He said we would have to barb-wire these people up as he wasn't going to take any chance on having his two children's throats cut. I told him that that was a rather un-Christian way of looking at it, but anyway this minister left the place shortly afterward.

Then we went on to Kaslo and got that fixed up and then New Denver and so on until they were all settled. Our problem was to house these people. We had to get them in housing for the wintertime, and it didn't look as though we were going to get any help from the other provinces like we thought we would.

So they called me down to a conference in Vancouver in July and asked what the situation was. I told them they would have to build about 700 houses. I said the main difficulty would be in getting material. We sent word down to Ottawa and the minister in charge was very anti-Japanese and he sent word back that we could only build 100 houses. One hundred houses. For thousands of people. Mr. Taylor, a very dynamic man, he said, "You go ahead and build as many houses as you need, but for Christ sakes, keep them covered up." So we had accommodations for all of them by the first of November. Where the material came from I never knew, but we used about 15 million feet of lumber. But Mr. Taylor managed to come up with the material.

The Japanese had big stoves in their houses and the wood was green and didn't burn too well, but they got along that winter fairly well.

There was some trouble moving them but we got the job done and there was quite a bit of paper talk about how inhumane it was, how badly they were being treated. I asked Ottawa several times if I could give them 5,000 good mechanics because workers were getting scarce. I told them all they had to do was put overalls on them and call them Canadians and they wouldn't have any trouble at all with the Japanese. It would have been a lot of much-needed help. But they wouldn't do it.

Another thing I did. We had about 100 veterans of the First World War—some had medals and were good men—and we made out very well with them. We used them as guards and other help around the camps. But we never had any problems with them. You can't take 27,000 people and move them and not have some hotheads among them, but we got great help from some of the elder Japanese.

It was a hard job to keep them employed. We only gave them 25 cents an hour and we did get some on the railway, about 100, and some got jobs in sawmills and they built a hospital at New Denver for more than 100 TB patients. Then the government called me in one day. They got the bright idea that they needed about 300,000 cords of wood for fuel because it looked like there might be a coal strike, a shortage that year. We set up a little mill at Roseberry and the Japanese cut about 200,000 cords that winter. Cut it, hauled it, and we were putting about thirty cords an hour through the mill.

And so the years went by. We got to know them, especially the younger ones, and it was a very real experience for all of us. We had charge of health and welfare and schooling and everything that virtually moved in a very large area, and there was no pattern to go by. If we made mistakes we did and if we did things right, we did that. But there was no precedent.

Some people say that it was cruel and inhumane treatment of a people. That is nonsense. We did everything we could for those people, the Japanese. Provided them with food and shelter and jobs and medical attention and entertainment and looked after the old people and the children too. It was a difficult time and the government had decreed that this was the way the Japanese problem was to be handled and that is the way it was. There was no other way.

It was a very personal experience for all of us and we all came through it together. When the camps broke up we, the administrators, got letters from the Japanese thanking us for the treatment we had given them, and I still see some of them, even now, some of those I knew in the camps.

If the only thing we did for them, that the war did for them, it got them out of the Powell Street ghetto. It got them away from each other and out through the country and they were no longer in a ghetto. Now they are not Japanese, they are Canadians, and they are far better off now than they have ever been in their lives.

A Mayor Named McArthur

One of the towns the Japanese were sent to was Greenwood. About 350 miles from Vancouver. It once was a booming town because the Granby Mine and its smelter were there, but in 1940 it was a ghost town. I think it once had 6,000 people, all along that main street and up on the side hills and there was about, there were twenty-eight hotels. But by 1940 it was a ghost town. Less than 250 people lived there. Only two small stores were in business. The rest were boarded up. In fact, most of the town was boarded up. When you drove through from Penticton to Grand Forks and on to the East you knew you were going through a ghost town.

Our mayor in '42 was a Mayor McArther and he had read in the papers about how the Japanese were going to be relocated, and he felt that these people from the coast could put some life into Greenwood. He read where they had thousands in Hastings Park and the problem was where to put them. And it appeared that nobody wanted to have the Japanese. He said conditions in the town bothered him greatly and if a lot of new and hard-working people could come in it would give the town a boost. Here's a chance, he thought. Help the war effort by taking the Japanese and keeping our place together. There certainly was a lot of empty space in town to rent. Old hotels, once some of the best, they were in a state of disrepair, but some were still livable in after a fashion.

So he held a public meeting and fifty people came. It was talked over back and forth and finally it came to a vote and forty-eight voted to ask the government to send the Japanese to Greenwood. Wrote to the powers-that-be. Offering Greenwood. So the Japanese came.

How Life Was in Greenwood

I was sent to Greenwood in British Columbia, which is a couple of hours' drive beyond the Okanagan Valley. It was a ghost town then.

I was a dentist in Vancouver when the war came and they told me that I was to be the dentist for the Japanese who would go to Greenwood. So one day in the middle of June of 1942 my wife and one daughter and myself were put on a train, along with a lot of other Japanese, and we began our journey.

When we got there I could see it was a ghost town in this long valley. As I said, there were about 300 Greenwood people there and when all the people from the coast got there, there was 1,356 Japanese there. So it became a Japanese town. Everywhere you looked there were Japanese in this old mining town of sturdy buildings, all brick. Built in the early 1900s.

Each family had one room. My wife and daughter and I had a room about this size, about fourteen feet by ten feet; but some families with five and six children—well, it got pretty crowded in there. This was in an old hotel and there was one toilet on each floor and in the hotel there was one washroom. The stove was in the centre of the hall on each floor and with all the families and all the people on each floor it was terribly crowded. It was hard for the women to cook. So many pots and pans on one stove at one time.

Some people wanted to put little stoves in their rooms but they wouldn't let us. Too dangerous. Besides, with a family in a room there was just no place for a stove.

And my, it was cold. The fall and winter of 1942 was the coldest it had been around Greenwood in a long, long time. Ah, one day it went down to 39 below and the building was old and the high ceilings, the stove in the centre couldn't hope to heat the floor and some people woke up in the mornings with frost everywhere, around the windows, on their blankets. The wet shoes the kids had had the night before were frozen to the floors. Like that. And some of the kids and people they had never experienced cold in Vancouver and they went around outside without any earmuffs or gloves and got frozen. There was quite a lot like that.

I had my office in part of the hospital they built in one of the old buildings. The camp authorities built the hospital. It was a put-up hospital so it was not well equipped or anything like that. When we called it hospital, that's about all we could call it.

I was able to treat the white people too but that was no trouble at all. But most of my work was with the Japanese people and I got my pay from the Department of Labour. My pay was 85 dollars a month and they paid me 15 dollars for all my equipment that I'd had in my office in Vancouver. They shipped that out for me. We could hardly live on the 100 dollars. Food was high. Rice was high when you could buy it, but the hard part was the clothing the first year. We weren't prepared for the cold winter and we had to buy all new clothing for everyone, and this was very hard on some families with no money and big families. Everybody had to buy warmer clothing.

People also had to buy blankets too. The winters were so cold and the building so unheated that the two blankets they gave each person were just not enough. Nobody froze to death but there was a lot of misery.

How did the people in Greenwood treat us? Hah! Well, at first I don't think the people in Greenwood knew what kind of persons the Japanese people are. They were very curious. When the first of us went there, about two months before I got there, everybody came down to the station to see us get off, to see what kind of strange people we were. Most of them had never seen a Japanese person before. Ha-Ha! But they found out that they were quite similar to the white people in their way of living, their way of talking and—well, behaviour, and we were able to communicate with each other very nicely and there was no trouble. The mayor, especially, was very good to us. The Catholic church was there, the sisters were there, and there were a lot of Catholic people among the Japanese and they helped us. The sisters started a school for us, so everybody integrated very nicely.

However, at first we had quite a hard time getting work for our men. Some of them first did maintenance work around the town, fixing up buildings for the newcomers and that kind of thing, and then because the war was taking men away all the time, some of our men got on the CPR section gangs. They started a little industry for the pit props for the mines and a few of the Japanese Canadians were able to work there. And there was a sawmill near at Midway and they hired a few.

When they first started to work on the maintenance they were getting about 22 to 25 cents an hour. That was working for the Canadian government. Nobody else was working for that low pay because wages were rising everywhere, but that's all the government would pay our boys. That's not very much money to raise a family on. Two dollars a day and a big family. No, it wasn't much money. But when they started to work cutting pit props and in the sawmill they started getting 47 cents an hour. I can't tell you what the Caucasians were getting for the same kind of work. But even 47 cents an hour out in the bush raising a family, with food and clothing expensive, that wasn't much money. But they had to do it.

A lot of people thought the war with Japan would go on just a short time and then we would go back to the coast; but as time dragged on and on, people could see that Japan was still fighting strong. So a lot decided they had to get their families out of the little cubicles in the buildings and they started to build their own small houses in Greenwood. Others decided to take the government's advice and go East, East of the Rockies, and find work there. Some had relatives on the prairies or in Ontario and they'd get letters from them saying it was much better. So they'd decide to go. But the majority did stay in Greenwood because they could work in the sawmills and that way they'd be closer to the coast and although most did move away eventually, there are still some Japanese living there.

But while this was going on, the people of Greenwood had long got over their curiosity about us and our group and there was formed a community association, with the mayor's help, and we built a library and a swimming pool and did other things. To make the town a better place. The mayor's name was McArthur. He's dead now.

So the community went along and things were okay, except there was the bitterness of some people. Especially the young people, the eighteens, nineteens, twenties. They had thought they were going to have futures down on the coast, that things were starting to look better for a Japanese in Canada, and then, boom, they were torn away from school, friends, shoved up in the bush. They were bitter. The children didn't care. The older people, well—the Japanese have a word and it means "can't help it." We have a war, can't help it.

That's how life went along in Greenwood, in the mountains.

"We'd Play the Food Game"

You know what we used to do? There would be all of us in the little room and maybe Pop would be drinking some of his beer he made and us kids would be studying and Mom would be mending or something, always busy, and the snow would be coming down on the roof and the only sound might be a lumber truck going up the road toward Grand Forks or someplace, and somebody would say, "Let's play food." So we'd play the food game.

Of course in Greenwood we couldn't get any of the Japanese food we'd got when we lived down on Keefer Street. There were so many Japanese people in Greenwood, hundreds of them, that you would have thought one of the stores would have got in a lot of fish—but no, they never did. Just round steak and bologna and potatoes and turnips and all the things the white people ate. Oh well . . .

This food game. It just meant remembering big feasts we'd had at home, some celebration, some banquet we'd been to or to somebody's house for a party.

My mother would never let her dishes go. When we went to get the train and my father wasn't with us then, we had a hard time carrying things because they'd only allow you about 150 pounds a person and I think seventy-five pounds for a kid, so that meant you took clothing and bedding and stuff like that. But my mother insisted on taking her dishes. All her dishes and there were a lot, all in a big box which some of the authorities looked at pretty hard, as if they weren't going to let her on. But finally a mounted policeman and a Japanese man helped load the box. Well, anyway, that's not part of the story but we were in Greenwood and having those dishes there helped us remember. Too, my little sister Hiroko would get out the sake cups and she'd fill the sake bottle with water and she'd go around and give everybody something to sip. It was all good fun.

Somebody would say, "Do you remember the Jujinos' party?" and we'd all laugh and cheer and then we'd start to name off the dishes we'd have. I won't tell you what they were in Japanese because you'd have trouble getting them down, but there would be all kinds of fish and some meat and all the other delicacies we have and pickles and tea and of course we'd start out with a broth and everybody would make the motions of drinking from the broth bowl.

Then somebody would say, "Remember the Katos'?" and we'd all laugh and we'd go through their party and somebody, like maybe my brother Koji would have remembered exactly how they had decorated the room because he'd been there to help and we'd go on and on. How it was cooked, boiled you know, and how it looked when the plates were passed back and forth, and how it tasted, and it used to taste so good.

I think the only one who really was upset sometimes was my father because he was Issei, you see, so he'd been to the road camps. He was about forty-five years old then and he spoke English pretty good and he'd had a good job in Vancouver, and then that war came along and it made him pretty bitter. He didn't like us listening to American records but we played them all the time. I used to get a friend of mine, Madeleine Roper, Vancouver, to send them to me. I'd send her the money and she'd buy them for me.

Playing the food game, it was something we never got tired of doing. We'd have picnics and banquets and just ordinary meals and breakfast and lunch and dinner and it was just like it was at home. Although it wasn't, of course. All we could get in Greenwood was rice. I think it was rice from Louisiana. The United States. I seem to remember the markings on the bag. It is a wonder our father let us eat it. But he had to have his rice too, just like the rest of us.

Sometimes when we're together again now, like when Tosh and his family drive out from Ontario and visit my family and Mom and a few others, we'll laugh and remember when we played the food game, just a little Japanese family lost up in the mountains of Greenwood and it was snowing. And we'd laugh at little Hiroko hopping about filling the cups with water and all of us leaning down and sipping so carefully.

Hiroko is dead now. Yes, she went to Toronto like a lot of others and one day my mother got a telegram saying she was dead. Killed in a car accident. We didn't hear much more about it than that. She was buried there. We couldn't go to the funeral. It is too bad, really. I start out telling of the food game and the fun we had, thinking of those wonderful meals, and I always end up thinking of poor Hiroko.

Bless Those Doukhobors

The first year at Slocan City it was hard because we had no fresh vegetables. Japanese live on fresh vegetables. Our diet.

The first year the Doukhobors would come up, with vegetables. They were a Godsend. People talk bad about Doukhobors but, boy, I'm telling you they were just simple people and they're honest and they sure helped the Japanese out that first year.

And the white people around there, Dutch, English, other races, nice people. One fellow, Van Dalken, he'd take me up in the mountains prospecting, treat me as a good friend; but yet when it came to the Doukhobors, he'd say, "Oh, those goddamned Doukhobors. They're thieves." I'd ask him if they'd ever stolen from him, why did he damn them, and he'd say, "Everybody says they steal." Ah hell. Human nature.

Yet those Doukhobors, these simple peasants, they'd leave they're homes at three or four in the morning in their wagons, horse-drawn wagons, and come down to our camp with loads of fresh vegetables, everything they grew, everything we needed for our diets, and just to make a bit of money, a few pennies. They didn't make much money. But they sure did give the Japanese a break because we got fresh vegetables that year because there wasn't time to plant our own gardens. Next year we had our own.

Nobody should ever talk to me about how bad the Doukhobors were because to us they were a fine people. Every Japanese will tell you that.

Some Guys Didn't Give a Hoot

I know there were some guys that didn't give a hoot about being in a camp. Evacuated. I knew some. Every camp had some. I'm sure of that.

Guys were no different in the ghost towns than they were in Vancouver. If they didn't want to work they didn't have to. One guy said he had a bad back. Got it in the mill at Alice Arm. Can't work. Who knows that? Can the doctor tell? No. So he puts him on the list that says he's not to work and he gets relief rates. I think this guy because he had a wife and two kids got about 35 dollars a month. That was the going rate. Not much, you say. Right. But this guy was a gambler. He always knew where the game was. Everybody knew where the game was, except the Mounties, who didn't care unless you did something wrong— and what was there to do wrong? So this one guy would gamble and he did okay. His two kids were nicely dressed and I never heard that they were short of food. In fact, I know they weren't short of food.

This guy was a born gambler. You'd watch him. Not a move. He'd take the cards one by one and nothing on his face. He'd bet or he'd fold and he'd play as long as they were willing to play and he always made money.

I guess he'd go to the hospital once a month or so and get things for his back. What do they give you for a bad back? Medicine? The rest of the time you'd see him walking around, going along the tracks with his two children hand in hand. He'd be at the bathhouse a lot, just lying around and making jokes. He was a real comic, that guy. He had a nickname. "Bugeyes." He didn't mind if you called him that. In summer you'd see him working in the little garden, which was actually bigger because a neighbour had given him his. So he had two. Then his back didn't seem so sore. But sore enough he couldn't go into the woods with the rest of us and cut trees for two bits an hour.

They say this guy was a big gambler in Vancouver. Well, you couldn't be all that big a gambler in Slocan Valley. He didn't have a lot of money because I think gambling is a day-to-day thing but he did all right. He just played cards. There wasn't dice or anything like that. Just cards. No Chinese games. Just the old pasteboards.

Anyway, when the time that the selective service was going around and saying you have to go East of the Rockies, this guy just laughed at him. He wasn't going to Toronto or anywhere. He was the kind of guy who didn't give a hoot. He had his little house and his family and he got his wood free, and if anybody got sick then they could go to the hospital or the dentist. He could buy all the food he wanted and the truck driver was bringing in beer from Nelson and if he wanted that he could have it. He told the selective service what they could do with their selective service. Didn't give a hoot and I'll bet he came out of it okay. Probably living in a nice bungalow right now in South Vancouver with the heat turned up and the television on and having a beer.

There Was No Place to Go

One of the bad things—ha, as if anything was good in the camps—but one of the bad things was that what we call Japanese, like the Japanese spirit, it doesn't hold up too well in a camp. Today it would be called a breakdown in morale. Then, I guess, when nobody thought much about it you could say that—well, almost everybody was down in the dumps.

Like my father. The first year he dug up and sanded and smoothed and made this lovely garden and really spent a lot of time at it, and all his rows were so well weeded and we had wonderful vegetables. You know, who would have thought he, a store in Vancouver, he could be such a good gardener? He put a little white fence around it. He even painted boards white and it looked nice. The next year he did the same and we had, gosh, golly, we had such wonderful vegetables. All we could eat and so good. But the third year round he just sort of collapsed. Quit. Said he wouldn't do it. "Them" was the government, the Labour Department. Let them provide the fresh vegetables and let them do this and that. Let them, he said, keep him in the prison and if they were going to do that, then let them feed him and his family. He just sort of quit.

I wonder if that's what prison life does to men? Do they have to be strong? Mind you, these weren't prison camps. Not like Tule Lake or Manzanar down in the States, where they had guards and barbed-wire fences and guns in towers. We knew about them. Don't ask me how. I don't know. The mail was censored and nothing like that would show up in *The New Canadian*, but they knew in the camp. They even knew what was happening in Japan. Somebody had made a short-wave radio. He listened to it at night. It was hidden, but he heard the Japanese broadcasts, how they were winning. That used to please some of the older guys. They hated Canada for what Canada had done to them.

But when you put this down, don't say we were in concentration camps. A lot of people had said that. It was no barbed wire, no guards. Just the police and a few guys, Nisei, young Japanese, who helped them. We used to call these young guys "dogs." The Japanese have a word for it but I won't say it because in Japanese it means more than "dog."

You couldn't travel without a permit. Sure, you could go to Nelson. There was a bus. I think there was a bus. If you wanted to go into Nelson that was your business. No, I didn't like going because the way they looked at you, the way they walked around you on the street. Like we were the enemy. But you couldn't really go far from the camp. Nobody tried to run away anyway. Where to? Where do you go?

My brother George wanted to sneak off to Revelstoke and work for a dollar an hour in a sawmill up there. Other Japanese were doing it. No, the government said. No, you can't go. So my

At Angler, Ontario, more than 700 Japanese Canadians were held behind barbed wire and guard towers. *(JCCC)*

A burial at Angler. The round patch on the back of the uniform was a bright orange target. *(UBC Special Collection)*

In 1942 hundreds of Japanese Canadian families went to work in the beet fields of southern Alberta and Manitoba. Living conditions were dismal and the work backbreaking. *(Top: UBC Special Collection, bottom: JCCC)*

Men were sent to work camps in places like Schreiber, Ontario *(above)*, and in the bush west of Jasper *(bottom, below) (JCCC; UBC Special Collection)*

Road gangs like this one worked for 25 cents an hour, building roads with picks and shovels. *(UBC Special Collection)*

Life in a road camp... *(Public Archives of Canada)*

Isolated from the rest of the world, thousands of Japanese Canadians were moved into the Interior of B.C., some places even unmarked on the map.

Greenwood, a ghost town . . . *(JCCC)*

Most families reached their destinations by train and truck, but many who
went to Kaslo took a sternwheeler from Nelson up beautiful Kootenay Lake.
(*UBC Special Collection*)

Slocan was just a collection of tents when the first groups arrived. (*JCCC*)

New Denver had a beautiful view of Slocan Lake and the
mountains. Many families cultivated their own gardens.
(*JCCC*)

Lemon Creek, another camp hidden in the mountains. Most Canadians did
not know about the enforced relocation of thousands of Japanese Canadians.
(*JCCC*)

Sandon was another gulch ghost town that closed down after the Japanese Canadians were dispersed across Canada. *(JCCC)*

Tashme in winter. *(UBC Special Collection)*

brother went. He left at night. Next day a car comes along the road and the door opens and a voice says, "Get in." It's a policeman. Back George comes. So you see, you couldn't go anywhere. But it wasn't like Manzanar, because there was green trees and hills and streams and fish around, and Manzanar was desert and they had army guys with rifles. Anyway, nobody wanted to leave. There were mountains this side of you and mountains that side and one road in and one road out and so there was no place to go. But like I said, most of us, after awhile, we just didn't want to go anywhere.

An Outdoor Cremation

The first time I was in the camp in the Slocan Valley and I saw a Japanese outdoor cremation it rather intrigued me. I thought it was rather sordid and morbid thing. This was about '43.

They cremated their dead. The body is in this picture. See the smoke? They would tend these cremations right through until there was nothing left of the corpse but just two or three little bones which were almost impossible to burn. They would take these small bones and put them in the urn with a few ashes. They'd have this urn right in their house.

The family would sit around on their haunches with their bottles of Coke and something to eat, because they were there all through the night, and they'd keep stoking the fire. When it was all over, when they figured the body had gone, they'd go through the ashes.

It was always so strange to me. Rather like the difference between them and us. I always felt it as so.

These were the bodies of the old people who died. They wanted their bones to go back to Japan. It is a Japanese way of life, and it is very important to them. I understand that on the first boat that went back to Japan after the war, those who had been cremated, their urns went on that ship. Land of their birth, their forefathers.

His Way of Saying It

Some Japanese were always harping that there was no Japanese drugstore and there was a man who had had a drugstore on Powell Street and he had managed to get all his stock up to Sandon and it was just sitting there so we said, okay, go ahead and open a drugstore.

So he did and there was a gala opening and everybody was invited and all us white guests got a small gift, and I remember wandering around the store and there was one section that was all French letters (condoms). So I said to the druggist that he seemed to have a lot of those things; I asked if Japanese bought many of them.

He said, "Oh yes. Japanese boys buy many, many of these. That means he doesn't have to jump off train before it stops."

Just his way of saying it.

"It Can't Be Helped"

Shikata-ga-nai. That is a Japanese phrase. You say it fast. *Shikata-ga-nai.* It means "it can't be helped." That's why we did it. *Shikata-ga-nai.*

That's why most of us didn't put up a fuss. It is part of our upbringing. When something happens, and it is what we pretty well expect and there is nothing we can do about it, we say

Shikata-ga-nai. Everybody knows what it means. Things are beyond our control. We couldn't fight the English from taking my father's fish boat and sending him away to Lucerne. They told my mother she couldn't be a dressmaker anymore. They put us in the camp. It was a long, long train ride and there was mother and four of us kids. I don't know where my oldest brother had gone. Then. He just ran and hid. We got to Sandon and we were tired, oh so tired, and all we had was clothes, some bedclothes, pots, my mother's sewing machine, and a box of patterns. I couldn't even have my air rifle. The bastards had taken it away too.

My mother was crying when she got off the train. Such a little poky place and the mountains everywhere and I think it was raining. There were Japanese people there and when they heard there was a train of Japanese coming they came down. To help, see that they got in the right houses, where to go. You know, how to do. They said nice things.

My mother was crying and one man came up to her and said, "*Shikata-ga-nai,*" and I remember my mother nodding her head and smiling a bit. It can't be helped. Well, it could be helped by me. I was fourteen and I was a tough little bird and I said to this man to shit on his *shikata-ga-nai.* You know, whether you know it or not, Japanese boys did not use words like that then. Never. Oh yes, in the back alley, with other boys—but never at home, never in front of the older people. Never. It just wasn't done. I had insulted my mother, the friend, everybody in that station.

I remember it well, the humiliation. He took one step toward me and he said, "You are contumacious," and then he hit me one alongside my head and that knocked me spinning. That man was educated. That's some word.

I had to go and apologize to him next day but I still didn't know what the word meant. But I never forgot it. No, I never forgot it. It was years later before I found a dictionary with it in, the ones at school were no good, and it meant "perverse, wilful." I'm not even sure I expected to find it in the dictionary. I think I even felt it was a high Japanese word I had never heard, but no, it was English all right.

Contumacious. I know that word now.

All I was was a fourteen-year-old kid who didn't know what was happening to me, losing all my friends, going out to this joint in the mountains, just trees and rocks and old buildings around, and I had enough sense to know that if this was *shikata-ga-nai*, then there was something wrong with all of us. I knew it then, fourteen years old, and I know it now.

It could have been helped. We were not cattle. We were human beings, Canadians, and I still say shit on their *shikata-ga-nai*. I do, although you talk to a lot of Japanese and they still say it. You see, to them it is fate. They had no control over the forces that control them. Fate. It can't be helped. Well, I just didn't happen to believe that, young as I was.

V-J Day

Near the end of the war we had moved from Slocan to Kaslo in preparation to moving to Eastern Canada and on V-J Day I was sitting in a Japanese bathhouse, and it was in the afternoon. Bells outside started to ring and this guy—he must have been about fifty —shot out a phrase in Japanese which means, "We've lost," and to show you how clueless I was—I was nine at the time—I didn't even know we were fighting a war.

I jumped out of the bath and ran out in the street and there were people selling fireworks and I thought that was terrific. Fireworks! So I ran home and got some money and I went back to buy some fireworks and set them off like the other people in the town. And this kid who was selling fireworks kicked me in the ass and said, "We beat you, you Jap. Get the hell out of here."

You know, until later I had no idea what it was all about. I just thought it was a celebration and I was going to get in on the fireworks.

That's how much a young Japanese person in a camp—well, me—that's how much he knew of what the whole thing was about.

Time Just Went By

I don't know who it was worst for. I guess the Issei. Our fathers, maybe grandfathers. Uncles. Those guys. Most of them had been big shots before Pearl Harbor. There was one man who had twenty acres of fully cropped land near Mission and a new house worth maybe 5,000 dollars. Well, you don't forget they just come and took it away, pffft, like that. They had been big shots in the country a long time and when they spoke it was like the old joke, people listened. Now all these old guys didn't have no say at all. If the government wanted something, they just said in a loud voice, "This is the way it shall be done." The old guys could only sit around and yak, yak. In the bathhouse you'd hear them. What they did. What they were going to do. What was wrong. They'd talk about who was winning the war.

Then they'd leave the bathhouse and go down to the store and buy some tobacco. I wonder what would have happened if the government had said in a loud voice: "No tobacco in the camps." They said it about liquor, beer, you know. That meant nothing. Houses had stills to make whiskey and they made it. Believe me, they made it. Lots of it. If you went into a house and you didn't see that contraption you looked for it because you knew it was there. You smelled the stuff. Whiskey. Beer.

Yes, it was kind of like a prison. You couldn't go anywhere and a guy in prison, he can't go anywhere either, can he? The younger guys didn't care. They, we played baseball. Just as good as we had before. I think one of the troubles was that we just looked at the old guys and said, "Okay, you guys got us into this and you'd better get us out of it and when you do, let us know. Okay?" See what I mean? We didn't care.

Time went by, each day at a time. Nothing new ever happened. Oh, maybe the school put on a concert. That was big news. There was the movie. They showed us movies sometimes. People used to yell at the screen in the hall. Shout. Ever heard of "banzai"? Well, I heard that. That was when the Jap bad guy shot down the American hero in his plane. Things like that.

Life went on. If you walked through New Denver or Slocan City, Kaslo, you'd say what a quiet little village it was. Clean, neat, Pretty scenery. People walking along the street. You wouldn't know it was a concentration camp. The people treated us fine. They were doing their job. I think they liked doing it. When we had a funeral they would even come. They'd stand back, of course. They came to our parties. At the concert. Those were mostly the church people. The Mountie was okay. There was more than one, of course, but nobody did anything wrong. The trucks that came in from Nelson, you could get to know the drivers and they'd sell you Hudson's Bay whiskey at 30 dollars a bottle. Then you had a little party. But it was dead in that nobody was alive.

I mean no ambition. Nobody saying, "I'm Barry Broadfoot and I'm going to make my fortune here." You couldn't go into business. You couldn't do anything but work for the government. Cutting wood. On the roads. Working for them. My sister worked in the office. Just paperwork. You could work as a carpenter. Somebody had to fix things all the time. The pay was just enough to live on. I think it was 30 cents an hour. If you were, well, maybe an electrician or could fix a pump you got 40 cents. At Revelstoke or Kamloops you could get maybe a dollar an hour. Just living took anything you made. Some people stopped using sugar and sold their ration tickets. Meat too. Lots of things. But whatever way you looked at it, the people barely, just barely, had enough to live on. They got by. If you complained, there was one guy in the office who would say, "What are you beefing about? They're eating rotted potatoes in Japan." As far as I know they don't eat much potatoes anyway in Japan. I don't know because I never was there.

Then they wanted us to move out. You see, we were costing

them money. A lot of money. What they wanted was to be able to get everybody out into the prairies or Toronto. Hamilton. London. Down that way. But the people wouldn't. You put us here, now we'll stay until the war is over. That's what you'd hear. People would come to my parents' home and sit around, tea and rice balls, maybe some whiskey, and this is the way they talked.

Then some guys who were in with the government would say, they'd pass on the word that there was a lot of good things in Alberta. Well, we knew different. Our mail might be censored but people were coming back for funerals and things. We knew what it was like in the beet fields. They just had to say that if you knew what it was like to work in the strawberries, then the sugar beets were ten times worse. All that sun, that dust. Ugh!

Why go? Why? They said they'd move us. Pay the way. I think they paid for sandwiches along the way too. Okay. But people would be hostile still. The only good place I heard about was Winnipeg. People seemed to do good there. But it wasn't my job to make a decision. Maybe I would have gone to Winnipeg. I had friends who went, are still there. But I was at home and I hadn't been taught to make decisions. You can't blame me.

So we sat in the ghost towns. We called it The Camp. Hellhole. Lots of words. It's like a village but you don't know anybody. Stick together, oh sure. Got to. Survive or perish. I mean, stand together or fall one by one. But people were different. Like a fisherman from Port Essington, he's always lived on the Skeena and fished. Then there's a farmer from Pitt Meadows. He knows crops. City guys. Country guys. Sawmill guys. All thrown in together. We couldn't chose our own society, so to speak. Not the way my parents wanted it. Kids too. Gangs. One bunch would walk down the road, Lemon Creek or Popoff Farm, and beat up other kids. There wasn't the friendship there should have been. People were sick of each other.

You saw the same old faces, heard the same talk. How many times could you hear that old man tell about how the three soldiers after Pearl Harbor had broken his window and stolen some rings and watches? The old fool shouldn't have had rings and watches in the window after Pearl Harbor. With the curfew on, nobody to protect them. The police didn't care. So there were soldiers around. But listen—I mean hear that story twenty times and you just feel like telling him, "Old man, shut up." But you don't. He's an elder. He's got wisdom. Oh yeah. They got us into that mess.

Well, anyway, until they actually booted us out, repatriation or move, the camp was okay in a way. Just the quiet valley, a bit of work, cutting firewood, keeping a few bees, making hootch, selling hootch if you thought you could get away with it, hoping the kids were getting some sort of education, which believe me, between you and me sure wasn't much—life went on. Nearly four years of it.

And yet, now we get together in the rec room with cookies and buns and cake and good things to eat and people talk about it and there's always somebody who says, "You know, it was a good time. I liked it." Always somebody. Usually a woman. She meant the peace and quiet, I guess. The do-nothing. Gardening. Shopping. Gossiping. The peace and quiet. The war sure was a long way away.

There Was Plenty of Booze

Sure, you could get booze. You could guzzle all day if you had the money to pay for it and some people did. Others would save up.

I was in New Denver for part of the war and then I was in Tashme for a few months after it was over and there was plenty of booze. We didn't have ration books but I don't think that mattered. They passed a law early in the game that we couldn't have booze. That meant whiskey and beer and wine.

Well, you could get it from the truck drivers. When they

brought in the supplies. Trucks were running all the time. I don't know if they bought up ration books but I do know that there was a big business in forged ration books. A truck driver told me so. He'd get mickeys and full bottles and hide them in his truck. It was expensive. A mickey would cost you $12 or $15. Just for a mickey. But as I said, people got the money somewhere. A man would get a mickey and go down by the lake and after a while you would see him staggering along the road.

It was a good idea not even to let any of the Japanese who worked in the office or the girls from the san see you because some of those people we knew were working for the English and they just might tell on you. I can't remember what happened to a person who was caught. They couldn't do anything to you if it was inside you but if the bottle was in your pocket they'd take it away, I'm sure of that. There went $10 or $15.

There were always people who would buy whiskey, just to sit around guzzling and forget what was going on. Next morning, who cares? They were all bad enough. But when I think of those truck drivers, I guess they were the ones who made the money. They must have made an awful lot. The war was awfully good to them, or I guess I should say the Japs were awful good to them. If you look one up you'll probably find they all live in big houses now.

Their Mail Was Censored

One of the big bugbears of the Japanese in the Slocan Valley was the censorship of their mail. You see, all mail would have to go to Toronto and it would take a long time to get back. It was ridiculous but that's the way it was.

We had teaching friends twenty-six miles up the road at New Denver and we used to visit them some Sundays and when our Japanese heard that, they'd come with letters to us and beg, plead that we deliver these letters to relatives and friends at New Denver. You see, they could not travel without a permit and you needed a good reason to travel. Apparently just visiting friends was not good enough, or maybe they didn't, couldn't arrange the transportation, I'm not really quite sure.

I'd take the letters. I wouldn't tell anybody. Why should I? I knew these letters weren't doing any harm and they just wanted to tell some family or personal business right away without waiting three weeks or so for the letter to go to Toronto. You see, although there were phones the Japanese couldn't use them, so letters had to do.

I'd take the letters and they'd be very grateful. I'd see that they were delivered at the other end.

Loose Lips Sink Ships

We got letters and sent them out but they were censored. We were the enemy. Remember?

We had cousins who went to Picture Butte to work in the beets and the first letter we got—oh, let's see, this was in 1942—they sent us a letter saying what an awful place Picture Butte was. At least they tried to tell us. But the letter was hacked up if it was a big piece of writing, and if it was just words or a sentence they used a kind of black paint on it. When our cousin Nina came to New Denver to the san because she had TB from the dust that blew on the prairies we showed her the letter and she told us what they had written. What they had cut out.

Censorship. Who made that decision? Didn't they know us, the Japanese people who were born in Canada or naturalized? And besides when you're writing from New Denver to Picture Butte or Winnipeg, what is there to tell anyway?

Of course, the Security Commission told us it was to protect the war effort, like that poster in the post office that used to say LOOSE LIPS SINK SHIPS. There were a lot of ships out on the prairie at Picture Butte. Near Lethbridge.

You had to turn in all your mail going out to the commission and all the mail that came through was censored. That took a lot of time. A letter I'd mail at New Denver for Picture Butte would first go to Toronto and be censored. Then it would go on to Picture Butte. That would take three weeks, sometimes more. If you wanted to send a birthday card you had to mail it a long time ahead. I think three weeks was about the time it took, at any time, and I don't think a month was unusual. All that travelling and then reading and cutting and blackening, and I don't think I ever put anything in a letter that just wasn't the ordinary things people write about. But that's the way it was done in that mighty war.

They told us to write in English. I can see why. The people who would have to censor it if it were in Japanese would be our own people, and who wants the guy working for the commission to know our family business? They said to not indulge in gossip. Well, what is a family letter? Who is living, who is dying, who is having a baby, who is going to get married, who is doing what, and why, and where, and how do you all feel? Isn't that gossip? I think so. In other words, say, "Hello, we are fine. Hope you are fine. Goodbye. Miki." Just the essentials. Japanese aren't like that. They like to gossip. They are strong on family. Family is very important. You just go to a Japanese party and see how important. Old people. Young people. Babies. They're all there. And they're telling us how to write our letters.

We got to do it though. In New Denver how do you mail a letter unless it goes through the office? You don't, that's what you do. You can't mail it from Nelson because you can't go to Nelson. You're in Jap, Japanese country, son. That's the way it was. From the beginning and right to the end, that's the way it was. Until Japan was beaten. All so silly. No, wrong. What could we say or do that would harm the war effort anyway? Not a damn single, solitary thing. But write in English, they said, but if you can't write in English write in simple Japanese. All these stupid rules. Why didn't they treat us like the Canadians we were?

I saw a submarine in Slocan Lake. I write that to my friend at Coaldale and I bet they take it out and then come around to me and tell me not to write things like that because loose lips sink ships. All so stupid.

A Doctor Reminisces

I was born here some—let's see now, October, 1900. My dad came here seven years before that. I was born on Hastings Street. Dad used to have a small store. I was born in that. All my life I wanted to be a doctor but they wouldn't accept me, so I went back to Japan, for the first time, and studied at one of the universities there. I interned there too. They wouldn't accept me in Canada because I was Oriental.

Then I came to Canada. That would be in 1928 and I began to practice. Just among the Japanese. Oh yes. I wouldn't accept any white people. No. Nothing to do with them. I was bitter. I certainly was. The way they treated me when I was small, you know. How they used to throw stones at me and call us Chink and things like that, you know.

So I was quite bitter when I was young.

I could have stayed in Japan and been a successful doctor when I was young but my mother wanted me to come back because we were Canadians.

In 1941? No, I didn't know there was going to be trouble. Not until we heard the radio. You know. Pearl Harbor. I couldn't believe it. I was living at 2725 Seventh Avenue East. That's where we bought our house. We had about five lots there, you see. But it didn't occur to me that they would really evacuate us. I just thought it was talk. We were allowed to stay until the last moment in our house because I was allowed to go to Hastings

Park to look after the patients there, you see. There were five Japanese doctors in Vancouver.

My mother and sister, when it came time to move, they went on their own to the Cariboo near Taylor Lake, and myself, my wife, and our little kid went to New Denver. My mother and sister were called self-supporting.

New Denver? Oh, the scenery was nice but the people first lived in tents until they decided to build shacks for the people. I had 2,500 people to look after in New Denver and Roseberry. At times I went to Sandon too and Kaslo for the Japanese there, but not always. They also had the TB sanitarium in New Denver and I looked after that with another doctor, a white doctor.

I got 100 dollars a month to live on, to buy food and everything. A hundred was not enough to live on and I asked for more and they wrote back and said it was enough. What more did I want?

The town? At first they don't like us. They wonder what kind of animals we are. There are only a few of them because it is an old ghost town and most people are gone. But they they start to make money from us, from 2,500 new people, and then they like us. They like our money. I was told that one Christmas when the Japanese got paid the drugstore made more, more in one day than in one year before the Japanese came.

In the end the white people didn't want to send us out of there, to see us go. Making so much money. Besides, then, then they treat us just like themselves. They find we are not animals.

There were about three Mounties. If I went to Nelson one would go with me. I had my car because I was a doctor and this Mountie is sitting beside me and there is this nice stretch of road and I turn to him and say, any cops around? and then I start speeding about forty-five miles an hour. We laughed like hell. I'd forgotten he was a policeman. But we couldn't leave the camp. Not without a permit from the police. But no barbed wire.

There was a Roman Catholic school for the older children and a government school for the younger ones, but my daughter didn't get a sufficient education. Only after we left New Denver did she get a sufficient education.

Funny, but that first winter we had an appendicitis operation every day for about four months. Something to do with the environment. When they'd get up in the mornings the inside of the houses were all covered with frost and we had an operation every day. Then after that it gradually ceased. I think the change of climate had something to do with that.

What I could never figure out was why people who were all established here in Vancouver were the hardest hit. Bought houses and furniture and everything and they weren't going back to Japan. Never. They were Canadians, established. And then the government told us they would keep everything for us. My daughter wanted Christmas trimmings for the Christmas tree, so I wrote the commission and asked them to send the box from the basement. That's where we stored everything we owned. That's when they wrote and told me that my house had been sold six months ago. To a white person. It was worth, at that time—we built it for about 6,000 dollars. When we finally got our money we got about 6,000 dollars, but when we tried to buy it back after the war they told us we'd have to pay 25,000 dollars to buy it back. I said what's the use.

When we moved back, after I had spent a year with my sister and practiced three years in Kamloops, I asked the real estate man if there would be any anti-Japanese feeling in this neighbourhood. He said no, there was none. There were Jewish people living around here, Canadian people, they all accepted us.

When I came back I rented two rooms in the Roosevelt Hotel and then I moved into the Dawson Building in a year. I had to start all over again. All of my patients were Japanese. I didn't change my attitude after the war. My patients were Japanese. I didn't look after Canadians.

You know what you experience in childhood sticks to you when you grow up.

His Garden Was a Marvel

There was an old man at Roseberry Camp and he had been a gardener somewhere near the South Dyke near Ladner there, and when he set out to create a garden he really did a good job. He did more than that, for I'd say that he created the best garden in all of British Columbia in those years.

The man was a wonder. I can't think of his name and I wish I had taken a picture of this garden and the flowers and the paths and the little structures he made out of peeled pine to make it look very Japanesy, but it was a marvel. He spent a great deal of time at it and the vegetables he produced, they were just out of this world.

When people used to come visiting or they came to the office on business, we'd take them down to see this garden and the flowers, and the old man we'd see him working in the garden and when he'd see us a distance away, quick as a flash he'd be in his house. We'd get there and start looking and then he'd come out, all dressed in white, white shirt, white pants, and highly polished black shoes and then he was ready to show us around his garden. He was an exception. He was so proud.

A lot of people put in a garden the first year after the year they arrived but most gave it up. Too much work. Too easy to buy from the stores and by this time a lot more of them were just too apathetic. There just wasn't enough to keep them busy, their minds occupied. Not in a place like Roseberry.

But the old man. He was proud as punch when we brought visitors.

"I'd Never Seen Bills Like That"

You know what a storekeeper in New Denver showed me? He
went into his cash register and he brought out a roll of big bills.
I'd never seen bills like that—1's, 5's, 10's, 20's. And old. These
bills were all wrinkled like they'd been around for a long time.

He said that many years before, Canada had changed from the
bigger bills which he was showing me to the smaller size which
we have now, and he said he hadn't seen a big bill for years.

But now, he said, they were coming out. The old people were
cashing them in and did I know what that meant? Well, I was
just about sixteen but I figured I knew. These were the bills, the
money, that the old people had hoarded for many, many
years—and now that they were in the camp they were starting
to spend their savings, which they had been saving for their old
age, or maybe to go back to Japan with to buy a little house and
die there.

If they were old, like if they were sixty or so, then he wouldn't
be able to work for the commission, so all they got was relief.
Japanese people hated to take relief, but in the camp they had to
take relief because the old boy wouldn't be fishing or anything
like that and the 25 dollars or what they got was not enough. So
every month they spent a few more of their dollars.

Of course, we could never know about those old people. The
commission didn't make them cough up their savings, and if it
wasn't in a bank, but say like it was buried someplace in the
house, then they might have had thousands saved. Now I doubt
that very much, I really do, but these old people were very
canny. They kept their business to themselves.

But that storekeeper. He sure had a lot of those big old bills.

That First Day at Tashme

If you were going to a ghost town, which was in the summer of 1942, you got all your stuff together that you were going to take and you put it into bundles and suitcases. They said each person could take 150 pounds. Sort of like they do on airplanes today. We had a couple of months to decide what we'd take.

Clothes. Lots of clothes. I told my husband, "Take lots of clothes. It will be winter there." We went down the street to Hastings and bought good clothes. We used the money we'd got from the Jew who had bought most of the things in our house. At the end we were sleeping on mattresses on the floor and just a few dishes, a table, and hardly anything else. The stove, of course.

The authorities said we should take our sewing machines. Now every Japanese person, woman, had a sewing machine. We took dishes and knives and forks and our dolls and sentimental things, and we knew a woman, a Mrs. Dietrich that Josie used to do domestic for, and she let us store some things in her attic which we couldn't take and wouldn't sell to the Jew. And then the big day came. Us huffing and puffing, and I can't remember how we got to the train. Did they come for us in a truck? Did we take a taxi? We couldn't have walked. I guess by that time my mind was in such a pickle I just don't remember.

But I remember the train. There was a desk there and a white guy and a Japanese guy behind it and a policeman standing there and my husband went up and we were ticked off the list. That meant we were present, like calling out the roll. I don't remember seeing many Japanese I knew. Just a few women I knew from shopping. None from our church auxiliary. My husband I think knew a few.

Then we got in the cars and away we went and along we went until we came to Hope station. This was the farthest I had ever been, except to Englewood once. Then we got out and there was our things to get, and when we got them, the trucks. I can't remember if they were army trucks or not but they seemed new. People were helped into the backs of the trucks and up the road we went. It wasn't a road, of course. It was like a trail you'd use for cattle. Down in one side, a hole, and everybody would fall over that way. Down the other. Bump. Trees overhead, pines and such, and all those mountains. The road went uphill all the way and along a river and I think it took about three hours to get there. It was a long time. I know I was very tired, just holding on to keep from falling. But finally we got there. First you saw the big barn and then you saw there were two of them and you were in this long valley. It's still there, you know. You can drive by today and see those big barns. Of course everything else seems to be gone. Still the mountains, the river, the meadows, but all the shacks and the staff house and the store and that is gone.

When the trucks came into the yard there were a lot of people waiting. All of them Japanese. You wondered where they came from. They were all looking at us, looking to see if they knew any of us, and we were doing the same. I saw a couple of people I knew. We got off the trucks in this big crowd and a policeman with a loudspeaker told us all to get over to this place and line up, family by family, single people with single people, and we did and that's the way we got the places where we were to live.

Then when we had the street and the house number, people helped you find your boxes and suitcases and they'd take us there, to the houses. The family that took us, the woman said that it wasn't so bad. She was older than I was and we spoke Japanese and she said it was good for the children, that there was lots of places to play and a lake and there were ball games to watch, just like in the city. I asked about schools and she said there was going to be a school. There wasn't a school yet. That didn't come for some time. Too long, I thought. The children missed their year. I asked about the house. I thought we would have a real house and she said no, just a kitchen that was shared, and a bedroom. I asked for everybody? She said yes, for everybody, but that the children were out playing a lot and there was work for the men. They were going to build the road. But I wasn't ready for what I saw. Just a little place. A shack. A chimney, a back porch kind of thing, windows, and that stuff. You call it, uh . . . tarpaper? Of course there was wood under that. But it wasn't anything, nothing. It was awful.

I remember this, When I was standing there and wondering if this was possible, this woman's youngest daughter came running in, up the steps and in, and she said that yesterday she and her friends had been up the creek and they had seen three bears up a tree. A big one and two small ones. You know, that is the only clear thing I can remember, really, today after all those years of that first day in Tashme. The three bears up the tree. I guess I was too shocked. I know we put our stuff away and we went to the store to buy things but I can't tell you what we ate. I can't tell you when we went to bed or anything. It was just too much, that first day. Just little Tsuyuko saying there were three bears up a tree . . .

All Those Japs Together

We lived up on the 3400-block Triumph. My dad was a donkey man, my mom and sister ran a dressmaking shop and I was going to school and I never did get downtown. Go to Stanley Park sometimes but I really never left the neighbourhood. There was plenty to do, playing with the guys, fishing down by the grain elevator, going to school and playing second base. My dad always said have your fun now because once you get out of school the fun ends. I had fun. I admit it. There were English guys and some Italians, lots of guys but you know, not too many Japs.

So then we go to Tashme. It's dark when we get there. We

don't know what's going on. I know what Tashme is now.
Everybody does. Then I'm not sure I did. Just the camp where
we were to go and be good until the war is over. That's what they
told us. Be good and when the war is over everything will be
okay. Okay? Okay.

We get a couple of blankets each to sleep in. A bunk. In a
shack, a kind of little house. That's okay. We're pretty tired after
that long day before.

Next morning I go out and there is this place. This Tashme.
Tall trees, like in Stanley Park. Mountains. Real big ones. All
these little houses. But you know what really struck me? Thing I
couldn't get over? All the Japs. Hundreds of them, doing this
and that, kids playing, women washing, guys walking around. I
was only fifteen at the time but I wasn't dumb—I just didn't
think there were so many. I'd never seen so many Japs together
at one time in all my life. I never went to the school-after-school
because my dad didn't believe in it, and the kids at school were
just everybody and our family just didn't seem to get mixed up
with the Japanese festivals and all that stuff with the dolls and
that. So I guess I thought that us and my friend Tak's family and
maybe a few others, like the old gardener who used to come
around with the horse and wagon—I guess I thought that we
were the only Japs in Vancouver. So here I am that morning
looking out and saying, "Jesus, look at all these Japs, will ya?"
Like that, and that is the first time I realized there were so many.

Then when I saw the rest of the camp, the other streets and
the barns and that—well that was something. I can't remember
now but I must have thought then that half the world must have
been us guys. And here I thought I was white. I mean I guess I
thought all the time at school and up on Triumph that I was
white and not different, like we used to throw rocks at the old
Jew who came down the alleys looking for scraps and we'd yell,
"Hey, hey, Jew, stay away."

It was a really funny situation. I was fourteen or fifteen and I
thought I was white.

I sure learned different later.

Snow at Tashme

Tashme Camp was a dreadful place, I suppose, but that first winter, which was so bad, it was also a beautiful place.

We came from Victoria where we hardly saw any snow on the ground and there it was in Tashme. It would come falling softly, falling softly when you turned the lights off when you went to sleep and next morning there would be a new world outside. You could see smoke coming from all the little chimneys in all the little houses and if you looked down the street you could see people walking along, all bundled up, and smoke coming out of their mouths.

And it was so soft and fluffy and so nice to walk in and I just loved it. The little kids would be going to school and rolling around in it and I'd be going to work at the hospital and kicking it and all the roofs had big blankets of snow on them and it was so still and quiet early in the morning. You might hear an engine down in the works yard or at the sawmill but that was all and when you looked up at the mountains it was beautiful. The sun would be shining on the snow and a lot of the men when they went to work would be wearing sun glasses. It made them look like aviators in the movies. It was quiet and peaceful.

You didn't think that because of the snow and the cold that that was why everything was wet in the house. You know, condensation. They build up the stove until it was very hot and then the heat would work on the outside snow and it would drip, drip, drip. Clothes got ruined. Blankets wet. Drip, drip, drip. It was awful.

But when you went outside and saw all the new and white snow lying there and no tracks in it yet, all clean and beautiful, why, I just thought it was the loveliest thing in the world. The most beautiful sight. That winter I hated Tashme for what it was doing to us, what it meant, but I also loved it for its soft, quiet beauty.

The Wood Was Wet

That wood. It was green, you see. It needed more time to cure and we didn't have time. The trucks used to come in and it would be cut up and we'd get it. There should have been better planning but in the summer, when it should have been drying, they were shipping it off to the city. Vancouver mostly but I think to other places too.

We'd put it in the stove and it would just not burn right, but even when it was burning it gave off no heat. You got a little if you put your hands or behind right by the stove, but it was no good. Too wet, Ice on it. Coal burns nice and hot. They should have given us coal. There must have been coal mines around.

It was so cold that the children used to cry at night. Nothing we could do. I don't think it was the stove's fault. It was just the wet wood, which would sizzle and pop.
And when we did get the stove going real good and get some heat out of it there would be dripping everywhere and it was awful. It spoiled things, clothes, books.

I remember one morning I had to do a bit of homework before going to school, just a bit, and when I put my pen in the bottle of ink I found that the ink was frozen. That's how cold it was.

The Anatomy of a Camp

No, Tashme wasn't bad. At times it was a lot of fun. There were a lot of kids there and we had school there and skating in the winter and in the summer we used to pick berries or go wading in the river or cross over by the vegetable gardens and try and catch small fish in the creek. We weren't allowed to catch fish, but nobody said anything.

It was different than in Vancouver, though. You see, it was in the bush. Mountains and bush and just the one road going out to Vancouver. To Hope and then to Chilliwack and then to Vancouver. We couldn't leave the camp except if we were sick. I got sick once and went to Chilliwack hospital and then my mother and then my dad got special passes and they came down to see me. Ooooh, but I was sick then. Something to do with my throat. I forget what it was but it sure hurt.

There was really lots to do. The second year I was in the high school and we went to school at night. On Saturdays we had a kind of school but it wasn't a real school. We listened to music and did dances and things like that. The Saturday school was best.

The houses were not very nice. They were over by the vegetable garden and they were made of wood and this paper you call . . . it's hard. Tarpaper! It wasn't very warm in those houses in the winter and the men were always in the woods cutting trees and bringing them in.

The Security Commission ran the store but most of the people in it were Japanese, and I remember some men in the store they smuggled in bottles of whiskey. From Vancouver. I don't know where they got it. But they'd put in a box or two of celery and when you pulled away the celery on top then you would find the bottles of whiskey. My cousin was one of these men in the store and he would sell it. He made a lot of money and he gave half or something like that to the truck driver. I think 40 dollars for a bottle of whiskey. Does that sound too much? Maybe. You see, Japanese weren't allowed to have liquor.

The same with beer. Once some of us kids were out along the road and we saw this truck come along near the gate and the driver got—he stopped his truck. He took two cases of beer and hid them in the bush. Us kids took one of the cases. They were for somebody in the camp. Smuggling. We opened the case of one of them but we couldn't get the top off, So we put it back because we didn't want to break somebody's beer on a rock. Besides, I didn't like beer. I had never had it but I knew I wouldn't like it.

The men worked, so there always were a lot more women

than men in the camp. Every family ate its own stuff. You shared a stove with another family. That was not so good because you didn't know that family and they might be something different from you. My father had a dry-cleaning shop and he could have made some money if he had his stuff there to do it, but they wouldn't let him do it. The other family with us was fishermen from somewhere up the coast. They were ignorant Japanese. Nothings. They knew nothing. But all the women did something. Some little, and some just looking after their family. There was a hospital there but that's not the one I was taken to because I was so sick that time. I went to the big one. The one at Tashme was small. Just maybe thirty or forty beds. For measles, ladies having babies.

School was fine. We had classes and the teachers were fine too. But they said that if we were to get a good education that after the war we'd have to go back for more school. A lot of the boys did, I think, but not many girls did, I think. What we got was good enough for us. Besides, quite a few of the kids then went back to Japan to help look after their parents.

We had bathhouses—I think two—and then they built another one. We had to have them. After a day on the road camp or working in the garden and it was a big garden, ooooooh, that sun used to get hot and it was dusty and a breeze would blow dust on you, then the bathhouse was wonderful. The men used to use it all the time.

Some of the people on the staff were fine. We liked the policemen. They were nice and one man just loved the Japanese children and he would pick them up and swoop them up in the air. The parents didn't get mad at this man because he was such a good man. He loved children. His name was Bill. I think he would be dead now as he was not young then. Some of the auxiliary policemen we didn't like. they weren't real R.C.M.P. and used to shove us around. But mostly the police didn't come around unless there was trouble in the Japanese houses. They were all in a row, row on row, like little neighbour places and you knew your friends on that row but you might not know them on the next row. Sometimes there were fights. Mostly it would be word fights but sometimes it would be worse. Somebody may pick up a stick or somebody would get hit. I think somebody would get stuck with a knife. I remember somebody in the camp getting stuck with a knife. It was something to do with buying something at the store.

There was fun too. We used to laugh at the staff. Some of them were fine and some weren't. We were talking about it one day a few years ago and somebody said that half the staff were unemployed used-car salesmen who couldn't get another job. You see, as I remember, they weren't making cars anymore for them to sell, so they got jobs with the Security Commission. We used to call the ones we didn't like, we said they were "pig-penners." That was because the staff used to live near the pigpens. There was pigs there and a slaughterhouse, just this side of the sawmill. Across the creek on our side.

Lots of people had money. Some were rich. I don't mean like today where people have a big house and two cars and a colour television, but when my father was in business in Vancouver he had money. He had his store and he sold that and he had money in the bank and I think he had bonds. He worked in the garden in the summer because that was easy and he worked in the sawmill in the winter because I think that was easy too. I guess you'd say my father had pull. He knew somebody on the staff. But he also had money that came in once a month. I don't know how much, but I think it was about 75 dollars that he took out of this account he had somewhere in Vancouver. So we never starved. I can't say that anybody starved in Tashme. I guess it was impossible to starve in Canada. There was so much food. Why, even in Tashme, there was the big, big Japanese garden and what we used to grow. Oooooh! Potatoes and onions and parsnips and everything and then there was the big government gardens. Two of them, I think. And they used to grow. The ground in that valley was rich.

I mentioned the *shoyu* (soya) and *miso* sauce place. It was a small factory by the garden. I think we got that sometime in 1943, late 1943. It was real welcome but that is something we love. *Shoyu* and *miso*. We made it ourselves.

We could buy rice but the price kept going up and up. It never seemed to stop. Talk about inflation now. There was inflation then too. It was a good thing we had the big gardens or it would have been too bad for some people.

There was a lot of things doing. Girl Guides. Boy Scouts. We'd go swimming or go over to the store and buy Babe Ruth chocolate bars or go and watch the boys playing softball and sometimes we'd just go for a walk and pick flowers. Once we were walking along this trail and just off the side of the trail there was a crossed stick and we couldn't figure what it was and then we knew it was a grave. From then on we called that Prospector's Grave Trail.

I don't think it was too bad. Remember I wasn't seventeen. I think I was fourteen when Pearl Harbor Day came and how shocked we were that Japan would do a thing like that. We were stunned. Oooooh! we were shocked. We didn't know what to do. And they said that we could stay in our house until we had to go to the camp. But we still missed Powell Street and going to the movies. Of course we had movies in the camp, but most of it was Japanese movies that were old. But still we'd go. Sometimes an American film. Fred Astaire and Ginger Rogers, I think. But we missed our friends, our school in Vancouver, the streets, going into the café and having a chocolate malted, but if you had to be out in the bush, interned because you were a Japanese—well, I guess Tashme was not too bad a place to be. To go to. You weren't lonely. That was one thing. You had plenty to eat. There was fun with the other kids. It would have been more lonely in Vancouver with no Japanese kids to see or talk to or go with.

That's Entertainment

There was this fellow who had these old Japanese movies. He used to show them in Vancouver, before the war, and he brought the stuff up with him to camp and carried on. They were really old. In fact, we'd seen them before in Vancouver and we saw them maybe three times in the camp. They were old and scratched and he used to do all the voices himself. The movie would be going and he'd be talking the parts so we would know what was going on. I can't remember if he charged a nickel or ten cents to see them but when you don't have anything to do, no other entertainment, then you do what there is. And that's what we did.

Like Living in a Zoo

If you thought anything about your neighbours, then you wouldn't want your children crying or them to hear any arguments you might have, just as you wouldn't want to hear their kids crying or their man-wife fights.

But in those little shacks, one room here with everything in it, a kitchen with stove and everything in it, and then another room, everything in it, things were awfully cramped. Let me tell you that. You could hear everything. Children crying. Sure, Japanese kids cry. Just like other kids. There is no difference. Why should there be? There are man-and-wife fights. I mean just because we're Japanese doesn't mean there aren't fights. Well, arguments. But some get pretty personal, I'll say that. Pretty personal.

Some kid wasn't doing well at school or not trying or the husband had a lousy job in the woods or making that Hope-Princeton road when actually he is a fisherman and the mother trying to make things work out—well, it got pretty bad. Pretty bad there at times. You don't want your neighbour to know, but how can you stop that when she is cooking at the stove only eight feet away in the next room? Thin walls. Or the other way about. You're cooking and you can hear them. All their problems. They fight. The kids yell, they want this, they want that.

Oh, it was awful. It was like living in a zoo. Some people couldn't stand it. They weren't made of stone, you know. Some people would do anything to get away. "East of the Rockies," they called it. The government would send you. And you went just to get away. It wasn't nice. It changed people forever. They were never the same. Friends came to hate each other. They wouldn't talk to each other at the store. Or they did lots of small, mean things. Yes, it made people mean.

But still we stayed in the camps. Most of us did. It was because we were afraid. We didn't know what East of the Rockies meant. That might mean Alberta or Manitoba but to the commission it didn't. It meant Ontario. Quebec. Other places. And we'd hear terrible things about those places. People would write a letter and it would get smuggled back. How people looked at you on the street. You went shopping at Eaton's and they'd look at you funny. "Who is that?" They'd be saying. "One of those dirty Japs, I'll bet."

There would always be somebody asking you why didn't you go, go back East. The administrators. Or sometimes the Japanese who worked with the office, the ones that some people called traitors. Go back East, they'd say. But nobody would go. They'd just sit in their houses and let the rain come down and then the snow come down and those mountains on all sides and argue. People would fight among themselves and you'd hear the next family fighting with themselves or even ones from one family fighting with another. There was no morale. You can't give morale by letting the boys and men play baseball and teach knitting to the girls. It doesn't work that way. We had to know what our future was and until we knew what our future was, there was nothing. Because there was always talk about how we'd all be sent to Japan or another place I'd never known or back East, but we couldn't stay in B.C. and we had nothing. Just a few trunks of clothes, three umbrellas, a sewing machine, some books, the children's records, and a clock and things like that. That is all we had. I remember I had some tea things, cups and other fine chinaware and things that I had got when I was married and I'd left them in my house in Steveston because the Custodian said he'd look after them. And when we wrote and asked for the trunk they sent it, but when we opened it do you know what was in it? Nothing. Just nothing. The trunk was empty. One of those Custodian people had stolen that lovely set.

Why did we cry? Why were we so upset? Why did we fight? Because we lived in little shacks no bigger than a big dog kennel, five of us, and nothing to do. How could I make a lovely meal when there was nothing to buy in the store and rice was about 13 or 14 dollars a sack and you couldn't get sauce or anything to do anything right? My husband, one day he'd be working on the road and the next day in the sawmill or in the garden in the summer and what was that for? I mean, what was the use of that kind of work? Just making a road that nobody would ever use. I'd look at my two daughters. They would skip and dance around and be singing the tune off the records they had up at the school where they had the gramophone, but there should have been a light in their eye and they should have been walking down Moncton Street and looking at life and laughing and instead here they were in the mountains.

So we lived in a little shack and we were strangers to each other and we were strangers to everybody else and there was no life to lead. My son. Maybe he was the best of all. He was too young to know but many years later, when he was a man, he told me one night, he said, "Momma, I knew what was happening. I knew."

Buy Victory Bonds!

I'll tell you something. Something that will surprise you. During the war there was this newspaper called *The New Canadian*. I think it went to all the Japanese Canadians in Canada and it told them about what was happening, and the government would use it tell the Japanese what was happening. There was also reporting in it. Yes, a lot of reporting. Sports. A lot of sports and news from the ghost towns and from southern Ontario and poems, short stories and just things that people wanted to say.

But every few months, every time the government was having a war bond drive, there was this big advertisement in *The New Canadian* telling how buying of victory bonds, war bonds, would help defeat the Axis. That was Japan, Germany, and Italy. It would say "Buy bonds to make the world free from tyranny!" Things like that.

Can you imagine it? Just imagine it. Here were thousands of Japanese in these ghost towns and on farms on the prairies and they couldn't do this and they couldn't do that and it wasn't all that much different from being in a concentration camp, if you look at it that way, and here they were asking us to buy victory bonds. People who had no money or just enough money to barely get by, to buy food and warm clothing and the Mounties coming around to check on you—and they were asking us in these big headlines to buy victory bonds and save us from tyranny.

I don't know whether the government paid for the ads or whether the paper ran them free because they had to, but how ridiculous can you get, telling people who virtually are behind bars to buy bonds to help with the war so they will be freed of those bars. I used to shake my head in wonder every time I saw one of those advertisements. A full page too. Buy Victory Bonds. Defeat the enemy. And as far as the government seemed to feel, we were the enemy. They treated us like we were.

Self-Supporting Japanese

It was a funny thing. You could go to the camps, Sandon, Kaslo, New Denver, Popoff Farm, Slocan City, and the government would do a lot of things for you, like giving you a small house, food sometimes, electricity, a pump. Some families went to those camps because they were so damn mad at the government that they said, "Okay, you put us into this fix, now what are you going to do? You got to support us." Like that. That was part of the story. There were thousands in those camps, the ghost towns.

But others, like my parents, they said, "Well, if we got to go we're going on our own. We will be as free as we can without some Mountie looking over our shoulder all the time." So if you had some money, a few beans, you could move to some places in the Interior of B.C. on your own and you were called self-supporting. It was a matter of pride for a lot of people, and they worked and made money and when the people in the town got to know them then it was fine.

We went to Lillooet. When we were planning to go there we heard that the people of the town were going to meet the train and shoot us with their rifles. It was scary and a lot of people were afraid. That didn't happen but they didn't want us in the town. They put us in East Lillooet. They said we had to be across the [Fraser] river from them. There was nothing there at first but sagebrush. No shelter. We had to buy our water. We had no electricity. They wouldn't let the kids go into town to school.

But that changed. We'd go into town to shop and the storekeepers got to know us. It took about a year. They saw that we were good workers and we talked like them, our kids acted like their kids, we did the same things as they did, that we were not much different. A few Japanese moved into town and started businesses and that kind of thing. There's a doctor still working in that town who was one of those people. It took about a year for them to understand that we weren't what other people said we were, but that was a pretty hard year.

There were Japanese who went to Christina Lake and to Taylor Lake and Minto and all around, and once everybody got used to everybody else then things got along fine. It was better, of course, if the townspeople didn't read the Vancouver *Sun* because there was one newspaper that was always trying to cause trouble. It had for years. But things got better, except for a few towns. Like Kelowna. That was a bad one.

There were other towns too in the Okanagan Valley, some of the small ones. I don't think Revelstoke was too happy about the Japanese either.

It was all hysteria. Everyone of us carried a bomb or something, so they thought. They didn't even know they were talking to self-supporting Japanese who were Canadians. What was the diff between a self-supporting German and a self-supporting Scotchman and a self-supporting Japanese? We hadn't done any wrong. In fact if the government had to take care of a lot of Japanese in the ghost towns even if they did have money, and a lot of them did, wasn't it a good thing to have some Japanese who were too proud to take money and wanted to support themselves? I've often thought that not too many people knew there were people like us.

"In the History of Human Warfare ...

My grandfather was the Spanish consul. My father. Myself. Three generations. Representatives of the Spanish government.

Shortly after I took over the consulate and shortly after Pearl Harbor I received notice from the Spanish Embassy that Spain was to act the role under the Geneva Convention as the Protecting Power for the Japanese interests. That means we were protecting Japanese nationals in B.C. and the Spanish Embassy in Tokyo would be protecting Allied interests over there.

My first task—it came awfully quickly—and that was to look after the Japanese consul here and Japanese dipolmats who were going to be exchanged on the Swedish ship *Gripsholm*. I handled it at this end and took over the Japanese property and then handed it over to the official Custodian.

The first phase, of course, was the removal very quickly of all Japanese from all coastal areas to a staging area in Vancouver, mostly Hastings Park, and their removal from that staging area to camps in the Interior of British Columbia.

Well, Hastings Park was crowded. I certainly wouldn't want to be there, but under the circumstances we found nothing to criticize the government for at that time. It was not only a matter of removing the Japanese from the danger area but it was also a matter of protecting the Japanese from the wrath of the Canadian citizen. Very quickly they set up the B.C. Security Commission and they appointed Austin Taylor as chairman, and ever since those days I have had the greatest admiration for Austin Taylor because he did a job that very few people realize the scope of, and the skill with which he handled it and the humanitarianism of it. Nobody knows because all they have ever heard is criticism of the man. But he did a fantastic job under difficult conditions in wartime.

They immediately set the wheels in motion of doing a survey of all the available practical camps in the Interior, and I saw more geography of British Columbia in those days than I ever saw again.

When considering a camp, many factors had to be taken into consideration. First, the practicality. The ready-made facilities that were already there rather than starting out in virgin territory. Then the other thing was the psychological—nobody wanted the Japanese near them in those days. So it was necessary to avoid that political friction, and where could you move them quickly? It was very good judgment, I think; those old towns had accommodation—old houses, old hotels, stores, doctors, retired people, carpenters, plumbers.

The point I want to come to is the philosophical end of it, because I feel very strongly on the matter. All that has come out is typical of everything today, self-flagellation for a job that we did very well.

I'll start off by saying that in my humble opinion—and you'll find out, too, from others—that never in the history of warfare have enemy aliens been treated as humanely as the

Canadian Japanese in the last world war. I'll start off with that. That's contrary to what all these left-wingers, bleeding hearts are saying.

To sum up my philosophy on the main points that are controversial: they say that they were robbed of everything and their standard of living was ruined. I can sum it up and I can prove it that 10 percent of the Japanese that lived on the coast before the war their standard of living dropped. Those were the wealthy ones and during the war their property lost value. It wasn't stolen. It all went into a pool and nobody wanted to buy it. But for 90 percent of the Japanese their standard of living was raised. This is a point that nobody wants discussed—for 90 percent and I can tell you how.

At the end of the war Canada benefitted enormously by eliminating forever the Japanese ghetto problem. They were scattered through the country and doing what they did they've solved that problem forever. We had 30,000 right here in B.C. and during the depression they said they were reducing our standard of living, working as slave labour and the white man can't get a job. That's eliminated forever. That problem is solved.

If you've ever studied the pictures or seen those camps during the war, they had things they'd never had before. First-class hospitals, first-class doctors, first-class nurses, and first-class schools, for everybody. They never had those before, except for the wealthy.

Every month I was accompanied by the superintendent of the R.C.M.P., usually by a fellow named Maag who was a representative of the International Red Cross, and we visited the camps. We had no standards to go on other than what our imagination had to go on, but we always felt they were very well built, very well run. I had jobs to investigate where somebody was very sick and didn't think they were getting the proper treatment, or they couldn't get communication with their families, they couldn't get messages to Japan—which was difficult in any case—and living conditions. Sometimes they were cold. That first winter was very cold. I urged and stressed and did everything I could to have something done about that winter and it was a big job and it amazed me what was done to make conditions more livable.

If I ran into something that was wrong I would report immediately to the head of the B.C. Security Commission, make a report to the Spanish Embassy which would go to Madrid and then to Japan.

There were ringleaders. Some of the leaders I had great respect for. Others I didn't. The Oriental mind is hard to study. I never did figure it out but I had to form my own opinions, whether they were legitimate or not. Some of the ringleaders in my opinion were anti-Canadian and subversive. Others were good strong leaders and were not trying to subvert.

Do I think some of them were actually anti-Canadian? Yes. Yes. If given the chance they would have gone back to Japan. No doubt in my mind. No doubt. What percentage I can't tell you and I had closer contact than 99 percent of the people. It is rather hard to fathom the Japanese mind and to know to what extent this feeling permeated the groups. There definitely was a substantial number that were subversive, in some camps particularly—some camps were bad, some camps were good. Slowdowns. Trying to make the people unhappy. Always pushing to the border of . . . ah, rebellion, ah, insurrection. No, there never was any real trouble. I would think 98, 97 percent of the people would never go for it.

Yes, I had to go to Alberta, to see the people who had gone to the beet fields, who had signed contracts to work in the beet fields. Lethbridge. Taber. I went to Manitoba once. There weren't all that many Japanese in Manitoba. They were living free. After they passed the security.

R.C.M.P. during the war, they'd check you, they'd check me, they'd check everybody, the Japanese, and if they were a good risk then they'd be allowed to go. The Japanese all had to be checked, their backgrounds. Of great importance in wartime.

Did I ever get the impression that they knew this was coming, that war was coming, that the Japanese knew the war was coming? No. I could never prove that. Of course, with the

Japanese, the Japanese mind, they would never admit it. Usually the only ones I could communicate with were the good ones, and I could never prove by any conversation that they knew that the war was coming. Some of them, at times, used to say, "Wait until the Japanese land here and things will be different." Quite a number used to tell me that in one way or another.

Canada has never defined what these people were known as. I don't think even the Spanish government did. They could have been enemy aliens, prisoners of war, undesirables. That was a vague line. Everything was done under the pressures of war and fear. Today, we would argue for six months on whether to do something, but when you've got the Japanese outside in the Pacific, and the philosophy of the people is "Kill the bastards," no politician has the problem in deciding. He knows the decision has been made for him by the public.

We thought they were coming. I was there. Some people are brave. The majority are not. And there were these thousands of Japanese in our midst.

In all the times I was in the camps I never saw one instance of cruelty, and that is why I feel so proud and feel so strongly about it and the men who did it, who administrated the whole thing. In their very able manner they took care of those Japanese. Such as they have never been taken care of before. In the history of human warfare—and nobody has ever disputed this when I tell them—never have enemy aliens been treated so humanely.

The 1943 Royal Commission Report

So in December of 1943, after all these complaints, the government in Ottawa decided to have a Royal Commission into the treatment of the Japanese in the ghost towns and camps in B.C. The government said it was because of the complaints the

Japanese nationals had been making to the Spanish consul, who was responsible for their treatment at the international level.

The Japanese were complaining that the provisions for their general welfare was not as generous as it should be, although how they could know what the scale should be I don't know. I'm just quoting from the report and what I read. They had also made complaints to the International Red Cross.

One thing I don't understand is this. What levels of welfare did the Japanese expect since there was nothing like this in the history of Canada? And how did the commission measure whether the Japanese were receiving more than generous, adequate, or less than adequate treatment as they, too, had nothing to base their decisions on? But let that pass.

It was a four-man commission, three men and a woman, and it was headed by a Dr. Jackson of the Manitoba government and it was sometimes called the Jackson Commission. I don't think it made much of an impact. I mean, it was probably read in Ottawa and then put away on a shelf and things went on as they had before.

One thing is certain—so I read—the commission made a five-day tour of all the camps in B.C. and that was it. A pretty quick look, I'd say. That's what the Japanese thought. And they wrote their report in two weeks or they handed it in in two weeks. They made this tour of Japanese areas and listened to some complaints from the Issei, those people who had made the complaints. I don't know how extensive a report they made as the only report I saw seems to have been a résumé as it was only fifteen pages. It must have been a résumé. It couldn't have been a Royal Commission report.

What they said they had done was visit each camp and talk to the camp supervisor and then meet with the Japanese Camp Committee and then visit all parts of the camp and situations which the Japanese said were undesirable and then talk again with the camp executives.

The report said "Your commission, as instructed, has made an extensive and thorough investigation of the welfare and maintenance of the people of the Japanese race in the Interior settlements. It records its admiration for the splendid piece of work executed by the original B.C. Security Commission in its task of evacuating twenty-three thousand persons from the defence area to temporary residences elsewhere. There was no precedent to follow. The construction problem alone, during the peak of war stringency of materials, was a gigantic achievement. The evacuation of these people with, so far as your commission can find, a minimum of hardship is a matter for congratulation."

There you have it. Right there.

One thing that struck me as funny was that in all this investigation, one of the most positive recommendations the commission made was that there was no provision for a restroom for the female staff for the B.C. Security staff in downtown Vancouver.

One thing that is important, and the Japanese and other Canadians may not have thought of it this way, but the Interior settlements were a temporary means of meeting an emergency and that the Department of Labour considered them to be "a step in the evacuation process and a training ground for employment in the prairies and the East." This is what the commission kept in mind at all times and in effect it must have had a considerable effect on their own findings.

The commission said it had received no complaints as to the food obtainable in the stores and the food they inspected was of average or better quality. There was a fair range of cheaper cuts of meat and fish. It said that the Japanese were encouraged to plant gardens wherever possible.

The commission said that every Japanese representative urged an increase in the food maintenance rates, and the commission pointed out that these rates were slightly higher than the regular provincial social assistance rates and other social assistance programs. The commission recommended that no increase be made in the maintenance rates for employable persons and their dependents, as it was in the best interests of the Japanese to accept work and so stay off the relief. It recommended a 10 percent increase in the rates for the aged, infirm, and unemployable people and their dependents, to be granted at the discretion of the welfare department.

The commission said that after inspecting all housing in the ghost towns and at Tashme it found no basis to the complaints that the housing was of unsafe construction. It pointed out that this housing was only of a temporary nature, but many houses had been winterized by the inhabitants with materials supplied by the B.C. Security Commission.

It admitted that a number of unsuitable, unsafe, and vacant buildings in some settlements had been converted into dwelling places "due to the urgency of the evacuation."

It said it had inspected the former Japanese housing on Powell Street and at Steveston and along the lower Fraser River, and said the new housing provided was superior and that even the old unsafe and unsuitable buildings divided into apartments were equal to the quarters previously occupied by the Japanese before the evacuation.

The commission admitted that some of the complaints of overcrowding, especially in the old remodelled buildings, were true, but said that, due to wartime, many Occidentals were also living in overcrowded quarters. It ended with the rather cryptic remark that " . . . Much more can be done in this connection [of alleviating the overcrowding] when the B.C. Security Commission has more co-operation from the Japanese." Possibly it meant that overcrowding would lessen when more and more Japanese families and single men moved East of the Rockies and out of B.C.

As far as employment was concerned, the commission felt the B.C. Security Commission had done a good job, considering all the factors of available raw materials, the locations of the settlements, and the skill of the residents. It noted that it was impressed with the fact that those who held the better jobs in the settlements were " . . . the better-educated and trained, the more efficient and generally more personable individuals." It noted that these people would best fit into outside employment, which presumably meant East of the Rockies, which was the federal government's main aim in handling the Japanese problem in B.C. The commission said that dispersing the Japanese in productive, self-supporting family groups or singly across Canada, where they would have the opportunity to be assimilated into local community life, was in the best interests of Canada and the Japanese themselves. It said the government's policy of withholding maintenance money from single employable persons eighteen years and over if they refused to accept employment elsewhere in Canada was "fair and sound and a necessary step in the re-establishment of the individual in self-supporting employment." The commission said it had learned there was plenty of work East of the Rockies for all employable males.

The Japanese representatives asked for an increase in the scale of wages—averaging 25 cents an hour—but the commission said that the Japanese were getting shelter, fuel, light, and medical care almost free and that served to bring the wages into line.

The commission recommended that the self-supporting employment program be accelerated and everybody be put to work whenever possible.

It also recommended that where it was practicable to increase the wage scale and that reasonable deductions be made for any services which were supplied by the B.C. Security Commission, which could be interpreted as paying more for work but increasing the deductions, thus leaving the Japanese worker in essentially the same position as before.

The commission did point the finger at the provincial government for refusing to provide kindergarten and high school instruction in the settlements when it was clearly their responsibility to do so before Pearl Harbor, and it recommended that negotiations be reopened with the provincial department of education "to the end that it reassume its obligation in respect to the education of the children of the Japanese race."

The commission found "an excellent program of medical care

including hospitalization, medical and dental services" at all Interior camps and there were sufficient hospital beds for the Japanese. Immunization programs were carried out against smallpox, diphtheria, scarlet fever, typhoid fever, and whooping cough, and pre-natal and baby clinics were all available and all well used. There were sufficient doctors and nurses. It cited the large TB hospital at New Denver. It noted that " . . . in the opinion of your commission the medical care provided at the Interior settlements for Japanese people exceeds that received by the average Canadian."

It said, "Your commission finds the Japanese people exceptionally healthy."

All Japanese complaints had included the lack of recreation facilities for children and adults, especially during the winter. The commission said picture shows were available, plus skating, skiing, and sleighing, and tennis, basketball, baseball, and swimming were available in the summer, and it recommended no further capital expenditures for recreational facilities.

The commission also recommended that when a Japanese and his dependents become established outside of the Interior— East of the Rockies—then the liquid assets that were held for him by the government could be given to him. Many would interpret this, of course, as another prod to get the Interior Japanese to move to the prairies or Ontario or Quebec.

Some Japanese veterans of the First World War argued before the commission that they should have preferential treatment, as no distinction was made between them and other Japanese, and the commission said, rather guardedly: "Your commission is sympathetic to their request that they be given preferred treatment if this is possible."

In summing up their investigation, the commission said: "Your commission is of the unanimous opinion that the provisions made by the government of Canada through the Department of Labour for the welfare of the Japanese in the Interior settlements of British Columbia are, as a wartime measure, reasonably fair and adequate."

Reasonably fair and adequate in regards to what?

Anyway, the commission dropped out of sight, never to be heard of again, and the report apparently suffered the same fate.

Commentators on the Japanese problem in the Interior settlements during the war barely comment on this Royal Commission, so minor and slight must its impact have been.

One writer went so far as to call it a "whitewash."

9 *They Learned a Great Deal*

Education is important to the Japanese. Even the lowliest peasant boys who came in creaky old ships to B.C. in the 1880s and 1890s could read and write. These first pioneers may have never mastered the English language, but they made certain the importance of an English education was passed on to their sons and daughters.

In a very real way an education was the open door to a different life, a better life, a life that hopefully could lift them above the hostility and racism they all faced and somehow managed to cope with.

Then came Pearl Harbor and the first movement of people into the Hastings Park holding pool—and not a classroom, a book, a globe, a pencil, in sight.

One of the major concerns of the parents who first were hustled into these barren buildings was educational facilities for the children. Of course there were none. But not for long. In a matter of weeks there was a school of sorts. By begging and borrowing, enough equipment was gathered and with the older students helping with the younger ones, each child in Hastings Park got half a day's school. It wasn't much but it was something.

However, as the summer wore on, children moved with their families to the ghost towns and camps. The B.C. government made arrangements for elementary education wherever space could be found. But what about kindergarten? What about high school? The government stood fast. No kindergarten, no high school.

Fortunately the churches—United, Anglican, Catholic— moved in and set up kindergarten and high school classes, usually under the most trying of circumstances, with little equipment and tattered schoolbooks. Amazingly, among those logged-off mountains under an indifferent sky, these crude methods of schooling worked rather well.

One teacher said the most important thing was not so much to give the students an education but to overcome the sense of loneliness, of deprivation that so many of them must have felt. In other words, in every way they tried to foster an atmosphere of real life among the students and not the artificial life of imprisonment which was their daily existence.

The knowledge that they had somehow succeeded against such odds must have made the poor pay, the frustrations, the sense of isolation worthwhile. Perhaps that is what teaching is all about.

The School in Hastings Park

In February they began to bring the first families down to Vancouver from Prince Rupert and all those islands and put them in Hastings Park and the first thing the parents said was, "Oh, my children are going to lose their school year."

You must understand how important education is for the Japanese. It is one of the most important things of all. They didn't want to lose time. Well, I was one teaching school at Steveston, grade one, and I was I think the only Japanese person teaching school in British Columbia, so it was up to me to organize a school.

In the Forum. Classes were there. Immediately after Pearl Harbor all the Japanese language schools were closed and they had their own desks and chairs and blackboards and we set them up in the Forum, which you know is a round building. We used the blackboards to partition off the classes as best we could. We got some good help from the Vancouver School Board but hardly nothing from the Department of Education in Victoria.

I would teach school in Steveston and then rush all the way out to Hastings Park and do what I could in the late afternoon, organize classes and what to do next day, but we couldn't do much. We did what we could though. We managed to give each child half a day's school. We didn't really have teachers, so I thought, well, the older ones will have to help the little ones. So we got a bunch of the high schoolers and including some from outside the fence, Vancouver, and they'd kind of give the lessons and mark the papers and do what they could. In this way there was some education being given to the children.

We had the lower grades on the ground floor and higher up the older grades, and it was then when I put my theory to work—that the parents didn't know much English and not how the school system worked, so I would use high school students with the correspondence school courses as their guide, although just the absolute minimum that they could give.

The Vancouver School Board was very good. They offered the services of a male principal for the whole setup. Stu McRae.

By May with families leaving every day, going to the camps, going away, I had only a small handful of my pupils in school at Steveston. So I went to the principal and I told him I would leave and spend my time at Hastings Park. That was where I was needed. He said I was employed for a year and I was entitled to my full salary if I stayed, but I felt I was needed more at Hastings Park, so I went in May.

In June a lot of children had lost some time in moving and getting settled in the camp, so we decided to continue on in July and we did, me laying out the lessons for every grade and the older people supervising and teaching and checking off what they had done. We managed that way all July but August became so unbearably hot and there was no air-conditioning, so we decided that we would terminate then for that time. So that is how the children got education in Hastings Park. It was rudimentary, I suppose, but probably no different than what the average rural child taking correspondence courses would get.

There was no money involved. Nobody talked about money in those days. Everything was voluntary, for the good of the children, for the good of the community.

They All Call Her Bartie

They kept dumping coaches, trainloads of Japanese from the Fraser Valley, Mission, Haney, Surrey, all farm workers, they kept dumping them into the Lethbridge area to work in the sugar beet fields, and there was absolutely nothing those.people could do. They had to go to farms, to little shacks, and they couldn't go into Lethbridge or Calgary, or Edmonton because these cities had made a deal with the B.C. Security Commission. They had been yanked out of their warm existence in British Columbia and dumped into southern Alberta. Slave labour.

It was the duty of the churches to do something but a chap, a minister I had known up north, a chap now at Taber, realized that the ministers were being hamstrung by their English congregations. While the ministers wanted to help the Japanese, and most of these newcomers were Christians, the English congregations of their churches wouldn't let them do anything. That was the sad part of it all. Pure and simple. We could do very little with the Japanese people.

The young people, they were the ones who concerned him and also concerned me because they were a dispirited, discouraged lot, you see. These young people had been planning to go on from high school and they were uprooted. Planning various careers. One wanted to be a journalist. Another wanted to be a lawyer. And so on. One highly intelligent girl who had been in first-year university at Vancouver, she located me and asked if she could get library books. You see, there was nothing for these kids to do in the wintertime. They couldn't go into the cities. In Edmonton. Therefore to sit in a little shacks out on the prairies, that was debilitating. These young people needed somebody to give them faith in themselves. They'd lost all ambition, all thinking.

The school trustees in Lethbridge slapped a 7-dollar-a-month fee on every high school student who was Japanese who wanted to go to school in Lethbridge. Well, at 20 dollars an acre, which is what the Japanese were paid for a year's work in the sugar beet fields and the average Japanese could only do ten acres, and if there were five individuals in the family, you add that up for yourself. That would be 1,000 dollars income for a year. The little children didn't count as workers and neither did the old people, but they had to be fed, clothed, kept warm, and a family, even in 1942, living on 1,000 dollars a year, why, it was insane. So there were no families which could pay 7 dollars a month for high school fees. So these kids were pulled out of high school and there was nothing for the mind, nothing for the development, do you see.

As one boy said when they brought them to Lethbridge district and they lined them up in the freight yards there and the farmers came in to get them, the farmers went down the line and asked each family group: "Whose Japs are you?" One boy said, he answered, "What does it matter? We're all cattle anyway."

You see, this was the feeling these kids had. Just when they should be learning about life, development, all the rest, they considered themselves like cattle. And what had these people done which was against Canada? Nothing. Absolutely nothing. Except that they had Japanese ancestors.

So these ministers couldn't do anything for this situation because of their congregations; but I was appointed from Toronto, you see, by the Home Missions Committee of the Women's Missionary Society and so my friend from Taber said, "Look, Miss Bartling is in a unique position. Let her do work among the Japanese." The committee bucked this at first but I got around the committee, but I remember one Anglican minister telling me after I had talked to them about the Japanese situation and what we should do, he said, "Woman, if I talked like you, I would lose my pulpit." Just imagine!

One thing I did, I started Citizen Forum Courses. They had them in Alberta. It was a form of adult education. They were radio programs that came from Edmonton. They would send out to groups pamphlets with questions ahead of time of the radio panel discussion, and after we heard the radio we would discuss the discussion and fill in the questionnaire. We'd send in our discussions, our conclusions. The following week they would announce over the air the opinions of various groups across the province. We had these discussion groups in Raymond, Picture Butte, and Taber and they gave themselves names, but not names so that they would know they were Japanese young people. Picture Butte called themselves the Picture Butte Chinooks and so on. Although the Taber group called themselves the Taber Ex-B.C.'s. We pulled our hair and had some marvellous times, and I wrote to the man who handled the radio discussion and I said, "Frank, please mention our groups over the radio as groups who were interested and doing well as often as you can," which gave them a sense of—well, their opinions mattering and that they had a part to play in the consensus. And this was one of the most important things I did do, this getting the young people together and thinking and talking and making them feel that just because they were sentenced to the war's lifetime out there on the prairie, that they mattered.

I also heeded their social life too. I felt that was important. These various groups would rent a hall and have a dance. I would be there right with them, taking the girls home after, and many a night I wouldn't get home until 4 A.M. That didn't matter.

Then gradually, as time went by and people got used to them, they formed what they called the Southern Alberta Youth Conference. They had a conference and met and talked about their problems, their parents' problems, Canada, their future. Things like that. That helped them too.

These are the things I did. I hope it helped. I know it helped. Somebody had to help those poor students. While Canadians slept well in their beds there were hundreds of young people, also Canadians, who lay awake nights just wondering, wondering, wondering what was to happen to them. Everything that could be done to assure them that one day all would be well, I tried to do. And those students, those teenagers, turned out to be as fine a group of Canadians as you will find anywhere in the land today. I think so. I keep in touch with a lot of them today. They all call me Bartie.

The School at Lemon Creek

I was a conscientious objector and after I'd graduated from the Ontario College of Education and wouldn't join the army they grabbed me and put me, shipped me to the British Columbia Forest Service. I worked there for a while. Fifty cents a day and my room and board. I kept hearing about these Japanese students up in the Interior without teachers and I kept applying, pestering for a transfer so I could teach these students, and finally they gave in. I hadn't taught a day in my life, except practice teaching, but if you knew how things were up there, you'd know that didn't matter.

So I was engaged by the United Church to teach in a high school that they set up. This was in September of '43. The government agency had set up elementary schools only, going on the premise that if they provided too many amenities like high school, then the Japanese people would stick in the Interior when they wanted them out of there, out to the prairies or Eastern Canada. So it remained for the churches to go in and establish high schools.

Of course, for a year these youngsters had been running around loose with not too much to engage their attention except that the more enterprising among them took correspondence courses. And of course they took courses in their favourite subjects, so we would find that someone had finished grade-twelve math and hadn't started grade-nine English. So, as you can imagine, it was quite a timetable.

The facilities were the ones used by the elementary students and we used them for the high school students on Friday nights and Saturday mornings. There were no lights in that school at Lemon Creek, so we took in gas lanterns and sometimes they didn't work.

In the second year, 1944, they managed to erect a two-room school and a small library and we were able to have day school from then on. This school was actually erected by the government authorities with Japanese labour. The B.C. Security Commission. We had blackboards. I don't know how we came by them.

Yes, it shocked me that several hundred, maybe a few thousand kids weren't getting high school education. Just elementary, and not enough to send them out into the world. It was the theory, almost, that these children were "just Japs." Yes.

Education. With us. They got as good as we were able to give them and so many had taken correspondence courses that we decided the first year to follow the correspondence courses as laid down—that they would be a fairly good guide as to what the kids would need.

The staff initially consisted of one of the missionaries who had been in Japan. She had run a girls' school. Her experience didn't fit her any too well. Some of the kids were rather a rough bunch, and also they let the resentment against the treatment they had burn inside of them. They found it rather difficult to distinguish between some Occidentals who wanted to help them and others. So they were quite a handful. We also had a young Japanese gentlemen from Vancouver who had been a storekeeper and he taught them commercial skills. I found myself, as the one university graduate on the staff, teaching them almost every subject.

I really can't quite say what I did expect when I went to Lemon Creek—whether a concentration camp atmosphere or a free and easy atmosphere—but I was glad to get out of that forestry camp. The first year I lived in a house that housed the R.C.M.P. constable and some administrative staff and found the atmosphere of that house a little stultifying. The last two years I had a separate room near the school and it was close to the work.

When I was allowed to go and do this work for the Japanese I was allowed 50 dollars a month. I got 65 dollars actually but I had to contribute 15 dollars a month to the Red Cross. When all this was over and I was able to take a normal teaching job, I jumped from there to the princely sum of 2,400 dollars a year. Well, anyway . . .

But these Japanese, these young people. We had problems. With regard to their extra-curricular activities. We wanted to keep some control and they wanted to run their whole—their clubs strictly themselves without any guidance from the staff, and this was, as far as we could see, just an outward manifestation of their feelings toward their situation in the country.

I remember one young chap, he was in grade eleven when he came to us, and when he was going to school in Vancouver he was a 98 percenter. Absolutely brilliant. And he went out there to Lemon Creek and started brooding about the treatment the Japanese had had and with us he was a 60 percenter. His name was Tony. His situation and the situation of the Japanese in the camps, it just eroded away his incentive. He was an extreme case. Some did well, of course.

We compared notes with teachers in other centres and we decided that there was a concentration of young people, teenagers, who took the whole thing about the Japanese as particularly hard. To some extent, three or four could infect 40. I can only associate the whole thing with the property situation. Everything taken. Everything they had, all those years of building up homes and businesses and the like, all gone. Gone forever.

We Sang "O Canada"

I said I wanted to work with the Japanese, so I was sent to Tashme in the mountains in early January of 1943. It was deep in snow. Mr. McWilliams, the head of the United Church, took me in and we had to walk up the trail for the last four miles. I remember my first glimpse of it. We looked down into this valley and it was all white except you could see stovepipes all over it with smoke coming out of the pipes, and two or three big barns. You couldn't see anybody. Just the smoke and the snow and the mountains. My impression, the smoke coming up.

Would I consider Tashme as being a concentration camp? Well, I've never been in a concentration camp, so I don't like using that word because it may imply more than it was. And yet on the other hand it was—they called it an evacuation camp to give it a more pleasant sound—and certainly the conditions at first were very bad. But on the other hand we had all the best in the way of food, just as they did outside the camp. That was one good point. We also had a hospital. That was another good point. But on the other hand you couldn't get out of it without a permit. There were guards. It was surrounded by mountains. You got into it by a narrow trail. You were certainly shut in, away from the world. You had the R.C.M.P. All those conditions.

Another thing, the Japanese value education very, very much. Very important. And the educational facilities offered them at Tashme in the primary grades was very, very poor. They practically had to teach the children themselves. There were only two Japanese who had any kind of training. And the government didn't send in anything to help them. These children were Canadians, born in Canada. You must remember that, and yet the government was denying them the basic rights of education.

The church, of course, took over the kindergarten and the high school, and there were a lot of things about the camp and a lot of people in the camp that I just did not know about because from morning to night we were on the go, teaching these youngsters and trying to prepare them for the world when they would get out of this camp.

Another one of the problems we had to face was recreation. There was nothing. When we went in that winter we found nothing and you can't have hundreds of people cooped up in tiny rooms through a long, long winter and nothing for them to do, so sometimes we got dances going in the upper floor of the barns. Something for these children, these youths, young adults to do. Anything at all is better than nothing and getting an education is the best thing of all.

I have not known, in all my years working with Japanese, known them to destroy property, but at Tashme that first year this is what they were doing. Cut up the piano. That sort of thing. Sheer frustration. The Japanese have a great respect for property and here they were causing damage. That was a very bad sign. Therefore, the high school we started was not only trying to give them an education but it was trying to create a whole new little society in the camp.

The first thing we did was to get the correspondence. We got the courses and the exams, and the exams were corrected in Victoria and sent back and so on. The first year that is the way we ran it. The second year we got permission to teach and mark and grade on certain subjects, although some subjects still had to go through Victoria.

And the books. Well, we had very few books. The few we did have were, well, scrounged, you might say. Found and brought in. The government would not pay for the books.

My first day. One of the administrators called me in to his office and he said that he was going to introduce me to some of the students who would be taught in the high school and we were to plan how we would run the school. We had to have it after the primary school was closed, so we began at half past four in the afternoon and, with time out for supper, we ran to half past nine.

So we decided on the soonest day that we could start the

school and then I asked them what kind of an opening would we have for each day, what would we do. And I'll always remember because they decided among themselves that first they'd sing "O Canada." It wasn't that they thought it was a lark up there in the mountains. They were very bitter about it, really. But they had been born in Canada and they knew nothing but Canada. They spoke English. They were Canadians and there they were, in a camp with guards.

And so on that first day, when they stood and sang, there were tears running down many of their faces. Because Canada had failed them pretty badly.

And the same thing could be said of us coming in, the church, the teachers. They didn't accept us very readily because our Christianity had failed them.

There were terrible things that happened there, the things that happened to families. Thousands of people drive that highway every month and go right past those big barns, they're still there, and they don't know what happened in there. But there were good things that happened in there too, you must understand. People, especially the school children and especially the high school children, they forged bonds of friendship that continue strongly to this day.

When I say good things, I really mean, I guess, the good things that happened in the minds and spirits of those young people. Well, I felt, when I hear and talked to them afterward, I felt that they had learned a great deal that their own children now growing in Hamilton or Toronto or Vancouver, in luxury and so on, are not learning. They feel that some of the most basic things and valuable things in life, which they learned in the camp, things that are really worthwhile, are not being taught to their own children. Not that they want them to go through all the miseries of that camp, but they themselves felt that out of it came some things that were worthwhile and purposeful to them.

Schooling at Tashme

After a while at Tashme the B.C. Security Commission arranged for schooling up to grade eight. After grade eight they said they weren't responsible. It was the same in all the camps in B.C. Now I wish you would explain that to me. Before we were evacuated we went to elementary school and then to high school just like any other kids. And why not? We were Canadian citizens and doesn't the law say that Canadian kids are entitled to go to school as long as he can pass the courses? Sure it does.

But no, there was to be no kindergarten and there was to be no high school and at Tashme there wasn't even going to be a building you could point at and say, "That is our school." But then the commission, which was acting for the provincial government in this matter because schooling, education, is the responsibility of the provincial government, they converted one of the big barns into classrooms.

We didn't have any regular teachers from the provincial school system. Teachers were hired and trained right within the Japanese community at Tashme. Like take my sister. She taught in grade one for a few years. She was not a trained teacher as we know a trained teacher—she had a grade-eleven education but she hadn't finished high school. So she was trained in the summer months the year of 1943 and she taught the little ones for three years. This is the way it was done right up through the grades. There were a lot of teachers who were Japanese and a lot of girls who were like teachers' aides.

But take myself. I was out of grade eight and I'd be going into grade nine—but there was no grade nine. The B.C. Security Commission said the government said no high school for us. In other words, why would a Japanese kid need a high school education? What would he need it for? To work in the mill, to work on the back of a truck, to pick berries? That's the conclusion you've got to come to, isn't it? So we just ran around loose.

Then the elders said, "This is bad. These kids shouldn't be running around doing nothing." But because of the shortage of building facilities the grades one to eight had the schoolrooms and there was nothing for us. So the churches started a night school for us. The churches must have got together in a gentlemen's agreement that they would help us out, and some pretty wonderful people helped the Japanese in those years.

Like take Tashme. The Anglican Church got hold of a small building and sent up a couple of teachers into the camp, and they took the kindergarten. Just to give the kiddies a little start before they went into grade one.

The United Church took the high school kids, ones like me. From about four o'clock we'd go into the barn schoolhouse and work. A couple of United Church missionaries came first and others later. So anyway we had night school for grades nine and ten from about four o'clock to seven, and then grades eleven and twelve would come from seven until ten o'clock—and that's how we got our education.

Each camp had different ways of doing things, but I think the first year most of them didn't have seats or blackboards or anything like that. But gradually the authorities eased up and they shipped in equipment from the Japanese-language schools we had before the war came. When the war came these schools were closed. The very next day. There were fifty-nine of them and we used to go to them after regular classes. So they used that equipment.

Tashme was a high school and they did high school things, like having bobsleigh rides and skating parties and picnics and volleyball leagues, and they even had a yearbook.

As a matter you should know, the Tashme High School Yearbook doesn't look much different from any other yearbook you'd see. You'd never know it was done by kids who lived three and four years in a prison atmosphere.

It was hard to say how good the schools were, but we all thought they were pretty good. An idea of how they were was if a kid, like my little brother, was in grades three, four, and five in Tashme, well, when my family moved out to Alberta after the war he went right into the sixth grade. That meant the standard was high.

The people who worked in those schools were wonderful. You never hear of them, of all the problems they faced and the low pay they had to take and the way a bunch of them would be jammed together into one small sleeping room and being far from the cities. But the sisters and the United Church men and women, the Anglicans, they sure were wonderful people.

At Tashme they had the right attitude too. At some places Japanese were treated as the enemy. I know. Friends have told me. At Tashme the teachers treated everybody the same, as Canadians.

You've got to hand it to the kids too. They studied hard. The only time a Japanese child is going to get his ears boxed is when he does badly in the classes. Education is very important. They didn't have any real places to study, just those crammed little huts—one family at one end in a room, another family at the other and the stove in the room between, but the kids studied. That was schooling at Tashme. Other places were different, but in the long run it was pretty much all the same.

"We Shared an Experience"

I think the greatest thing that happened was that we, the missionaries, shared an experience with them, the students, and gave them not just the education in the books they did have but a chance to acquire some basic attitudes toward life. You see, we had school from Monday to Friday at night, but we also had school on Saturday mornings and on that morning we had special subjects.

For instance, we had music. We got records, the very best music, and a pretty good record player for those times and they studied music, they listened to music and they discussed the music and what it meant, and that was something that was not being done in other schools in the province at that time.

And then, we had the studies of books. One book was on the basic meaning of life and we made copies of the different chapters and then the students broke up into groups, after they had read the book and the chapters, and they discussed each chapter and talked it over until they understood the meaning, the philosophy of it, what the author was trying to tell them. This particular book I'm speaking of was *What It Means to Grow Up*. A very fine book. I can't remember the author's name.

Using that as a start, the Japanese students expressed themselves and their views along these lines and were able to see their own experiences better, the meanings and values of life, and with better understanding they grew greatly in their attitude toward life. This was something that other students in the ordinary schools were not getting.

I met with a group of my pupils years later in Eastern Canada and they told me they were anxious about their children. Their own children were getting a very superficial idea of what life is. And yet they are going to schools today which could be called super-schools. They have everything but understanding.

Out of that schooling they got in the camp, and because the students and the teachers were able to share so closely, I feel it was a great experience, not only for the students but also for me. It was all a growth in character, a growth in thinking about life and out of that high school there are so many men, and some women too, who are putting great things into the life of Canada.

It Was Good for Their Morale

The kids were always well dressed. I mean the students. They'd see newspapers and magazines sent in, and if there was pictures of fashions of young people, and I mean especially the girls, well, they would try and make clothes like them. It was pretty well the skirt and blouse or sweater and bobby-sox era anyway.

You must remember that the mothers were all good seamstresses. Some of them had been in the business, little shops, working at home in Vancouver, and they could do the work or they could have taught their daughters. Most of the girl students could do some of the work and we did our utmost to encourage them.

You see, it was part of the morale of the school that they look good. No, I don't quite mean that. I mean the schools, the high schools, were such run-down places, old barns, buildings just thrown up, that it was good for the morale of the students if they wore good clothes. To my knowledge they always wore good clothes to school. They got them somewhere. They could order through the catalogues—there was nothing that said they couldn't do that. Dozens of big parcels used to come in in every mail. Clothes. Cloth too. They often started right from scratch, making a dress from the beginning, or a suit.

It was good for their morale. They may have been locked away in a camp with no hope for any kind of future in the near future, but they could still dress as well as any city girl. That was one thing. The boys were not as fashion conscious, as I recall. Of course, boys never are. It was mostly shirts with a sweater and slacks. But they, too, dressed neatly. There is no doubt about that.

Let me put it this way. If you saw those students, judging from the way they were dressed, the way the girls did their hair, and even their talk—like their slang, the phrases they have among each other, the things they did—I'm quite sure that if you didn't look up at those mountains and realize that you were in what amounted to a prison camp, you would think that they were in a high school in the city of Vancouver.

Of course, this went for the little ones too. I was only talking about the high school students. But the lower grades, kindergarten, they were always well dressed. Neat in appearance. So in that way they did not suffer. Just like ordinary children.

"We Prepared the Way"

Now of course there was a reason for everything we did. The children, and most especially the boys and girls of high school age, would soon be moving out into the world, on the prairies, in Eastern Canada. To work maybe, to go to other high schools perhaps. But what our job was as teachers and administrators in these relocation centre high schools was to prepare the way. In a word, even though we were locked in those mountain valleys and the children had no communication with other schools, we somehow had to make the schools we had as close to the Canadian system as possible.

This was done in many ways, but first you must consider the hardships because our schools were very crude. Classrooms were hopelessly inadequate, and books were scarce and the ones we did have were battered and torn. There was nothing that matched anything a city high school would have in the way of chemical and physics laboratories, sewing rooms, home economics facilities, teaching area for typing. Everything was done almost on the level of the little log schoolhouse of pioneer days. But we managed. How we managed, so far from civilization, so far from any news of new teaching techniques, so far from any fraternization with other schools, always made me and still makes me wonder. But it was done.

Of course, you must understand that it couldn't have been done without the full support of the student body. And you must understand the Japanese in this regard, for they regard education as almost a sacred trust. I'll go further. They regarded it as the most important thing in the world, for they knew, young as they were, that they were going out into an alien land when they left the camp, and that is why they knew they had to have a good education to survive.

Oh yes, there were some dropouts but not many. Just a few.

And you must remember that at Tashme a lot of the students were working a full eight-hour day, on the roads and in the sawmill or on maintenance for the boys, or in the store, the post office, and so on for the girls. So they worked during the day and the church, we in the church, taught them at night. So there were bound to be a few dropouts, because of this heavy workload for one thing, although some of the boys were taking correspondence courses in subjects which we could not teach. After all, while we were a high school, a private high school I should say, there were no facilities for shops and things like that.

And then there were the parents. We mustn't forget the parents. It was mainly from the parents that the students had their great desire for education in that they had seen the narrow and grasping and poverty-stricken lives their parents had led before the war, mainly because they were restricted because of lack of English training. But these parents were enthusiastically behind the school. I think we had forty or more parents for our first Parent–Teacher Association meeting, when there probably were no more than sixty or seventy students in the school at the time, and I often wonder how many of those parents were able to understand the proceedings in English. But they wanted education for their children. It was the way out, you see. They could see it and so could the children.

It carries over to this day. Why do you think there are so many successful Japanese Canadians? It all goes back to the one thing. Education. Doctors and lawyers, architects, writers, administrators, government people, people at every level of government. And all those who have their own businesses. Gracious, I've heard it said, without any figures produced, of course, that beyond the Jews the Japanese are Canada's most affluent minority ethnic group, and that is in competition from the Chinese, who are no slouch at this kind of thing.

But back to the main point, high school. That other was just a bit of my mind wandering around. High school. It was painfully apparent—and I mean painfully apparent—to the Japanese that they were going to lose the war. You could tell just by reading the newspapers. And what of these children after the war? They didn't want to be labourers. They wanted to be teachers and office managers and have their own businesses and be nurses and teachers and doctors. But if we kept them in such an atmosphere as a camp—and let us not forget it was no different in many respects from a prison camp—then when they did go back into civilization where would they be? They wouldn't fit into the schools, whether at the elementary level or at the high school level, or for those who were to move onward and upward, at the university level. So we had to create something for them that was not there. We had to give it, for lack of a better word, the atmosphere and the reality of a big city high school.

That is why, in that remote mountain valley we had our Sadie Hawkins' Day Dance. We had our chess club. We had our music appreciation courses. We had our field day using the house system for competition. There were dances and we made every effort to get the most up-to-date modern records by the big bands. Those children, grade nine and up, knew more about the big name band leaders and the different types of music and the Hollywood scene than most city children did. We taught them to dance. They had their own dances, of course. Jiving. Jitterbugging. Remember them? But we also taught them to waltz and fox-trot. Someday they would come in handy. We had hockey teams even though half the players would be using sticks they had cut out of the woods, and we had skating nights. My, how those children loved those nights on our little mountain lake. Under a moon and stars. The world of reality and the camp seemed far far away. Although I wonder, I sometimes wonder, just how many of those children thought about it. What I mean is, did it do something to them, psychological to them, from which they have never recovered? I don't know if it can be measured but if you do take one yardstick and that is success, then you might say that it did them no harm. But I often wonder.

But back to the school. The school and their social life was one and indivisible. There was no corner store hangout for them.

Noplace to go. And so they had judo classes, which is natural for Japanese children, and informal dances where the hep-cats cut the rug, as they would put it, and a Pre-Spring Frolic with a grand march and the works, all in that building. It was rather a glorious sight to see what a bunch of children could do with bits of coloured paper and some strings of Christmas tree lights and their imaginations. It was the era of the bobby-soxer. I'd almost forgotten all about it. Of course we teachers were honoured guests and they danced us into exhaustion.

The other side of it, of course, was more intellectual, for that was a type of preparation too. There was the current events club. The teacher in charge would read an article from one of the news journals or newspapers and then the students would discuss it. From the point of view of almost being prisoners—well, I guess you could say they were prisoners—and having been away from civilization for about two years, they all did remarkably well. That is one thing. They had exceptionally good minds. There is no doubt about that.

Let's see, what other clubs. There was a public-speaking club, debates with the "yeas" having it over the "nays" just like in any public high school—except with us it was in a large barnlike room, often quite chilly because heating was a problem, rather than in a beautiful gymnasium with polished hardwood floors like in some city high school. There also were public-speaking courses, which I'm sure proved invaluable to students when they left. It gave them a chance to get up on their feet before their peers and organize their thoughts on a subject and present their opinions logically and forcefully, and that was a good thing because the camp atmosphere did have a tendency to make those who were already shy a great deal more shy.

A glee club, of course. Very popular. They just sang their hearts out.

There was a handicraft club where the girls were taught tatting and crocheting and knitting. Then the boys wanted to get in on the action, whether to actually learn or just to be near the girls. I remember one fisherman I met years later who told me that on the long nights when he was going from one fishing ground to another off the coast he would pass off the hours knitting socks, and he said he'd learned to turn a heel at the handicraft course in the camp when he was a lad.

There were the usual quota of romances, of course, or should I say it was something like a square dance at times, changing partners and so forth. This was something that couldn't be stopped, and we no more tried to stop it than any principal in a city high school would try. Of course it would have been impossible. But I don't mean to say there was much trouble. These were unusually well-behaved young people. Unusually well behaved.

And, of course, they had their high school yearbook and that is something to read. That really is something that opens your eyes.

First of all, it was the product of the young people themselves. They were not a lot different from those being put out by high schools in the city or a town with photographs of the classes and literary essays and what you would call "in" jokes and profiles—short, mind you—on every student, and literary essays. Now the literary essays were something to remark upon. They almost always dealt with Canada, patriotism, their love of Canada, and to a lesser degree the involvement of Japan. As I recall, this was hardly mentioned. But almost every essay reminded the students of who and what they were—enemy aliens—and when they graduated, went East to find work, that life would be a great deal different than they had ever known. Most of the essays and valedictories were cautionary and there was a measure of bitterness to them in that they seemed to always ask the question "Why Us?" Now that was a very good question. Why them? It was something that the teachers often had a hard time answering.

Well, they had their high school annual. One of the male teachers made the printing arrangements. They were even able to get a few advertisements to pay for the printing. The annual, of course, always gave full marks to the thirteen or fourteen teachers who taught them. As I remember, four or five of us were white and the rest were Japanese.

But the fact that they had an annual and they put it out on their own showed that they were close to being like a city or noncamp school, at least in spirit. I say that again, at least in spirit, because if you turn the coin over and talk about facilities and convenience and even the capabilities of some of the teachers, then you are talking about something entirely different. I've often thought it was well that they so engrossed themselves in sports—baseball, hockey, mountain-climbing, badminton, basketball, and others—and their clubs and picture-taking expeditions, so they wouldn't have to think about the quality of the education they were getting. Because with the facilities we had and the difficulties they faced, working during the day, school at night, no place in their crowded homes to do homework, it is a wonder that they succeeded at all.

But they did. Oh yes, they did. Many have told me that when the war was over and the camp was closed down and they went off to other parts of Canada that they were able to slip into the school systems without any trouble at all. In fact I do believe that a few were even able to skip a grade upward—and that is all the more remarkable.

We weren't just teaching them English literature and chemistry and history and maths and keeping their bodies and minds full of activity so they wouldn't brood upon their position. I like to think that we were preparing them for going out into the world and to accept the Canada they would find, and not to let despair take over from the spirit of their hearts, to let despair gain control when they ran into difficult situations over which they had no control. What I mean is, I hope we sent them out into the world of Canada without hate in their hearts for what had been done to them. That, in the over-all way, was the objective of the schools in the relocation system, and that was what we as teachers all strove to impart, even though it was not something that was really talked about, brought out into the open and dissected in a matter of speaking. We tried to do what education has tried to do from the beginning of time, I suppose, and that was to send them out as good people, good citizens, and with love and freedom and honour in their hearts, to practice liberty and equality among all people. I think that is what we tried to do. I guess we were trying in our own way to teach them the secret of true living, and I sometimes wonder if it wasn't the students themselves who taught each other this spirit while they were among those hills, cut off from the world they had known.

10 *East of the Rockies*

It is vital to understand that the federal government had no intention of ever allowing the inhabitants of the ghost towns and camps to move back to the West Coast. On the contrary. The Japanese were to be scattered across Canada, each province taking its share—and thus would be eliminated the Japanese Problem in B.C.

However, it would appear that this decision was never made clear to the Japanese. Or if they did know, they chose to ignore it with the attitude, "You brought us here and it's up to you to put us back in our homes." But what they didn't know, or chose to ignore also, was that their homes, their farms, their businessees, did not exist anymore. In any case, some of them didn't have enough confidence or money to start afresh in Ontario or Quebec, which was, as far as many were concerned, an alien land. And some were too old, or too young, to move.

Attempts were made to force single men to leave B.C. by cutting them off from employment. Families were cajoled. Promises were made. Jobs were guaranteed. It was a slow process, but there was a trickle going East.

It has been said that the more determined, the more sophisticated, the ones who understood the whole picture best went East of the Rockies. Let that be. By January 1, 1943, the number of Japanese in Ontario had swelled from 130 to 1,650. By January 1, 1944, there were 2,424. A year later there were 3,742, with the majority in and around Toronto, while another

263

532 were in Quebec. Those who took a chance and made the move found a new life and, most important of all, freedom.

The Long Trip East

Of course, one of the features of camp was that every three or four days one of the families would come to some sort of arrangement and decide to move East, to Toronto first usually, and then perhaps into southern Ontario.

Then many people, a great many, would meet and see them off and there would be a great deal of emotion involved. Some of these people might be relatives, of course, but mostly they were just friends, friends they had known in Vancouver or maybe even in Japan, but certainly friends in the camp. There were gifts given, food for the trip and advice and a great deal of emotion on both sides.

No, they wouldn't take the train. There was a daily bus service from Nelson and back and they'd take that. Then they'd take the Kettle Valley line from Nelson.

No, they didn't have banquets. It never went as far as that. Banquets cost money and these people had very little. No parties either. Those little tarpaper shacks they lived in were not for parties of that sort. Crammed in like sardines. People who had been friends in Vancouver and shared a little shack with each other, they might not be friends when one left. Human nature.

But it was still hard on them. They were leaving friends behind and going into the great unknown. No matter how many letters they got from people who had succeeded, or rather, who were doing well in the East, there always was apprehension. Apprehension about the language, about the job, about schooling for their children and how they would be treated.

Leaving the ghost town and the camp, it was a very emotional experience and probably the biggest decision a father and to make.

Eggs, Herring, and a Box of Bread

When they moved us to Ontario to work that first winter they said they'd pay our way and feed us and there would be a guard to look after us in case we wanted something.

Well, we—or I, I never saw that fellow. Not once. Not in three days. I heard he was on the train but where he was I don't know. We were in an old Colonist car with the smoke stack sticking up and the little stove, and by feeding us they meant they put on a couple of cases of eggs, a couple of cases of canned herring, and a box of bread. It was every man for himself, and by the time I found that out, maybe at the end of the first day, the food was all gone. Maybe that's why the guard never came around. He was enjoying himself in the dining car.

Then we had to get off the train at stations and buy what we could. Sandwiches, egg sandwiches or cheese sandwiches, and I think maybe ham. A piece of pie and a cup of coffee.

Some fellows had no money. The rest of us looked after them. But that's how the government said they'd feed us right across the country—some eggs, some herring, and a box of bread.

I remember one of our fellows was asked at a station counter by a girl if he was Chinese and he said no. "Indian?" No. "Negro?" No. "Well, what are you?" He said Japanese and she said she'd never seen a Japanese before. An awful lot of people we met on that trip had never seen a Japanese before. We were certainly strange to them.

We met no hostility or anything like that. Just a lot of stares and some smiles. Prairie people are different from people on the coast.

Treated Like Just Ordinary People

Dad said that when he was going from Kaslo to the beet fields of Chatham I think it was. He had his family with him and they were on the train. They were travelling on the train just like anybody else, just going, but after being in camp for a bit and in Kaslo with guards and police and so on, he felt a bit touchy about it.

I remember him telling me later that he couldn't understand it. It was so strange after a couple of years in camps, called enemy aliens and not allowed to travel, not allowed to do this or that.

He said there were the ordinary passengers on the train but there were some soldiers too, going from one camp to another. Maybe on leave, he said. Funny thing was they bore no animosity. They didn't mind if he was Japanese. On that train, the people on that train bought candy and oranges for my little brothers and sisters and they'd talk with my mother and father and ask them how they were, where they were going, and all this kind of talk.

It was not as if they were in Canada at all, or what I mean is that it was not like it was in British Columbia. People seemed to know there had been trouble with the Japanese, but it didn't bother them—everybody ·treated my family as if they were ordinary people. Which they were, of course, but after all, when you've been living under the conditions they had lived under for a couple of years, you feel that you are prisoners.

Not on that train, they didn't.

Dad said that by the time they got to Toronto those words "exclusion" and "segregation" and "expulsion," why he had just about forgotten what they meant.

How I Got Out of B.C.

After I got my B.A. from the University of B.C. and completed my work for my diploma in social work, then I went to Hastings Park where the families were. I can only say that I was very distressed. The women and children in cattle barns, blankets separating families. You could say that they were all in a state of shock at what had happened to them. Oh, it was a dreadful time.

Well, now that I had my diploma I made a commitment to carry on and to try and help these people as much as I could. My family were very distressed that I would agree to work for the government, the government which had betrayed us, and I made a complete break from my family. They never looked on it that I was working for the Japanese community. They just felt that I was just being a stoolpigeon for the government. Of course that was not the case. I really made a break with my family at that point, but later they did welcome me back.

I know that my mother and father never trusted the white people again. They had spent really a number of years prior to that trying to establish some kind of meaningful relationship with people they thought would support them, but when it came down to the crunch those people didn't support and they never trusted the whites again. That was one of the really difficult things for my parents to experience. They told me later, when I was working with the CCF, they said, "Political activity is useless. You can't trust any government that is established by those people." And they never established any kind of friendship with people who were not Japanese after that.

Now I'm back to when I got my diploma. So I was sent into the ghost towns and I went from ghost town to ghost town helping. There was a supervisor named Bunny Moscrop and she developed the welfare service and I worked with her.

The main problem was financial. And there was always this business of families who were separated, this business of wanting to get together again. There were always families who were making plans and leaving and we had to look after the arrangements.

This movement to the East became more and more, and that's when I quit. The welfare office personnel were asked to help speed up the movement of these people to Eastern Canada, to force families to make a decision. So I said to myself that rather than asking people to make a choice when they weren't sure what was ahead of them, I would go East and see what the situation was. I could not remain and work in a situation where I was asking people to make choices which were just impossible. The Security Commission was putting pressure on us to get these people to make a decision. I thought it was tough pressure. Yeah.

I came East in April of 1943. They told me I could sign up as a domestic servant and commit myself to a home for six months. No work as a social worker. No, to work in some woman's house. That was the only way they were going to let me go. So I signed a contract with a woman in Forest Hill, Toronto. To be a domestic. When I arrived she had already hired someone and Mr. Ernest Trueman, who was replacement officer, government, for the Japanese said, "Oh well, Kay, there are all sorts of jobs available." And I told him to hold on. I said they were all domestic and really I was not suited for that. I was a social worker.

I told him I had only signed up with this one woman and if she didn't want me, then I considered the contract null and void. I did have some money saved up, having worked at the highest paid job for a Japanese within the B.C. Security Commission— 65 dollars a month I was getting. I said to him that I could get by on my own for a month or so, and was it possible for me to look for another job. Dressmaking, a social work job. He said it would be like bumping my head up against a stone wall. Japanese girls were only accepted as domestics. However, he said, okay, go out. So I found a job with a Finnish dressmaker. I did try the YWCA for a social worker job but the person that interviewed me said I had a chip on my shoulder and that perhaps I needed time to adjust to the new environment of the city and freedom, become more stable.

But this woman did recommend me to the Farm Service Camp, which was run by the Y, and when I was interviewed they said I could go as a recreation person to the Farm Service Camp in Vineland in the Niagara Belt, my room and board and 45 dollars a month. So I said okay and I went there and gave up my job as a dressmaker. But when I got out there it wasn't really a recreation job. They had, on second thought, hired somebody else and I would be a kitchen assistant. But that would be better than in the city with the Finnish dressmaker. I thought, maybe, if I could prove myself with the Y, then that would lead me to something else. So I went and I scrubbed and got up at five in the morning and started the hot water and I peeled the potatoes and I—that was really hard work. But I was the best kitchen assistant they ever had.

One of the funny things about it was that the director was the widow of a man who had worked with the YMCA in Korea. His name was Patterson. She was asked as the wife of a missionary to address church groups in and around the area and she would say to those church groups that to talk about Korea, really, is out of date, but that there is a Japanese Canadian girl on the staff of the camp and would they listen to her story? So she would take me to these meetings and I would talk about the Japanese Canadians. I would talk about what they had been through. They knew nothing about the evacuation. Nothing at all. But their reaction to all this was quite different. Their first reaction was about what beautiful English I spoke, as if they expected me to speak broken English or some other language. She speaks English, isn't that wonderful? And then of course they would remark what a sweet little girl I was, as if they expected that anyone of Japanese parentage would be something very much different. I suppose some of my message got through. I hope so.

I appreciated the support Mrs. Patterson gave me and one day some important people from Toronto came down to visit the camp. I met them and they learned my story from Mrs. Patterson and so my name was mentioned to the board of the

University Settlement House. One woman who helped was a Mrs. Jaffray of the National YWCA. She came down. Her husband was a professor of social work at the University of Toronto. So I got this invitation to apply for the job of adult worker there, at the settlement house. And I did and I stayed there for four years.

Once I got the job I found there was no antagonism whatsoever. It was a multi-ethnic neighbourhood, near where the art gallery is, on Grange, and people didn't ask me if I was Chinese or Japanese or what. I don't think people with problems bother about the colour of the skin or someone who is helping them. There was just one incident. A funny one. Every Saturday night there was a military night. A dance. The head resident of the house was a little leery. Felt that some of the military boys might be hostile but then she said, "Oh, let's try it." And one chap, an air force man, asked if I came from Haiti. That was the only time anybody asked me what I was. There was no trouble. None at all. Everybody thought there would be trouble for the Japanese Canadians, but I never knew of it.

And that is how I got out of the B.C. camps and out of being a domestic servant and out of peeling potatoes and back into social work, which was my profession.

The Chinese Said, "Out!"

They were always trying to get us to move to Eastern Canada. To us, that meant anything from Lethbridge to the Atlantic Ocean, you know. We really knew nothing about Canada. Cooped up on the West Coast for all those years.

But one thing they said, we wouldn't get any Oriental food. They said it because they couldn't go into Lethbridge and go into a restaurant there. So word would come out of Toronto and they'd say it was okay except for the food situation. Well, in 1943 they fired a bunch of us from working on the woodpile and there was nothing else to do, so a friend and I decided we'd go to Toronto. That was where they wanted us to go. When we got to Toronto I said to my friend that here was where it was going to get rough, none of our food in restaurants.

We pick out a restaurant and go in and order and eat and pay and nobody says nothing. This went on and on. There was no trouble. None at all. All that worry for nothing. Except in the Chinese restaurants, the ordinary restaurants and the chop suey joints. Do you think we could get Oriental food? Not on your life. Those Chinese guys were really against us. They'd come running out of the kitchen and chase us off as soon as we stuck our heads through the door. The English and the Greeks and the rest, they just didn't give a hoot. But the Chinese, guys we figured we could get along with and enjoy some greens and noodles and rice, they were so much against us it wasn't funny. In fact, a lot of them still are. Still against us. This is 1976 but they're still that way. We're a funny bunch. You talk about an elephant having a long memory. We Orientals don't get in a scrap and shake hands and forget all about it. No way. We remember a long time. That was the only discrimination in Toronto, from guys we thought might be on our side.

A New Life in Toronto

In November of 1944 I decided I would go to Toronto. I wanted to go because things weren't getting any better and in fact they were getting worse. In our family, at least. But in most families. I would do anything. I would sew and cook and look after babies and wash, so I knew I could get a job. That's what they told us at the administration building. But I was the only one who decided to go that particular time.

So in about two weeks the welfare officer called me up to the office and I said I would go. She said there would be a job. They gave me a ticket for the bus down to Nelson and a ticket on the train to Toronto and some money. For sandwiches, fruit, chocolate bars, and orange crush.

When I got to Toronto there was a woman named Mrs. Emmelman, or Emaline, who met me at the booth at the train and she took me to a woman who lived in a big house in Forest Hill. It was all so simple. I had a big room in the basement and there was a bathroom down there and it was all so nice. I mean the place was warm and when I went outside—like I'd go downtown every Sunday to the Church of All Nations for the Sunday night service—there was no trouble. I mean it was nice. Snow, but nice. As warm as it had been in New Denver. There was also no discrimination like people in New Denver said there would be. That you'd be spat on in the streets and called a dirty Jap and things like that.

The Masons gave me Thursday afternoon off and Sunday night off and I got 30 dollars a month, which I thought was fine because it was the most I had ever made. I didn't get that when I worked in the hospital in New Denver because they took things off you, like laundry of uniforms and unemployment insurance and your meals and things like that. So I was happy and on Sunday nights after service we would go to one of the girls' places and have cakes and tea and it was nice. It was better than home.

Then one day when I opened the front door there were two policemen and another man standing there and I was scared because in New Denver we were always afraid of the police. I knew somehow that they were there because of me and they were. It turned out that nobody who was Japanese was allowed to work in Forest Hill—Forest Hill was like Shaughnessy. It had a lot of people in it who had a lot of money. Mrs. Mason talked to them and then she closed the door on them and she said I was not to worry because her husband would fix it up at the office.

But he didn't. The next week Mrs. Mason said she was sorry but I would have to go, and I really think she was sorry. I'd only been there a little while but I'd liked her and I know she liked me and the children liked me. But there was the rule then, the law. Other places in Toronto but there, no.

So. Well, I didn't know what to do. I wouldn't go back to British Columbia. I was through with that place—if they didn't want me, then I didn't want them. So I said I would go downtown and see my friends and Mrs. Mason said, "We're about the same size. We'll see what you can do with some of my things." I had been wearing a uniform, a maid's uniform, at her place, and if I was to go out and work I'd have to have other clothes. At New Denver we just wore skirts and sweaters and bobby sox and those flat shoes and Mrs. Mason said those wouldn't do. So we went up to her room and she put a lot of things on the bed and said I could sew them to fit myself and there were a lot of good things there. Expensive things. Wow! I thought. But I didn't have anything to carry all those new things, so she gave me a big suitcase. It was so big it would have taken a man to carry it, but I'd have carried one twice as big to get all those nice clothes. Everything. Skirts, dresses, shoes. Everything except nylon stockings. Nobody gave those away. They were too hard to get.

Then I packed what I had in my other suitcase and she got me a taxi and I went downtown to this boardinghouse on Pembroke Street where some of my friends lived and the lady let me in. When my friends came home from work were they ever surprised to see me. Boy, were they ever? And all those clothes!

I needed a job and I guess I looked worried, and everybody laughed because getting a job was nothing in those days. So I went to work in a place where they made parachutes. We wore white coveralls and our hair in snoods and the money was so good. Better than at Mrs. Mason's although when it all worked out, the food and rent, I guess I kept more at Mrs. Mason's than I did at the factory. Nobody said anything about me being a Japanese. A Canadian of Japanese ancestry, I should say. I didn't think of myself as Japanese. There were all sorts of people in that factory. All people who had come to Toronto for better jobs. There were even people from Newfoundland there. I hate to say this because it's not fair to judge a lot of people by a few people, but I found them to be ignorant. They seemed to know nothing. Maybe it was the schools they went to. One girl had teeth that were all cracked and rotten, black. But she was a nice girl.

One day, this was in the spring, a girl came to me and asked me if I would like to go to a dance. Well, that was one thing I could really do, dance. That's all we ever did at home, dance or watch the boys play softball or just walk around. So I said yes and she said the armed services club put on a dance on Saturday night and the fellows in the army and navy and air force came and we were called hostesses. We would dance with the boys and there would be Cokes, cookies, hot dogs. You know. Just like at home. I was a little worried. After all, you know, I was Japanese and there was a war on and, you know, suppose somebody said something like, "What's that dirty Jap doing here?" or, "I won't dance with that Jap." I was twenty then, but something like that could hurt just as much as if I'd been sixteen. Or fifteen. But they all said come on, come on, and so we went to this place and were picked up in this little bus and away we went, about twenty of us from the factory. Oh boy, I tell you my heart was in my mouth when we got into that hall and put away our coats, but everybody was saying how good I looked because I had fixed up Mrs. Mason's dress and I did look good. That was one thing about the government. They could have taken lipstick and powder and nail polish away from us because there was a war on, but they didn't so I knew I looked pretty good.

You weren't supposed to dance every time with one fellow, but if you found one that you could really jive with, you just naturally went along with him and there was this big lean fellow. Today the kids would call him a long drink of water. But, boy, he was something. He had *Australia* on his shoulders of his uniform and he sure was Australian. His talk. His line. And we danced and people would form a circle around us and we'd just cut loose. Boy, let me tell you something, it was something. Finally, and I knew this was coming, he said, "Say, what are you?" Or something like that. I told him I was a Canadian-born Japanese and waited for the roof to fall in. I knew he'd never seen a

Japanese before. Not many people had. Just in pictures, in movies. That fellow just laughed and said, "Well, I'm an English-born Australian," and we both laughed. And here all the time I thought he would hate me after finding out that because of what the Japanese and the Australians were doing to each other. But he didn't care. He was a free-and-easy cobber. "Cobber" was his word. It meant guy. His name was Jeff.

I was with him for every dance even though other fellows wanted to dance with me, but I wanted to dance with him. When we left to go back to the bus he said he'd see me at the next week's dance, but I never did. He never showed up again and because I knew I'd be seeing him next week I didn't give him my phone number. We weren't supposed to give the fellows our phone numbers anyway but I would have, but I didn't and I did a lot of thinking about him for quite some time. I used to look for him at the dances they had but two or three or four months, make it four months, went by and he never showed up and of course I wouldn't ask anybody about him.

So, after awhile I wouldn't think of him much at all. I'd say to myself, after all, what would a four-foot-eleven Japanese girl be doing with a six-foot-two-inch Australian? But for a long time I liked to think that he had been sent to some other station far away and couldn't write or phone me because he didn't know where to find me. Oh, these things do happen, you know. You read about them all the time in books.

"I Jumped in With Both Feet"

When we left Nelson there was a woman missionary whose name I forget but a lovely warm woman and she said, as the train was pulling out, she called, "Now, George, remember, both feet now."

I laughed but I didn't forget what she said when I got to

Toronto, for she said the only way to handle this whole thing of moving East to a strange land was to jump in with both feet, get in the swim, and become a Canadian as quick as possible. She meant that in Steveston we'd not been Canadians except we had been born in Canada but we . . . whatever we were, we weren't Canadians. We weren't Japanese either, although a lot of us thought we were.

At Toronto, a man, a minister met us and after he shook hands he said he was going to take us to a hostel, but after a couple of days I left there because I didn't like it there. Too many smart guys, too much big-shot talk, so I went and saw this minister in his big church downtown. A big old church. His name was the Reverend Finlay. People called him The Chief. I went to see him and he told me where to go and find a job. He said this factory making uniforms didn't hire Japanese just as cheap labour—if you could do the job you got the same pay as anybody. That was something. That's why some of those fellows were just lying around the hostel—they didn't want to hire out as cheap labour.

So I was following the advice. Jump right in. Over the waist, so to speak. I was working in a factory with English guys and in a roominghouse with all sorts . . . every type of people. Men and women. It was sure different from Lemon Creek and Slocan City and everybody sitting around talking about the good times that never—won't be again because they are all gone.

I went again to see The Chief and he said I should join the Young Peoples' Group, so I joined the YPG and got in with a bunch of people, good young people, who didn't care if I was Japanese or Chinese. Maybe some of them thought I was. Then I went down to the YMCA because I got some swimming tickets and I joined the camera club. The equipment wasn't as good as I had in Vancouver but I found myself helping the instructor teach the new people in the class. We'd go over to Centre Island and take pictures. Go to the C.N.E., what they had of it, as I remember, and take more pictures. No, there didn't seem to be any trouble getting film. No, I could have a camera. Not like in B.C., where they took them away from us. Oh yes.

I went to church too. I liked going to church. Especially Mr. Finlay's church. A wonderful man. He was wonderful in the pulpit. I think in those days that the newspapers used to send reporters to some sermons and they'd send one to his once in awhile. He could thunder. He was against oppression and discrimination and his church was in an area where there were, was, a lot of different people and he'd preach on this. I liked it. He was against people who exploited us.

Well, I was doing what she said—jumping in with both feet. I was in a house with other people and I worked with white and dark and coloured people and I was in the YMCA and in the church and I found I liked city life. It wasn't like Steveston, where you took the special downtown to Little Tokyo and all you heard and all you talked with was other Japanese and all the fun you had was go to the show or the ice cream place or the Jap noodle house and talk.

I felt I was becoming a real Canadian. I was speaking better and going to the public library and taking out books and nobody was saying anything to me about it, like they sometimes did in Vancouver. I found that when I tried that other people were kindly and friendly and if they wanted to know what it was like in B.C.—what is it like to be in a concentration camp or in a ghost town—then I could tell them. But if they didn't ask, I wouldn't tell them—I didn't think it was part of what I should do.

When I would go down to Dresden to see my cousin Kishio, who was working on farms around there, I would say for him to come in to Toronto. I could get him a job and everything would be better and pretty soon he would be able to send for his wife and son. But no, he said that would be no good. He was always expecting to be allowed to go back to the coast and I said to Kishio, old boy, I'd say, that just isn't going to come about and you know it, and he'd call me a liar. He used to get mad. Then he'd say he was doing fine because the farmer let him live in a little house and drive, and I'd say that wasn't living. I said we had a whole new life to start living and if he was going around the country on Sunday picking up other Japanese guys in the truck and just going to some place and drinking some beer, maybe some whiskey, and talking about old times on the coast, then he wasn't making a new life for himself.

He said I could have my life and I said okay, so that was the last time I went and saw my cousin. He didn't want to jump in with both feet like she said and instead he wanted to be stuck in the mud. It worked out fine for me. Everybody was friendly and kind, wanted to help. I just had to show that that was okay with me too. Not enough Japanese would do that though. Too many . . . their training, let it be always like the old ways. But the old ways were gone.

A Cabbie Named Tom

I could never get over those [Japanese] guys. This was just after the war. One, Tom, had worked somewhere down near St. Thomas for a couple of years on a farm and he was kind of slave labour the way he told it. He worked for this farmer. The man fixed up an old chicken coop or a shed like that and that's where Tom slept, and when he got his meals that was the only time he was allowed in the house. This farmer had kids and relations used to come down from Toronto or out from London or wherever, and they were told not to speak to Tom.

This is what Tom told me when we were driving cab. He'd decided to come into Toronto. Remember, he wasn't a prisoner or anything. He could have left any time he wanted. But he stayed because I guess he liked the farm life and it was near the lake and he could go swimming and he was a great one for using a camera, he said, and he liked to walk around the country taking pictures.

But then the government had some policy and they let out a lot of German prisoners from some camp in northern Ontario to work in the fields in southern Ontario. These weren't Afrika

Korps guys or anything like that but mostly, as I understand, seamen who had been picked off German ships which had been captured. In other words they weren't hard-trained Nazi soldiers but just guys who worked on ships. Well, this farmer applies for one of these guys and he gets one to come. I think their main crop was onions and things like that. So along comes this German. This would be sometime in the summer of 1944, I guess. And what happens to him? He's given a bedroom in the big farmhouse. This is what Tom says, and there he is out in his chicken coop on a cot. The German guy eats with the family, but when they're sitting on the porch at night in the evening there is Fritz or Hans sitting with them and playing his harmonica and everybody is having a fine time. Whether Tom would have had the guts to go up and sit with them I guess I'll never know because he never told me.

Another thing Tom said. This farmer lent this German a pair of slacks and a sweater once and he took his niece from Toronto into St. Thomas to a show. God, if the Mounties had ever caught him. But he did it. That German must have been the one with guts. Of course he spoke damn good English.

Another thing Tom said. He'd been down to the lake and was walking back this Sunday late afternoon and the farm truck went by with everybody on it. They'd been down swimming too. Did they stop for Tom? Not on your life they didn't, and when Tom got back to the farm he said they were just cleaning up the tablecloth from a picnic on the lawn, so there was nothing for him.

And he worked like a dog. Seven in the morning to seven at night, meals and then to bed. That's the way he worked. He got the right pay, he told me, because the man from the Farm Labour Bureau, the Ontario government thing, used to see to that.

We'd be sitting in front of the Eddie in my car just smoking and he'd be telling me about this farmer, this Dutchie, and how he'd been treated and I used to say, "Well, Tom, why did you take that kind of shit? Why didn't you just go down the road and catch a bus into Toronto?"

He could have, you know. Nothing was stopping him. He wasn't a prisoner even though the German was and the German was living the life of Riley, dates with this niece, a nice room, playing his harmonica and probably not caring a hoot whether Hitler won, lost, or jumped into the Rhine River.

He was a funny little guy. This Tom, I mean. He'd just sit there in the corner of the cab and he'd pull out another Sweet Cap and light up and he'd say, "Well, I just can't really say. I've been through so much these last few years that I guess I just figured that Dutchman's farm was like a monastery." Words like that, something like that. Then he'd giggle that funny little giggle and say that besides he was getting forty dollars a month and I'd tell him that for Christ sakes there were people making sixty dollars and more a week in war plants, and probably even around St. Thomas or London or Hamilton and he could have cut himself in on that heavy dough. No, he'd say, he just wanted to be in a place where there was nothing doing, where he didn't have to think and he could weed those onions for days at a time or throw those sugar beets onto the wagon for days at a time and not even have to think.

One time he turned to me when he'd been telling me some of the things that had happened to the Japs out on the coast and he said, "You know, the fact is that I was so scared of what happened that it took me all those years to get over it and the farm was the best place."

That was the time I asked him what he was doing driving a cab. If that isn't the lousiest job there is, being hassled all the time, drunks, whores, even robbing, going here, going there, traffic, long hours, lousy shifts, always somebody bitching, poor pay, no fun, drinking lousy coffee. You know, the whole thing.

And he said, "When I came up to Toronto I figured I had to catch up on life again. I hadn't had any life. I had to know what it was all about, so I got a map and I studied it for about five days and then I went and got a licence and I got a job driving cab."

The little guy figured that the quickest way he could get back into life again was driving cab. After a while he disappeared. Somebody said he'd quit. I don't know where he went but I wished him well because in the few months that I knew him I thought he was one of the swellest guys I'd met, and I can't tell you his last name. Kakawama or something like that.

But he didn't hate the Canadian government. He didn't hate that lousy farmer who paid him forty dollars a month and wouldn't let him sleep in the house. He certainly didn't hate the German, arrogant bastard that he sounds to be. I couldn't understand this. If somebody had taken away my old man's grocery store and packed us all on trains out of towns to live in the bush, what would I have done? I used to get mad and I used to say, "Damn it, Tommy, you'd have seen me with a rifle, that's what you'd have seen me doing." He used to look at me and smile and he'd say, he'd shake his head and he'd say, "Naw, Steve, naw. It was wartime. Nothing you could do. Just wait until it goes away."

I wondered that time if the difference between me saying I'd be grabbing a rifle and he just sitting there smiling and blowing out smoke and saying, "Naw, Steve, it will go away," is the difference between me being a Scotsman and he being a Japanese. I wonder.

A Real Surprise to Them

During the war there was this United Church missionary at Tashme named Miss McLaughlin and she and some others were looking for people in Eastern Canada to take young Japanese students into their homes and she wrote a Mrs. Bott in Ottawa who contacted the Bowell family, W. F. Bowell, a very fine man, and he said his family would take me in as a student. I was sixteen.

Now whether I had lived two years in the camp at Tashme or in my own home at Sapperton, I had never really been out of my front yard, and at Tashme I had met these United Church ministers and workers and they struck me as wonderful people. So although we had been Buddhist in Sapperton on the coast I became a Christian at Tashme and it was the Reverend McMaster said to me, "You're going to Eastern Canada. It is a very strange place for you, you are young, there are temptations and dangers and I think it would be best if you were baptized before you went." So I was baptized just before I went to Ottawa.

Now this was the surprising thing to me. We had been through the evacuation and going to the camp and living with all the hate and discrimination on the coast and being branded an enemy alien and taken from our homes and dumped into the mountains, all this. But when the Bowells took me to church, McKay United Church right behind the Governor General's residence, people I met at that church, important people, in the government, other businesses, those people I'd met didn't even know about the Japanese being evacuated. This came as a real surprise to them.

Another thing, they hadn't even seen a Japanese, or hardly any. Well, maybe embassy people before the war. They thought I was Chinese. I'd say, no, I was Japanese. Japanese. That surprised them.

Then when I'd be talking to them they'd look at me and say, "You're talking English. Where did you learn the English?" I'd say I was born in Canada and that surprised them too.

They really didn't know what went on on the coast, about the Japanese, about the evacuation.

She Just Couldn't Take It

When the war came and we knew we were going to be sent into the camps in the mountains my sister, the one younger than me, she said no, she wasn't going to do that. She'd do anything but that and she decided she would go to Toronto. I don't know where she got the idea but she decided to go, so she went to the commission and said she wanted to go and they said, "Wait! Wait! We don't even know if women are going to be allowed to go East." But in two weeks they made up their minds and she went.

She went, even though she had a deep inferiority complex. I remember once we went shopping for meat in the old Spencers' Store and the man that waited on us, he talked to us in simple English. Oh my, but she was affronted. I mean deeply affronted. I didn't really mind as I thought he was just trying to accommodate us better, but she was deeply affronted about this.

She went to Montreal and she worked in a big house as a domestic. I have never seen the house but I know it was a big one. She lived in the basement, cellar, and it was like the English way. She had worked as a domestic in Vancouver but it was a nice house and she was part of the family. But in Montreal she didn't know anybody.

She worked there for a while and then she committed suicide. She hanged herself. There were no pills in those days.

Later on we found that she had been deeply depressed. She had a scrapbook and she had collected all these stories about the Japanese, the relocation, the Black Dragon Society, and all that. It would have made anybody desperate.

In those years, all the families all scattered and all that separation and no, she just couldn't take it. It was very tragic.

The Plan That Failed

I'm not sure how it came about. It was at the time when the government was really working, getting the Japanese to move out of B.C. They wanted them distributed. Scattered. So many in the Maritimes, so many in Quebec, so many in Ontario, the prairies, and for all I know, the Yukon. Anyway, you get the idea.

Somebody got the idea that if each town, each district, county, or township or whatever you want to call it, if each of these geographical locations would sponsor one Japanese family from B.C., then the problem would be solved. Anyway, this was called the placement plan, or the church placement plan, but all the churches were supposed to join in and find farms, homes, and jobs for the Japanese. The government probably paid the shot, but it wouldn't be much, I suppose.

The road to hell is paved with good intentions. You've heard that. We could say the road to heaven, for the Japanese, was also paved with good intentions. I think there were enough Japanese willing to go East if they were guaranteed a home, a job, sponsored. Church and government. A good combination. But somewhere the whole thing just fell to the ground dead. All the good words spoken from pulpits and magazines didn't necessarily mean that they would be carried out. And carried out they were not. The Japanese were ready to be welcomed, but the communities, the towns, the districts didn't want the Japanese. They were willing to sympathize with the Japanese when the Japanese were in B.C. or on Alberta farms or in Toronto, but when it came down to them having the postbox next to you on your lane, that was another matter.

I guess it was the church that was partly to blame. The United Church and the Anglican Church. The dogans. Lutherans. They all said, like, well, we've got a church in every district and every church has a congregation, and they'll listen to the pastor or priest and quick as jolly jump jack, there will be people glad to give the Japanese a job, to help them resettle.

Nobody knows what happened. I can't remember. I wasn't that much involved. All I remember was that this church advisory group and all these ministers working to find farms and jobs for the Japanese, they didn't do so good. In fact, they didn't do good at all. I don't know why.

It might have been that there was too much bureaucracy, which you can have in a church as much as you can have in government, and if that was the case, then you've got church bureaucracy and government bureaucracy—and that combination is far too much for anybody, even the Lord, to beat. So all the good intentions, all the plans, everything apparently went to nothing. And too bad. It should have worked. Except it didn't. Bureaucracy. That's probably why.

And besides, people didn't know the Japanese. I don't know what they thought they were. Some kind of devils. There are the East Indians of today. Well, they are the Japanese of thirty years ago. There were people, you know, and still are people today who believe that if given half a chance a Japanese will pull out a knife and cut your throat from ear to ear. I'm not kidding.

So, when the minister in the pulpit asks his congregation who will take in a Japanese family, you could see everybody looking sideways at his neighbour. He's waiting for his neighbour to put up his hand. If he won't, then I won't. It was a tough situation.

And all the time, there's the Japanese sitting back in B.C. waiting for the call. It never came. Some plans look good on paper and that one did, except—well, except people still weren't ready to trust the Japanese. They'd never seen one. Maybe that was the reason. If they'd talked to a few they'd have found some pretty decent people. But, people just did not understand the Japanese and the Japanese were not very good about making themselves understandable. White skin versus yellow skin. Blue eyes, black eyes. Potatoes twice a day, rice two times a day. I wonder if we'll ever learn.

Overcoming Prejudice

When I was working in Ontario during the war we go to church. I am not a churchgoer but the people I am working for they say for me to go to church, so I go. These people say why don't I come and as I was United Church in Vancouver, I say I'll go. That's how it began. Then other fellows start going with me to this church in this town.

And as we go, a lot of white people look at me and look at the lady and her husband I go with and they say, "What the hell you doing with him?" That's their attitude. So we keep on going and going, week after week, and the people I'm living with they get telephone calls saying haven't they learned anything yet? They'd tell me and my friends that some people are ignorant, you just can't teach them anything. They were right behind us all the way.

Then one day we go to church. The minister was Mr. Johnson but this day they have a man named Reverend Preston. He came from Toronto. And, ah, his nephew Dave had some relation with my boss and his wife, so he told Reverend Preston about all this talk going around, going on.

This time, I'll never forget it, we walk into the church, St. Andrew's, and he is the guest preacher and I'd say about 90 percent of the congregation are against Japanese. So this Doctor or Reverend Preston he made a speech or sermon about us. You know, about what kind of people me and my friends are and what ignorant people live in this town and go to this church and they're talking about something they don't know anything about and that these boys, us, are here not because we wanted to be here but because we were sent here. And when the hour sermon is over, we go out on the porch and down onto the walk and every one of those white people, they want to come over and shake hands with us Japanese fellows. They told us they had learned something they never knew before. One man said he had been told something by a neighbour and he believed on it and he told somebody else and so on, and that is how it went through the whole town, everybody not knowing about us and thinking things, making things up and passing on, and none of it is true—until they hear the actual truth. Then they know the truth. That'a a good story.

Victory at Chatham

When we got to Chatham from the bush camp there were twenty-one of us and we went to the Harwich labour camp, which was about two miles out of town. The beets weren't ready because of the rain. They told us just to wait. We couldn't go to town—confined to camp, they called it. They had Royal Canadian Mounted Police guarding us.

The first Sunday we were there there was a special welcome for us, and a lot of different churches, I think it was about thirteen, came to the camp and brought lunch baskets. There were special religious, church, services for us and as most of us were Christians, well, that was okay. The minister gave a sermon and one of the fellows who visited us had brought his accordion and that was good for the music part of the singing.

Then we went out in the beets later and worked hard, but we did good work and when people got to know us they let us go into Chatham. Sometimes when it was too wet to work we'd go in during the daytime, but a lot of times we went at night. You get awfully bored in camp—you can't play stud poker or read or write letters all the time.

Soon people began complaining. People said that Canada was at war with Japan and here were Japanese roaming the streets. We weren't doing anything but spending a little money on coffee and ice cream and maybe going to a show, but some people didn't like that at all. Some people thought we should be locked up in camps all the time, let out to do the farmwork and then locked up again for the night.

Well, we'd all been born in Canada. We were Canadians. Newspapers who would come and see us would be amazed, and say so, that we could speak English. Why, we could speak English as good or better than they could. But people with husbands and sons overseas, they were complaining. People thought we should have been fed bread and water. Well, we were working hard, saving their crops for the money we earned, and we were paying board for the food we were eating, so why shouldn't we have good food?

One of the outfits that got into the act was the legion. The Canadian Legion. They wrote a letter to the Chatham paper and that stirred up things. It said that a lot of people were dissatisfied with us and that even though we were Canadian citizens we shouldn't be allowed to roam the streets day and night, and if we did come into the city it should be under supervision. We had done that before but it was just a waste of time. There was nothing said about how we were saving their crops, because there was no local labour or no good local labour, and that we had come as volunteers to Chatham. Nothing like that. Just roaming the streets.

In another letter to the *News*, a woman wrote in and said that she had been uptown one afternoon and she saw nine Japs on King Street. Oh my. Then she went on to say that Japanese soldiers were raping girls in the Far East and using bayonets on the prisoners of war for fun and that if Japan wins the war all the women and girls of Canada will become slaves to the Jap soldiers. She wanted all the Japanese guys in the whole district working on the farms to be kicked out.

She didn't say that only ten guys from our camp were allowed into Chatham at any one time. She didn't mention that we lived in a camp and that we didn't qualify for a driver's licence or that we couldn't have any liquor or go into a beer parlour. She didn't take it into consideration that we were well behaved. Neither did the legion and all the others who protested. We couldn't even go swimming at the public beach because people complained.

Our transportation was cancelled. We couldn't play softball all Sunday.

The City Council even got into the act, and then the fat was in the fire. They even had a special council meeting. What the council had done was send a letter to Ottawa asking that we be confined to our barracks while not working. In other words, be slaves. But they wanted more than that. They only wanted single men in the district. No families. Then when the harvest was over we should be taken back to camps from which we came, or somewhere else, for the winter. That would mean the northern Ontario bush. Then next spring and summer, be carted back like a a bunch slaves. And then when the war was over, out we would go. No Japanese would be allowed to remain in Kent County after the war. That caused the hullabaloo. Some of our guys quit working for a bit. A little kind of strike.

Of course, the farmers and packing plants knew what would happen and if we wanted, we would just all refuse to work, and then what about all their tomatoes and sugar beets and all their other vegetables? They'd rot in the ground. Just rot.

It got pretty tense, but the fight was mainly between the City Council, which apparently had no jurisdiction about what went on in the county, and the farmers and industrialists, who knew we were saving their bacon.

We were just the guys who were saving their skins. I think there were about 300 of us in that area and with no local labour—they didn't count high school kids as any good, or they had to go to school when the picking time came. And all this because we were going into town—roaming around, as the writers of letters to the editor said. If you had no friends, and there were some places you couldn't even go in, and you would have nothing to do, wouldn't you roam around? To keep from going back to a lousy camp? Sure you would.

I won't go into it but the whole thing came to a head, and we were given the okay. More meetings, a lot of talking, but what happened was this. The Board of Trade laid some weight on a few hard heads and passed this resolution that said an injustice had been done us and they and everybody else was so glad to have us there to save their vegetable crops. This resolution actually praised us. It said we had shown ourselves to be of good character, industrious and capable, and were responsible for having saved many thousands of acres of valuable food crops, thus adding to Canada's war effort. And so on. And it said that the Board of Trade of Chatham and the City Council regrets any injustice done to the Japanese Canadian workers through statements, rumours, and it wanted the public to thoroughly understand this. That we were good guys. They even sent a copy of the resolution to the Prime Minister of Ontario and the Minister of Agriculture for Canada. That was on September 25, 1942, and you could say it was quite a victory for all of us. Even the R.C.M.P. signed the resolution. And the resolution, I must say, also mentioned that in all the time we had been there, not one Japanese Canadian got into any trouble.

So it made us all feel a lot better. But there is one thing I should point out, because others did. We were the only labour available, and we were good labour.

It was just one incident, really, something that happened in one small area of southwestern Ontario, but you can get the idea. And Chatham, Ontario, is an awful long, long way from Vancouver.

He Made the Right Moves

When we got to Toronto in 1944 we were sent to a manning pool just outside Toronto, a big house rented just for Japanese sent from the ghost town. I was desperate to get out of there and get work because every day we were in that big house the children were missing school and one of the reasons we had come out from Slocan City was because I wanted a regular school for my kids.

There were Japanese people in that house—they were there for months. They wouldn't do anything but lie around. Not me, I wanted to get out and get work and get my children in school. I only stayed there, what, three weeks.

So then this man came, he was an orchardist. He had a peach orchard. I got talking to him and I asked how's the house and he said it was a big house and I asked how the school was and he said it was a good school, right on the corner of his 100-acre plot. His grandfather had donated the land for the school. He said, "Why don't you come down and take a look at it?" So I did, by train, and gosh, it was really nice. I was thinking only about accommodation and school and this was fine, so we pulled out right away.

Then when I did that, others from that manning pool came down and they got jobs in orchards around Leamington too. You know, they sat there for weeks and months, no initiative, but when one does it, then they all do it.

I think I got paid 100 dollars a month, and house. That was very good in those days. A free school, a good one. So we had a few years there and it was very nice, but you see, this man, my boss, was a Jewish fellow but he was tight-fisted. He was a nice man, he treated us fine and he'd let me take the truck to take my kids to the beach on Sunday when he wouldn't give the truck to any other of his workers. But he was tight-fisted.

But . . . my wife got sick once and he said, "If you need any money, don't hesitate to ask."

But I just couldn't save any money and I'd say to myself that there is no future if you can't save any money. So when New Year came and he didn't give me a raise, and I didn't like to ask him for a raise, I said there's no future here, so I give him two weeks' notice and I quit.

Another thing, I felt that I would like to give my son a better education and there were better schools in London, so that, I guess, was another reason that we moved. I went to work for my brother, who had a contracting business in London.

From then on, every move we made was a very, very fortunate move. From then on. You see, in Ontario, that part of it, there was no discrimination against you if you were Japanese origin. No, we didn't find anything unfriendly at all. They were all friendly. After all, you smile to a person, they smile back. There's no unfriendliness if you yourself feel friendly toward a person. Anywhere I went. Detroit. Windsor. Tilbury. It was, "Hello, how are you?" Everywhere.

Now I'm back in Vancouver and I don't know. One example,

even now. There's one person, I don't know who he is but maybe he was a Japanese prisoner of war. He sends me clippings. If there is anything derogatory about the Japanese, here or in North America or in Japan, he sends me the clipping. he writes: "Do you expect anything better than this after how you treated us?" Things like that. I don't know who he is.

Some little things like that worry me about Vancouver.

Free at Last

My brother Kinsey was born in Japan because my mother and I had gone back there for a visit during the First World War, so he was a year or so old when we returned. That handicap stayed with him because he was classified as an alien, an Issei, and it was very difficult to become naturalized in those years. My mother tried several times to get him naturalized but every time she got him before a judge, the decision was no. He was just a child then too. You'd go so far and then no further.

So when the war came along my brother was put with the other Issei in building . . . up to the road camp of the CNR at Red Pass near Jasper and then my mother followed. She went to Kaslo, the old ghost town.

Then I followed, but instinctively I had a feeling of some foresight that this, this business of the work camps, the moving of the Japanese Canadians out of the coast, that that was going to be it. As far as the future was concerned. So it would be better if I paved the way and went out East and there was a certain amount of curiosity, too, about what it all was about. But as I said, that instinctive foresight that nothing was ever going to be the same again.

So I went with a bunch out to Schreiber, out in the northern Lake Superior country and we worked there on the so-called Trans-Canada Highway, getting 25 cents an hour. After three

In a small, crowded house a little girl takes her bath in a washtub. *(UBC Special Collection)*

In Tashme camp, families, living two to a hastily built shack, had to share a common kitchen. *(Public Archives of Canada)*

Young children at the Tashme school. *(Public Archives of Canada)*

The Tashme store. *(JCCC)*

In their remote locations, the Japanese Canadians made their own entertainment, devising costumes and sets with their customary ingenuity. (*UBC Special Collection*)

Pretty as a picture, this little girl posing in kimono and parasol spent the war years in a camp in the mountains. (*UBC Special Collection*)

Like teenagers everywhere, these young people gathered around campfires at night to have cook-outs and sing their favorite songs. *(JCCC)*

Christmas, 1945, at Slocan. *(JCCC)*

Children celebrate the *bon* festival in the ghost town of Sandon. *(JCCC)*

Baseball was a popular game, even in a camp like Lemon Creek. *(Public Archives of Canada)*

In Vancouver's Stanley Park the War Memorial honoured the Japanese who fought, and sometimes died, in World War One. *(JCCC)*

A Nisei soldier visits his parents interned in Slocan. *(JCCC)*

Arrival and departure: In 1942, internees watch for familiar faces as trucks bring another group of people to Tashme. *(Top) (UBC Special Collection).* In 1946, Japanese Canadians await trains that will start them on their long journey to Japan.*(National Film Board)*

School children gather to celebrate Easter at Lemon Creek.
Where are they now? *(UBC Special Collection)*

weeks we had an opportunity to come south and work under the Ontario Farm Service Force and we came down to Valetta, near Tilbury. We were housed in old huts there with an old First World War Veteran as a guard, but still we were there under the supervision of the R.C.M.P. The huts were regular tarpaper, wood frame barracks of army huts that were put up in a hurry, wooden floors, double-tiered steel beds, showers, and it was like a camp like in the old days in B.C., logging camps.

Farmers would require help for a day, a week, ten days on some crop and the farmer would come in his truck and take you back, standing up on the back, and you'd stay there. Twenty-five cents an hour—that was the standard pay the government had decreed for all evacuees, wherever they were. And out of that we paid room and board.

After working May, June, July, September, October, I was then allowed to come into Toronto but only because I could claim I knew a friend there. I arrived at Union Station November 10. A sleety, cold November day. We came out and there was a Murray's Restaurant across the street and we went in for breakfast. When the waitress had taken our order she asked, "What are you?" I said we were Japanese Canadians and she said, "Oh, this is the first time I've met a Japanese." It was a friendly comment, so my first impression of Toronto was one of warm friendliness.

And then we walked up Bay Street and I shouted to myself, inside, I said I am free, I am free. Because for the first time I had this release that I was on my own, I can do whatever I wish and no one to order me around every minute of the day and to me, this was freedom evermore.

11 *How the Nisei Went to War*

Prior to Pearl Harbor no Japanese Canadians living in B.C. were called up, and no volunteers were accepted. When Hastings Park began to fill up in early 1942 any number of young Japanese pleaded to join the army, even if they had to serve in a lowly labour battalion. They were refused. Instead, they were sent to road camps and ghost towns.

But in 1944 the tide of war was changing in the Pacific and the British desperately needed men who spoke Japanese to be translators, interrogators, broadcasters. The Americans had a large pool of men, their own Nisei, but the only British source was in Canada. Consequently, a British Army captain was sent across Canada to interview possible recruits for the important jobs ahead. They were to be inducted into the British Army, given a minimum of training, and then shipped to the Far East. It seemed like a workable plan. After all, the Canadian government wanted no part of the Japanese.

The news quickly spread among the Japanese and there was great commotion. One man recalls two tumultuous meetings in a church hall in Toronto, attended by virtually every Nisei in the city, at which the whole issue, from the philosophical to the practical, was thrashed out again and again until eventually the majority decided enlistment was the right thing to do.

The captain eventually found about 150 volunteers. But an odd thing came to light. The British found that only a handful of the volunteers could be shipped right out. The rest of them had

294

to be sent to a training school, S-20, in Vancouver because they either could not speak Japanese or could not speak it well enough.

And then something strange happened. The Canadian government suddenly decided that these men could not go overseas in "a foreign uniform." They would have to go as Canadians. This was all right with the British; they wanted the men. So they went, and performed the job expected of them, often working in combat zones, and did the job well. They went overseas under a cloak of secrecy. No bands played for them, but of course, at that stage of the war, no bands played for anyone. When they returned, they came home in ones and twos and without fanfare.

And as a footnote, it was not until September, 1945, with the war over, that the Canadian government released the information that Japanese Canadians, those "enemy aliens" of 1942, had played a small but vital role in the Allied victory in the Far East in 1945.

Few people know this even to this day. Many Japanese Canadians know it. The families of the veterans know it. The veterans know it. Somewhere among their possessions they have the medals to prove it.

Volunteers Not Wanted

Let me tell you about the Japanese soldiers in the First World War, the 1914 one. There's a statue down in Stanley Park there saying about these 200 Japanese Canadians who went overseas to France and it lists their names, or maybe it is just the names of the fifty-three who were killed.

People say, "My, isn't it wonderful that these men from Vancouver went overseas to fight." Well, that's not quite the way it happened. History and time has a strange way of playing tricks on people.

Sure, there were Japanese Canadian volunteers in that war, and I think the number was 200. I know that fifty-three were killed and all but twenty or twenty-two or so were wounded. That is quite a record.

So these men wanted to join up, go and fight Germany, which was also at war with Japan. They formed a group and had three or four army officers and sergeants to drill them and they spent three months, two months, something like that, drilling, and people said, "My, isn't that fine."

I should say that the money these men cost, the expenses, was paid by the Japanese themselves, the men, the community and the Canadian Japanese Association. And then when they figured they were ready to go overseas they couldn't get anybody in Ottawa or army headquarters to do anything about it. One of the association men, the president, went down to Ottawa and all he got was the run-around. Finally somebody told him that 200 men was not big enough to make a battalion and that volunteers were not wanted. This is really baloney, you know, because the Japanese knew that they didn't have enough men for a battalion, but they did know that any country that was fighting a war—and especially one like that 1914 war—needs volunteers. All it can get. So they said, "We do not need you." What Ottawa was saying is that the British Columbia politicians were telling them, "Don't take them Japs."

So there was nothing to do but stop training until an officer in some battalion of the Crowsnest Pass in southern Alberta heard about this and he said, "C'mon, you can join my outfit any day." So they did. They got their uniforms, because they didn't have uniforms yet, they got their uniforms sent from Calgary and they went to Alberta and some got put in this battalion and some in that and some in the Princess Pats, which was pretty well known. And some of those men, when they went up against those German machine guns could hardly speak a word of English.

You know what it was all about. The B.C. politicians had it all figured out. They knew that when the boys came home they would have to give them the vote. All war veterans got the vote. And the Japanese Canadians didn't have the vote, not provincial or federal. And they were afraid that if the veterans got the vote then there would be agitation and talk and all this business in the newspapers about giving all the Japanese in B.C. the vote. This was only in B.C., of course. Japanese Canadians could vote in other provinces but there were so few of them. So rather than give a few Japanese the vote they campaigned against them getting into the Canadian Army.

If you really want to know, it wasn't much different in the Second World War. Japanese Nisei and Sansei could join up in other provinces, but they couldn't join up in B.C. and they wouldn't be drafted in B.C. either. In all those years, between 1914 and 1939 nothing had really changed. It was a terrible thing. It made the heart sick at times. That is what hatred and fear and suspicion of things you don't even know about does to people and it did it right here in B.C.

Something Was Wrong

When the world war started in Europe in 1939, the Japanese like everybody else got registration forms for the military service, all the young men in their early twenties. Only the notification—but nothing after that. We thought that was funny because other young men, white men, were being called up—but nobody in the first call-up was Japanese. That made us wonder.

Some of them went down to volunteer in the army or the air force or navy, and they didn't get anywhere. They were just turned away. Yet we knew these young men were okay for military service because they had been checked by doctors and were okay. There was even a picture of one of our young men in *The New Canadian* being checked over. *The New Canadian* was the English Japanese newspaper that started about 1938.

No word. Others were going off to the camps for their training but no Nisei. Somehow we were not eligible. At least we didn't seem to be eligible. But why not, we asked? We're Canadians too, born in Canada. Uh-huh. Our young people, a lot of them, they felt pretty bad about it.

Then I think one of the military men said that they were not taking Japanese in the second draft, which was along in 1940, but to wait for the next big draft of their age. So we waited.

Then along came the next call-up and there was no Nisei in that draft either, and then we knew something was really wrong. "What's wrong with us?" people asked themselves. "Why can't we participate in Europe?" The fact is that we didn't even think of Japan in the Pacific. We knew what Japan was doing. We could read the papers like everybody else, but we somehow didn't connect. Maybe we didn't because there were no Chinese called up in the first two drafts. But we didn't concern ourselves with the Chinese. That was their problem. It was our problem we were thinking of.

No, it wasn't exactly a feeling of dread. It was just a feeling that something was wrong. But no young Japanese anywhere in Canada, not just in B.C., were called up, so we didn't know whether they had an inkling of what Japan was going to do—make war.

So we had to come back to the thing that it was discrimination of the Oriental because of the franchise problem. Well, we thought, oh, it's discrimination again.

To this day I don't know what it was. Nobody has ever said, that I know of. Nobody.

A Lot Were Itching to Go

Lots of guys wanted to enlist. Even when they were in the jug, in Hastings Park pool, or out in the camps. Shout "You Japs want to go?" and you'd have got a lot of guys.

Some guys even went to the government and said they'd like to form a Nisei battalion. I forget the reply but it was a kiss-off.

You want to know why they didn't want us in the service? Simple. Simple as this round cup here. In the First World War guys joined up and went overseas and when they came back the government finally got around to giving them the vote. So a few, maybe fifty Japs had the right to vote. Because they'd fought King George's war. Now there was another King George's war and the Japs want to go and the government says, "Oh Christ, let these guys go and when they come back we'll have to give them a vote because we gave it to their daddies." Something like that.

The truth is, in B.C. they just didn't want to give anybody the vote, whether you were Jap, Chinese, Hindu, anything Oriental.

Sure, the Japs in B.C. wanted the vote. We were not a bunch of dumb savages. We knew what the vote was. In Japan the lowest peasant has voted for a long time. We knew. And it made us second-class citizens without it. For some reason, and I don't know why, the Chinese guys didn't care about the vote. Making money, I guess. That was all they wanted.

They said we couldn't understand Canada's ways well enough to vote intelligently. Excuse me, but bullshit. I was born in Canada, right up there at Rupert, and I went to school down here and worked in my father's store and talked to English people 50 times a day and read the *Province* newspaper every night—and some guys said I haven't the intelligence to understand what's going on. Again, and pardon me, I say bullshit.

I'll bet a lot of Japanese don't even vote. It's just that they wanted that vote so they could say they were first-class citizens instead of second class. It's human nature. That's what it is. And that's why our boys couldn't join the army when a lot were just itching to go, and even fight against Japan, mind you. Because they would have to get the vote when they came back and wouldn't that be horrible for poor B.C.

Why I Joined the Army

The war went on and of course, the R.C.M.P. had a record and I guess on it were all the times I'd tried to join the army. When the going got tough in Southeast Asia, the British came out to Canada to recruit because they saw how well the Japanese Americans, the Nisei soldiers, were doing down there and they heard there were persons like that, like the Japanese, in Canada. So Captain Don Mollinson came out here to recruit.

Mind you, it wasn't the Canadian government that was doing the recruiting. No, it was the British Army which was fighting that war in the Pacific and they needed men to interpret and translate and broadcast, and they wanted us. The Canadian government didn't seem still to want any part of us.

The R.C.M.P. came with Captain Mollinson and I said that's fine, and I signed on the spot. I'd go. On that trip I think Captain Mollinson signed up twelve other Japanese, but one was rejected so that made twelve of us. The captain said, "We got to sign you up so they don't know you're in intelligence work, so we'll put you down as volunteers." I think the "they" he was talking about was the Canadian government. The government knew we were being asked to sign up but not in intelligence work, which was pretty good. So instead of going into intelligence right off, they put us down as corporals in the

British Pioneer Corps. The ditchdiggers. Well, that was fine. We didn't give a damn which way we went as long as we went. So this was in mid-1944 and we waited and waited, week after week, and nothing happened. We wondered what in the world had happened.

Then we heard there was a big pow-wow in Ottawa and the Canadian government was saying, "These guys aren't going overseas in a foreign uniform. They're Canadians." You see, being signed up by the British we'd wear British flashes on our uniforms. And anyway, since when is a British uniform a foreign uniform? But the ironic thing, here for three years we were considered the enemy, aliens, not to be trusted in any way, shape, or size—and now they were arguing that we couldn't join the intelligence corps of the British Army. Anyway, weren't we all fighting the same war? Against Japan.

I thought to myself, "The whole thing is very peculiar."

And so the upshot of it was, no way would the Canadian government release us to another army. If those guys were going to go, they'd go as Canadians. And after all they'd done to us. But we didn't care. We wanted to go, no matter who sent us. So anyway, we were all called back, demoted to privates in the Canadian Intelligence Corps. By this time it was January of '45. All this fooling around.

Then they called me in to Toronto and said okay, "You're going to leave for overseas tomorrow." We had no training, no uniform, no nothing. Just standing there as bodies. I said, "After all this fooling around, can't you give us six hours to go and say goodbye to our wives?" So what they did was give us the six hours and I went down to Brantford where my wife was, said goodbye, and then came back again next morning, got on the train, down to Windsor, Nova Scotia, or somewhere around there, got on a ship to England, and in the few days, about a week or ten days that we waited in England for a ship to take us to the Far East they gave us a bit of instruction. Well, you know, you don't make a soldier in a few days. A year, maybe.

In less than ten days we were on another ship out of Southampton going to the Far East, just rushed through and receiving training as we were on the ship. They gave us a few books and training manuals and there we were trying to make head and tail of all these things a soldier must learn. Well, you know, nobody can study on a jammed troopship. Impossible.

Then we got jungle training in Poona, India. Only lasted about ten days. Then they split us all over, they were so short, and it didn't take us long before we were all over the Far East. We were supposed to interpret, interrogate Japanese prisoners, that sort of stuff. Translators, although we weren't very good as translators because none of us had very much education in the Japanese language. Interpreters, yes. Nobody could fool me on a Japanese dialect because the structure of the Japanese community had been such that we had people from the south of Japan to the north of the country, which is like the difference between the Sicilians and the Norwegians. No accent could stump me, so I was able to help out a lot in interpreting and questioning.

We didn't get into action. Not action as such. But we did go as close to the action as was considered safe, as we were considered pretty important. There weren't too many of us, you see. The British were very short of guys like us. I worked with Japanese prisoners, making a study of their psychology.

I also had another job. I and another fellow were doing news and commentary on the radio for Southeast Asia Command, from Kandy in Ceylon for a while. I was a sergeant by this time.

I also met a Mr. Black and a Mr. White and they were like no other Japanese I had seen before. After about five minutes' talk I realized they were Japanese who had turned traitor on the Japanese. They were well educated, very formal, wore civilian clothes, pants and white shirts, and that was the first time I realized that it was all baloney that no Japanese would surrender. The two men, they got their nicknames from the British, were making propaganda leaflets. Our boys would drop them over the Japanese lines.

I think there was about 150 in service in the Far East during the war. Then there was the Japanese-language training school in Vancouver toward the end of the war, whites and Japanese, which they should have started right off the bat of Pearl Harbor. They would have got lots of volunteers and those fellows would really have helped the war effort with propaganda and radio broadcasts and things like that. But they didn't, of course. If they had of, they would have had hundreds and hundreds of Japanese volunteers and maybe would have saved an awful lot of lives by really understanding the Japanese and their culture. It is a hell of a language to go and pick up, and not many whites can do it. There is man's talk, woman's talk, language of the various classes, all the accents. Those volunteers if they had had a Japanese language outfit early in the war would have done a lot of good. But of course, nobody thought of it. They were all too scared of us. They didn't realize we were as good Canadians as they were.

I was in Ceylon, India, Burma, Malaya, Singapore, and last before I came home I was with the Australian War Crimes Investigation Team.

I got home in late 1946. I did my two years. When I got home restrictions as far as travel was concerned, restrictions as far as moving back to British Columbia, they were still in effect for Japanese. Being what I am and having served in some pretty tough places in the jungle, I said to myself, "Oh, is that so?" As I said, being what I am and being still in uniform I left my wife and my little fellow and came right out here by myself on the train. Just to see what they would do, if these stupid laws still were in effect, and how they would affect a Canadian soldier. Nobody stopped me on the train. I don't know why.

When I got to Vancouver I went over to see the R.C.M.P. officer in charge, the one I'd known when we had been evacuated into the Interior. He was still in charge. A hell of a nice guy. I said, "Hey, Blackie, I'm back again."

Well, you should have seen his face. But he said, "Hello, hello," and his secretary welcomed me, but they felt very, very uneasy. I knew damn well why they were uneasy. The police are police, regardless, and all the rules and regulations and orders-in-council said I shouldn't be in Vancouver. I could read his mind. He was thinking, "Oh-oh, here's a soldier, a friend, a

Japanese, and he's in the 100-mile zone and he hasn't got a permit. What will I do?"

I let him off the hook and I said, "If there is anything you want me to sign, Blackie, just give it to me and I'll sign it." I meant a permit which would legally allow me back in Vancouver.

So he looked at me and he pushed a sheet of paper across the desk at me and it was a permit, which I don't think he was allowed to give out, but here I was. I just signed the darn thing without reading it. I trusted the man and he was horribly embarrassed. Then we chewed the rag about old times.

Then after a few days I took the train back to Brantford and that was that.

I came out to Vancouver because they told me you couldn't come back, that it was still barred to the Japs even though it was our home. What I was saying was: "Okay, what you going to do about it? I'm home."

I wanted to go and break the ice, to show them I wasn't afraid of them.

As a matter of fact, maybe that was why I joined the army. To show them we could stand up for them. Not for myself but for everybody else.

Dad Thought Me a Traitor

When this British Army captain, Mollinson, comes around getting us to join the war as interrogators, well, naturally I joined up because I wanted to. By rights, by the way we'd been treated, maybe I should have told them to go to hell.

My parents had been before in New Denver, in that concentration camp there with all the other Japanese people from the coast, so when I joined up, my dad, boy was he mad. Wow! He disowned me just like that. He thought me a traitor.

He could have come to see me off on the train. I think my mama wanted to but he wouldn't let her. Only my brother came.

Right here in town we had a few Japanese people too, and when they hear I join up the Canadian Army they never say good luck or anything. They just ignore me. Even my own friends, they just look at me and they say, "Okay." That's all. Just "Okay." Some are pretty damn bitter about it all.

But as I go, after, my parents, my friends, these people you make enemies with by joining up, they realize that I'd done the right thing.

Why Should We Volunteer?

Sure, about joining the army. Sure, they came to me. Wanted me to join up too. I felt that under the circumstances, why the hell should I? Now, why the hell should I?

I feel the ones that joined up, most of them did because of their own personal reasons. I think they were aware that getting those veterans' credits, they could go to university later on. Or they just wanted to be big shots.

There was a lot of talk back and forth about it. Some pretty big meetings. Should they join up, go overseas, or should they not? That was the question. Everybody was talking about it. It was all anybody could talk about for quite a time there. Go or not. Some went. I don't hold it against them. Others didn't go. I think maybe they were the better ones.

Sure, prove yourself to be a good Canadian. I was a good Canadian before and they tried to do everything they possibly know how to make me into a non-Canadian. They kicked me around. They kicked my brothers around, my father, cousins. My friends. Does it make it more loyal for you if you put on a uniform? In those days? I think that's a lot of crap. I do.

And a funny thing. The ones that joined up, to be interpreters, most of them guys were the least proficient in Japanese. I know some of them who can't speak three words together in Japanese. For personal reasons. That's why.

But it was a long time ago. I guess it is all forgotten. Who remembers those times when there used to be all that talk about it?

Why, the Canadian government didn't even want the Canadian public to know that there was a bunch of Japanese Canadians going overseas to work in Malaya. That's how much they thought of us. When the Americans were boasting of their Japanese troops, the Nisei rifle team in Italy, the Canadians under that Mackenzie King were trying to keep it all quiet. Hah!

A Chance to Prove Loyalty

They came around and they came to me: "Will you join the army? You see, I am out in the field and they came and they came to me and they say this is the British Army they want us for, and I say why should I join the British Army when the Canadian Army don't take us, eh?

I says that much as I'd like to I got to think this over. Think it over.

So at this time I'm working with this couple and they're just like a mom and dad to me. So I went back and told them and he says, "Well, it's up to you, to prove yourself you're a good Canadian. Well, this is a chance to prove it." You know.

Well, I say okay so I just took the opportunity and joined up. We went to Halifax, then England and from England, then to Bombay and then Singapore. Our headquarters. Interpreting and interrogation. Rank was sergeant. Fastest sergeant in history.

I should say we don't go as British soldiers. We were

supposed to, then the Canadian government, they change their minds and say that if Canadians go to war they go as Canadian soldiers in Canadian uniforms. So that's what we did.

First, they won't let us join up when we're in B.C. Then they kick us out of the place like we're no good and spies and put us in camps all over the country, and then when the British say they want us, they raise a fuss and say, "No, these men are Canadian citizens. They go to war like Canadians." Funny business.

12 *Some Chose Japan*

Repatriation. Most people did not even know what the word meant. But it was to be a terrible blow for all Japanese in Canada, whether born in Japan or Canada.

On August 4, 1944, Prime Minister Mackenzie King told the House of Commons that no act of subversion or sabotage had been found before or during the war by the Japanese. That was the good news. The bad news was that the government would now institute a voluntary system of deportation to Japan, regardless of citizenship.

In short, it was the government's final solution to its long-planned program of dispersal of Japanese across the country.

First, every Japanese over sixteen was asked if he wanted to stay in Canada or be voluntarily deported to Japan. Those under sixteen would automatically follow their parents' decision. The Japanese in B.C. were told that refusal to go East of the Rockies if they did not wish to go to Japan could, in effect, be looked upon in future as an act disloyal to Canada. In the first step, the signing, 81 percent of the Japanese in B.C. volunteered to go to Japan. Of course, 40 percent of these were children who had no say in the matter. Nevertheless, this figure, 81 percent, astonished many Japanese East of the Rockies, where only 15 percent, including children, had signed for voluntary repatriation.

A total of 10,632 signed for repatriation, including 3,740 dependent children. An interesting fact is that of those dependent children, 3,416 lived in B.C. The figures show that of the 7,000-plus East of the Rockies, only 1,371 signed to return to Japan, indicating that they were settling in their new homes.

The repatriation, or deportation, was to be carried out under three orders-in-council, issued under the terms of the War Measures Act, that all-embracing piece of legislation with which the government carried out the war. Inspired by the valiant efforts of the Co-operative Committee on Japanese Canadians, civil rights groups, university clubs, churches, and individuals went to work in an all-out effort to overturn the orders-in-council. Letters and telegrams flooded the Prime Minister's office, Newspapers joined in.

Meanwhile, the Japanese were having second thoughts and in the B.C. towns and camps, 5,598 persons, adults and children, revoked their voluntary "yes" vote. East of the Rockies, another 715 withdrew.

After the war the issue continued to reverberate, until Mackenzie King quietly announced on January 24, 1947 that the hated orders-in-council had been repealed. The long fight was over, but some had not won. Nearly 3,700 Japanese nationals, naturalized Canadians, and Canadian-born had voluntarily gone back to Japan. They found a war-torn, starving land. Nothing was as they had hoped. Strangers reviled them in the streets, looking at their American-style clothes and saying, "What are you doing over here, taking our food?" For most it was an unhappy time. The young people longed for Canada, even the Canada of the ghost towns, and their parents looked back and regretted the move. For some there was no returning, but for others a strange trek began. Over five, ten, fifteen years, many hundreds of Japanese Canadians—the figure is unknown—returned to Canada.

One woman said, "Everybody, you know, who could get their Canadian citizenship back, get a sponsor, they came back. We hated Japan. We were Canadians."

King's Master Plan

You've no idea what a blow in the guts that was when that came up. Repatriation. We just couldn't take it all in. Some guys just went to pieces. Well, it's my theory that they had repatriation back to Japan in mind from the very first. They just kept it quiet. And it was Mackenzie King all the time. All the time. Taking it from the beginning, Hastings Park and then the ghost towns and then East of the Rockies, it was all a master plan.

Except it didn't work. It did in a way but in another way it didn't. Thank God there was enough democracy left in this country, even if it was hanging by shreds, to see that repatriation didn't work all the way.

Finally – Government Policy

August 4 of 1944 was a day a lot of us remember because that was the day Mackenzie King stood up in the House of Commons and finally talked about us, the Japanese, and what was going to happen to us. Some of it was good, and some of it was bad. I guess more of it was . . . well, I really don't know.

At least we knew what our future was going to be.

First, you've got to know that for years there had been talk around the camps and among all of us that we were going to be sent back to Japan after the war. He spoke in 1944 and that was a full year before Japan surrendered, so you can see the Allies were pretty sure they were going to win the war. In fact, it was a cinch. But there had been all this talk. A lot of people who were in the ghost towns of B.C. said there was no point in going to Eastern Canada and resettling if they were just going to be sent to Japan. And a lot of Japanese who had gone East, well, I guess they said what is the use of working hard and buying a house and all this stuff if they're going to send us all to Japan. No matter what. No matter if you were born in Japan, not naturalized, naturalized, born in Canada. Get out, we don't want you!

The Prime Minister, he finally said what the Canadian policy would be. He put a lot of minds at rest. First, those who wanted to go back to Japan, fine. They could go. The government would see to it. No trouble. Just say you want to go and ships will come into Vancouver and take you back. I think he said that there would be no trouble with Japan. It would be a beaten nation and what the Allies said would go. Everybody could understand that.

Next, there would be a commission set up and this commission would look at every Japanese, or every Japanese family, and decide whether they were or had been loyal or disloyal to Canada; and the ones who had not been loyal, then they would have to go back to Japan. Whether they liked it or not. He said the ones who were found to be loyal, and that would be all but a few, I think, they would be treated justly and fairly. He made that quite clear.

If they'd done this at the start, just after Pearl Harbor, it would have caused an awful lot of less heartache and sadness and terror. Just pick out those who were disloyal and put them in camps and let the rest just keep going as they had. But they didn't segregate at the time, and so 20,000 people were kicked out on their ass.

There were people who came around and talked to us about the Prime Minister and his speech. One thing they said was that not many—darn few was the way they put it—would be allowed to return to British Columbia. By that I mean to the fishing grounds and to their farms and their stores in the city.

So they'd have to go East of the Rockies. The government was pretty definite about that. That was why so many decided to go back to Japan. On a voluntary basis. I don't know how many bad guys were deported, but I do know that most who went back to Japan went because they were mad at the Canadian government, or they just were too old or didn't have any money to start again.

As it turned out, most of the people who chose repatriation were from the camps in B.C. Those who had gone to Alberta or Toronto, they had finally got settled down one way or another and they were starting to do okay. Nothing great—restaurant work, gardening, on farms, dry-cleaning plants, but they were settling in and getting on with the job.

One speaker said one thing though. I remember it. He said that there would be no support from the commission to Japanese if they indicated they would like to go to Japan, see what it was like and if they didn't want to stay, then they could come home. This was definite. Make up your mind and that is it. They changed this later, of course, but that time, about late 1944, they were quite definite. You've made your bed, so you can lie in it. In other words, the Canadian government still wasn't on our side.

One speaker said that race prejudice is as old as man. It always has been around. Anything that is different, people fear it. He warned us this: If you go East, don't all go to Toronto. Don't all go to Montreal. He warned us not to set up all in the same neighbourhood with our own stores, our restaurants, a bathhouse. All of that. No, that's where we made the big mistake in Vancouver. The ghetto life. While it is our tradition in Canada, go to different places. Spread out. Go to smaller cities and towns and start there. There is always work. A Japanese works hard and he will always get a job. But don't be all together. He said we would have to be wholehearted in our acceptance of this dispersal attitude or we would find ourselves in trouble again. Canada is a white man's country. It is true, he said, and remember it. You can live happily and well in Canada, but not too many people together.

I think we did it. Now you'll find Japanese in every place in Canada. In other words, old Mackenzie King wants us to assimilate. That is, grow in with the rest of the population. He asked us to show him that it can be done and we did it.

Some People Were Bitter

When the police came around, they would go to a widow whose son was in the bush and her daughter was working in a hospital in Montreal and they would say, "You have twelve hours to sign this." What is that poor woman to do? Saying "yes" means she goes back to Japan with the repatriation and saying "no" means she leaves her home to go to Eastern Canada.

Look at it this way. It was impossible. Yet I tell that story because I know the woman it happened to. Anyway, she said no and it all worked out fine, but for the others? How many finally went? Close to 4,000 and that was a lot of people and a lot of those people were Canadians, born in Canada. Some were naturalized.

But people were hot about everything. It was a hard time in the camps. The papers told us the war was nearly over and what was going to happen? Nobody knew. People were bitter. Some awfully bitter. Not so much now, but then, a lot of people in those camps really hated Canada.

Some of us, we knew that the war was going to end soon and then things would change. They did, of course. We weren't fortunetellers. We just knew things had to change. Things would get better. So some of us didn't want them to sign yes. We went around and talked to people and told them not to sign. We argued. A lot had already signed. But some hadn't. Maybe the Mountie hadn't come back to them, or I don't know. And those who were bitter, being locked up in those camps all the years, they called us all kinds of names. Names the Japanese call each other when they are really mad. But this just wasn't mad as if I punched you and you got mad. This was real mad. You might say burning anger. They smeared our windows with dog shit. They'd yell at us inside our houses at night. The Nisei weren't too bad. It was the Issei who did this, the old people. Even though they put dog shit on my windows I didn't get mad at them.

Take you. A man comes and he says I want that television set and that car and that chesterfield and house and you can go out to the bush and live in a shed. And you can't have anything back, and you've got to live in that shed for four years. What would you think? Well, that's what they thought. They thought that. I mean, to hell with Canada.

One Man's Strong Opinion

We were in Kaslo and when I decided to take my family to Toronto I went to the commission and told them that first I wanted to go to Tashme camp to see my father and mother-in-law because they had signed to go back to Japan.

One thing, I was tired of fighting all those people who had signed to go back to Japan. They thought because me and some others wouldn't sign that we were traitors or something. Crazy.

All the people, most of them, who were going to Japan were at Tashme then but the war was over, Japan was finished, and people I had known in Vancouver and the camps were coming up to me and saying "I've got my signature cancelled. We don't have to go to Japan now." And they're fearful, they don't even let their neighbours know that they've got their signature cancelled and everybody is doing it. Now that Japan is beaten, they want no part of Japan.

Even to this day I have no respect for those kind of people, those who jumped from one side to the other. What are they anyways? They're not even Canadians, they're not even loyal to Canada. Just as soon as Japan surrendered—they're even lesser than rats. To this day I still have a feeling of contempt for them.

Turmoil in the Camps

The Mounties came around and said we had ten days to sign, one way or the other. So I didn't sign. In our area just three of us, just a handful of Japanese, didn't sign. The rest did.

And then when everybody had signed or not signed, then came repercussions afterward. My children, my sons used to get beat up at school, after school by the kids of people who had signed to go back to Japan. One time he came home wet and wouldn't go out to play anymore, so the next day I went down the railroad tracks to meet him coming home from school and a bunch of other kids were chasing him through deep snow, and hitting him. Then I understood what it was all about. He'd go to school but he wouldn't go out and play anymore.

They insulted my wife, too. The women's . . . uh, some association, club, they called her that she was an Indian, that she was an Indian because she wouldn't sign. To repatriate.

Sure, all the others signed because they felt—well, at that time they thought that Japan was in its glory and all the stories about victories for Japan's enemies were just so much baloney. They figured that these stories were being printed so the stories of Japan's victories wouldn't be believed.

So when that atomic bomb was dropped, a lot of people who had signed up took back their signatures but for a lot, they were sent to Japan anyway. Men, wives, kids. I don't know but I think a lot of those people still wouldn't believe that Japan was beaten. Those that went back to Japan and then came back to Canada, I talked to some of them and they sure found out things weren't so good for them over there. The Japanese would say to them, "You're Canadian. What the hell are you doing coming over to our country?" They found out all right.

"*I'm a Canadian*"

Uki was a friend of mine. I never thought of her as Japanese. She was just a friend.

Uki's parents were old when they had their children. The children were comparatively young for their parents.

When the repatriation order came—sign up for Japan or get out of B.C., you remember—Uki thought she had them persuaded that it was the best to stay in Canada, and they went to this room where they were to sign one way or the other. Uki was with them, of course, because she interpreted for them. They sat in the room with others who had decided to go back to Japan, and by the time their turn came to come up to the desk her father decided he was going back to Japan. She was a dutiful daughter. She had to tell the policeman that they had decided to go back. She saw everything going from her. Going back to a country that was beaten, or was being bombed into defeat. Going back to a country that none of them really knew anymore. She had to tell the policeman that her parents were going back to Japan and the tears were streaming down her face because she knew it was her duty to go back with them because they were old and nobody to look after them. But she didn't. She wouldn't sign for herself.

And I'll always remember . . . she came to my place and I was washing in the basement and we sat on the basement steps and the devastation, the complete utter shock, and she said, "My parents have signed up and, Nancy, and I . . . I couldn't go back, I couldn't go back. What will we do?" She was devastated, completely devastated. She was only eighteen then.

She said, "I couldn't go back. I'm a Canadian."

What Happened to the Little Kids?

It was the little kids. We'd be mooning around, feeling awfully sorry for ourselves that some were going to be shipped off to Japan. Like cattle, said one of the kids. And there were the little kids, down by the lake, playing near the water, throwing stones, sticks, splashing. You know how kids do. Me and my girlfriend were walking down there this day when everybody knew about the papers that had been signed and what families were going to Japan. My girlfriend said to me, "Look at them, playing there, and they don't know that in a year or so they're all going to be little Japs." You know, I had to laugh. I asked her what the hell she thought we were, right then and there. She said, "I am a Canadian." I said oh no she wasn't. She was a Jap too, plain and simple. We were all Japs. We were all damn Japs. Because the Canadian government said so.

I said that just because her father hadn't signed the repatriation paper that didn't make her any less a Jap. She started crying and she kept saying, "I'm a Canadian." But I thought of an old saying, and I mean I just thought of it now, but it says that if you fly among crows, expect to be shot as a crow. And that was us. That was happening to us. When you were in a camp, in the ghost town, you were a Jap. That's all you could be because that was about all that was there. Japs and Japs and more Japs.

So those little kids playing down by the water, making water rings by throwing stones and laughing and getting their feet and leggings all wet, they were no different from me and my girlfriend. They didn't know anything about the repatriation, which is something we don't talk about much now. It is pretty painful and it's long and gone. They didn't know and I think it is a pretty good thing they didn't. I don't often think about it, but I wonder how many of those little kids did go to Japan. I mean is one running an elevator in a Tokyo department store now? Is one an engineer? A teacher? What? What did happen to them? There must have been a thousand kids that went.

One girl who went although she wasn't in our town, she went and when she came back when she was about thirteen she went to a school in Kitsilano. She said she remembered nothing about Canada, and she had been away only seven years or so. Those little kids, those ones still in Japan, I guess they don't even remember they once were Canadians. Too bad.

The Young Felt Betrayed

A lot of people wondered why so many young people—call them teenagers whether they were under sixteen or over—would sign to go back to Japan. In other words when they were Canadian citizens, why would they go to a country, Japan, where they would be foreigners even though they were of Japanese ancestry?

Well, does anybody have to be so bloody stupid about it? It's obvious. Without coming out and really saying it, because young people really aren't that articulate, they knew in their own hearts that Canada had betrayed them. They didn't have to be the brightest to see that.

For three years, not counting what had gone on before Pearl Harbor, they had had a rough time. In the ghost towns. Moving from place to place. No education or poor education. Working for peanuts when the country was booming and others were making a dollar an hour while they were stuck in some ghost town getting almost nothing an hour and that having to go into the family pot.

They, in effect, had been denied all the opportunities that are so important to Canadian boys and girls. A good home. A good education. A good job. Freedom.

And another thing. Well, let's accept it. They had a Japanese heritage. A lot of the things their mothers and fathers and older people did were still Japanese. But before the war they could get away from that. They'd have some of the Japanese business at home but in the schools, at play, recreation, everything, they were mixing with Canadians, English, Scottish, Germans, Norwegians, Italians, Chinese, and they were benefitting from this. It was helping them to become more and more Canadian, and consequently they looked more like Canadians and thought like them, enjoyed the same music, laughed at the same jokes. Some even dated white girls. And so on and so forth.

And then, then you put them in camps. Well, they still have the language and the music and some of the education, but there are maybe 200 pupils in the school and they are all Japanese. See what I mean? I'll bet the same thing would work if you did it to Norwegians or Irish. The Norwegians would start being more Norwegian again and so on.

They had three years to sit on this, three years to see the disintegration of family life, home life, bickering, fighting, the coming and going of people—and all the time the authorities telling them they're going to have to move East. Or else.

I used the word "embittered." I'm not sure that's the right word. Maybe there is another, but after awhile it must have gone through their minds that nothing was ever going to change. In Canada they were always going to be Japs and the dice would be loaded against them. No matter where they went, people would say, "Jap" or "Chink" and it would be like it was for their father's generation. No good jobs. All the stinky ones, all the hard-working ones, all the lower-paying ones, all the rat shit in the world. Pretty dismal.

So then the government comes along with its repatriation thing. Anybody who wants to will be sent to Japan. Well, the kids, they look in the mirror and they shake their heads and they say, "Well, I guess I'm a Jap," and they figure that maybe over there they can get a fair shake. They don't know what it is like. They don't know the rigid cultural and social standards which will or would be stiffening to them. They don't know that the police and the authorities will look on them as foreigners. All they think is what the hell, what's the point in going on in Canada?

Then there were the parents. Some were naturalized but if they didn't get in under the wire, then a lot were still Japanese. Enemy aliens, so to speak. They'd put their two bits' worth in. Naturally they'd want their children to come with them to Japan. They figured Japan would be better than Alberta or Ontario. So they'd order the kids or nag them to sign. Of course, a child under sixteen did what his parents did anyway. Signing, I mean.

Another thing you've got to remember. After three years of living in those camps and ghost towns, some of the kids were getting out of hand. Yes, I know that Japanese children, so to speak, are supposed to be marvels, but I've heard teachers refer to them—or some of them—as real roughnecks. Toughies, one teacher called them. You see, the camp brutalized them. Everything about the camp brutalized them, just as it brutalized their parents.

One thing that has bothered me a little and it's that word "repatriated." Now if a person was born in Japan, then he can be repatriated. That means going back. But if a person was born in Canada, like about 60 percent of the Japanese were, how can they be repatriated? Wouldn't they be patriated? I don't even know if there is such a word. Must look it up sometime.

But no, they were just children. They'd sort of lost their way. Nobody was showing them a future. Their dreams, I guess you could say, were shattered. They had hopes and dreams just like any Canadian high school kid. One wants to be a doctor, another an engineer. This girl a nurse and this one just wants to marry Tommy Wakayama and have five fat kids. You know what I mean. It was a terrible experience for them. It came at the worst time of their lives, or I mean the best time of their life. But it was the worst. Shut off, locked off from the world. Living in what would pass as slums in any slum city of the world. No contact. Just jitterbug music drifting in from the outside world. Goddamn it, can't you get mad when you think of it? The hope fading from their eyes, like the eyeballs drying of a person who has just died. That's what it was. Those young people were dying inside and nobody was doing a blessed thing to help them. It should make people angry to still think about it but they don't. It's all over now. It happened to other people a long time ago.

Certificates—Up in Smoke

The night before they were to go to the coast to catch the ship for Japan they had a big bonfire in the centre of the camp and they burned everything that said they had anything to do with Canada. Birth certificates, documents, everything. A great whoop-te-do. They weren't having anything to do with Canada. To hell with Canada.

Then they got to Japan and a lot of the young people who spoke Japanese were a great help to the American forces in administration working in the offices, and they did well until the Americans finally decided they would not hire Japanese anymore. Or maybe there just wasn't that much work anymore in the offices.

So those young people who had gone back to Japan, to hell with Canada and all that, figured they would have a better chance of being kept on by the Americans if they could prove they were really Canadian citizens. Well, they had no certificates. That had all gone up in smoke. So we were inundated with requests from these people asking us to get them duplicate certificates. In the letter they used to say they didn't like the food, the fish they had to eat, or the country or the people but they were stuck in Japan, but if they could work for the American Army things would go easier for them.

To Japan—and Back

August, 1946. That's when we got out of the camp. That's when we went back to Japan. Actually we didn't have much choice. We only had two choices and my father wasn't that well enough to start up a business or go to work in Eastern Canada and they wouldn't let us stay in British Columbia. My mother wasn't much behind him in age and he was in his sixties and then she became sick. Not bedridden but not well either. Now I hadn't finished high school. I was in grade eleven.

Everybody talked about repatriation and I think one thing that happened—well, it split up many families. Quite a few. Either the mother or the father wanted to remain in Canada, but the other one was quite disgusted with what had been done to them, and besides they had nothing. No business, no nothing. To go back to the old country, half of the family went with the mother and half with the father, so there was great sadness.

My father said that at least if he went to Japan he had a house there, a property, and his relatives were all out there. So, ah, well that was his decision. My mother was for remaining in Canada. You know where I was. Well, certainly. I didn't want to go to a country I did not know. But this was my father's decision. So the three of us went back. Yes.

We were terribly disappointed in Japan. They put us in this army barracks. They weren't using it so it became a reception centre. The first night a lot of us cried. The food was, for one thing, awful. At least we were able to eat in the camp in Canada. Nobody starved. But in Japan the food was awful. I heard some people couldn't eat it at first. Then they realized that was all there was going to be.

And the people. The feeling. It was about us. The Japanese were saying, "Why are they coming back here for?" Well, in a way you couldn't blame them. A defeated country. They didn't have enough food for their own people and we were coming out there from a country of plenty. You know. It is a natural feeling. We were strangers to them, foreigners. Canadians. Standard of living was very, very, very low. They were starving. You'd see them having a bowl of rice, bowl of gruel. And we came to take some of that. A bowl of soup.

We were very fortunate that this reception centre wasn't too far from my parents' village and his brothers were there. We had written to them that we were coming and my father had a house there because every so many years before the war we would take a trip back there and he wanted somewhere to stay. So he had this house so we only stayed at the reception centre for four days. But there was families that stayed at the centre for four weeks, I heard.

My parent's relatives were farmers and after the war the farmers were better off than the city people. At least they had food. As far as food was concerned we were very very fortunate. Meat, of course, was out of the question. But fish, always been a staple food, you could always get fish. They brought food over to us until we got going.

I was the only one who was well enough to seek employment, so I went out to a company . . . this Japanese company as an interpreter for the Americans, the army. I wasn't very happy there. I was Japanese, but when you've been born and raised in another country, in another culture, you almost feel like a stranger. I was so desperate to be able to communicate in English because that was my language. I was just fooling myself that I could really speak Japanese.

So a friend got me a job with the American occupational forces. That only paid me a very small percentage of my first job, but I was a lot happier because with the army I heard English spoken all the time and I could see things that were familiar. It was kind of like I was back in Canada.

We were classified as foreign nationals by the Americans, and they wouldn't let us buy things in the PX army store. The only privilege we had was that we were able to eat in the army messhall, which had Western food. Well, I consider that I was very lucky in that respect because I at least got one good, big meal a day—but to this day I have no liking toward chile con carne because we used to have that many times a week.

The Japanese. That's another thing. I think a lot depends on the individual. If you're looking out for trouble, are biased, or have an idea that because I'm a foreign national, a Canadian, and I'm superior, well, they will retaliate and they'll give you the same feeling and they say to you, "What are you doing over here? Why don't you stay in your own country?" The people, Japanese, who I had some contact with, they were very nice and if they ever asked me why, or what we were doing over there, we would explain to them what had happened. We would say, "What would you do?"

I came back in '49. I spent three years over there and all the time I wasn't very happy. It was against my will to go over there in the first place and after a couple of years I didn't see much future there.

So I tell my parents this but they do not want to come, but they say that if there is a family I can stay with in Canada, look out for me—if I'm going to be happier in Canada, then go. But I had repatriated—I had renounced my Canadian citizenship, so I had to get new Canadian citizenship. It took quite some time but between the Canadian Embassy and Ottawa it was done.

My future husband's parents and my parents were very, very old friends and so they kept in contact and so my father wrote to my father-in-law-to-be and he said his daughter wanted to go home, but she couldn't come back to nothing. So he said fine, we'll vouch for her, come on home. So I came on an American ship, a passenger liner not quite converted back from a troopship. And I eventually married my husband in Lillooet.

Well, it's been an experience. It is hard to say that if it hadn't been for that, how would my life be. It's hard. And what has happened, it has turned out quite well. But for me, no, because my parents both passed away in Japan; because I never did get to see them again.

The Forgotten Committee

I don't suppose many people remember now about the Co-Operative Committee on Japanese Canadians because it was a long time ago, starting during the war. But it worked very hard, did a great deal, and the people who worked on it and the people who responded to it have every right to be proud of themselves.

It all began in June of 1943 when a small group—well, actually, it began with Ernest Trueman who was placement officer for the Japanese division of the federal Department of Labour. He had been a worker in Japan for many years with the YMCA and he was sympathetic to the plight of the Japanese from B.C. who were coming to Toronto, especially the girls who were coming out to work as domestics. These girls were having difficulties, resettlement problems, as you must imagine, and Trueman thought it would be a good idea if a group of church people and other Toronto workers formed a committee. How they could help these girls. The little group was made up of some people from the YWCA and the women's missionary services of the United Church, the Anglicans, the Church of All Nations, and other people who had had dealings with the Japanese. In Japan.

This committee met with the local representative of the B.C. Security Commission and discussed the girls and how they could find suitable jobs, homes, recreation.

The next step was bringing in people from the YMCA, the Student Christian Movement, which was in the universities and colleges, the Catholic Church and others and they decided they could do work among the Japanese men too. At the same time the Japanese men and women in Toronto were asked to form into separate groups and send two representatives each to the meetings. It should be noted that these two Japanese groups later joined to form the Japanese Canadian Committee for

Democracy, which later became the Japanese Canadian Citizens' Association, which speaks for almost all of the Japanese Canadians in Canada today.

During the fall and winter of 1943 and 1944 the committee was spreading throughout southern Ontario with advisory councils being set up. The committee, taking the lead from a similar movement in Vancouver, sponsored a petition which was distributed throughout Vancouver which urged the government to take some constructive attitude toward the Japanese and resettlement. During this time they reprinted in part an article which had appeared in the magazine *Saturday Night* dealing with the problem, and about 10,000 copies were distributed and it drew up other petitions and sent delegations to various municipal councils and even to Ottawa, all with the idea of giving the Japanese Canadians a better break.

But as the months went by, the political side of the whole question became foremost for the Co-operative Committee. Little did the organizers realize when they started out in such a small way that they would end up challenging the government's policy and taking the case of the Japanese to the Privy Council, London, the highest court in the British Commonwealth. But they did.

It all began on August 4, 1944, when Prime Minister King stood in the Commons and spoke of the policy of the Liberal government toward the Japanese in Canada. He said that no Japanese of Canadian birth had been suspected or convicted of any acts of sabotage or espionage, and then he went on and said no further Japanese immigration would be allowed into Canada. He also said that those Japanese in Canada who were found to be disloyal to Canada would be deported. Saying this after saying that they had found no acts of disloyalty in the first three years of the war. Then he said that those left, the Japanese, would be dispersed across Canada. He also said that a type of commission would be set up to examine the background, loyalties, and attitudes of all persons of the Japanese race and thus would be decided who would be sent back to Japan and who could stay. The Prime Minister said that only a set quota would be allowed to go back to their homes on the West Coast. Quite a mouthful for one speech.

The Co-operative Committee agreed that it was perhaps best that no more Japanese be allowed into Canada, but it felt that a commission to look into the Japanese loyalty, attitudes, was unjust. Things went along pretty much the same for months after that, and not many people moved out of the Japanese relocation centres in the fall and winter of 1944 and 1945.

Then came the crunch. The government decided it had to clear the Japanese out of B.C. They wanted them out of the camps and ghost towns and so in February of 1945 they announced a voluntary repatriation plan. It was simple. The Japanese—nationals, those with citizenship, those born in Canada—were offered the choice of making a voluntary application to go to Japan after the war or move East of the Rockies. Of course it was aimed straight at the 8,000 or 9,000 Japanese still in B.C. The government announced that unwillingness to head East of the Rockies might be seen at some time in the future as a lack of co-operation in carrying out the policy of dispersal. It was pretty direct.

The survey was finished in May and about 10,300 people of Japanese ancestry were involved. The Co-operative Committee had been watching the situation and when the results came out they knew they had a fight on their hands because they saw the whole thing as a threat to civil liberties. They knew they'd have to go into action quickly and that the committee would have to be expanded to include more lawyers and other persons, and that money would have to be raised if the people of Canada were to know what was going on.

At a meeting of about twenty groups interested in the Japanese problem, a resolution was drawn up protesting the government's repatriation moves. At the next meeting the name Co-operative Committee on Japanese Canadians was officially adopted and Reverend James Finlay of Carlton Street United Church became chairman. He was chairman of the committee for the next six years, when it disbanded, its work finished. He was one of the many clergymen across Canada who devoted much time to the work.

In July the committee sent a high-powered delegation to Ottawa to interview government officials and the upshot was that the government officials defended the policy of repatriation and, besides, they said they had heard of no complaints about deportation. This convinced the committee that the people of Canada would have to become aroused and articles were sent to the press and a pamphlet printed and distributed.

Then, with the war in the East over, in September of 1945 the government announced that it was ready to ship the first of 10,000 Japanese Canadians back to Japan just as soon as shipping arrangements could be made. And the committee really swung into high gear. Time was running out.

One of the first steps was to draw up a leaflet which they called *From Citizens to Refugees—It's Happening Here!* and 50,000 copies were sent out. It emphasized that Canada, a signer of the United Nations Charter and the Atlantic Charter, would have to deal fairly and justly with Japanese Canadians, not only because none of them had ever been proved disloyal, but also because repatriation would be a black mark on Canada's reputation. It also pointed out that no action had even been considered about nationals or citizens of German or Italian nationality and those countries, too, had been Canada's enemy. Therefore, this was pure and simple discrimination toward a people based solely on racial origin. The leaflet urged all Canadians to write to the Prime Minister and their Members of Parliament.

Things started to happen. During that autumn regional committees were formed in Vancouver, Calgary, Edmonton, Lethbridge, Regina, Saskatoon, Winnipeg, and major cities in Ontario as well as Montreal. People were beginning to see what was happening. Public meetings were held. Newspapers took up the cause. On university campuses there were many meetings. Another pamphlet was printed and distributed and then another 25,000 copies were printed and passed out. Sworn statements were taken from Japanese Canadians who had signed to go back to Japan, showing just why they had signed—and the reasons were rarely because they were disloyal to Canada. The Prime Minister's office said it received more mail on the issue than on any other issue. And so it went.

Then in late November the government changed its stand somewhat. The Minister of Labour said more than 10,000 had requested repatriation, but nearly 4,000 were children under sixteen. The minister said the government felt that in general all Japanese nationals and those born in Japan, but naturalized, should be sent back to Japan because they had showed their disloyalty by signing. It said that those Japanese who had signed the forms before September 2, the day the peace with Japan was officially signed, those would be permitted to withdraw their applications. Their repatriation would be cancelled. It also said that those who had signed after September 2 could have their applications reviewed. This applied, of course, to those born in Canada. So the committee welcomed this statement, but it still left the future of about 4,000 Japanese in doubt—those born in Japan and not naturalized and those naturalized.

The government insisted that all the statements taken were voluntary, but the committee insisted that coercion was involved in that the Japanese were threatened with imminent separation from their families and the danger of being considered disloyal. The committee said the applications formed no basis for determining who was disloyal or loyal. It said the applications did not actually show how many people actually wanted to go to Japan, but only how many who felt they could not leave B.C. for a strange land East of the Rockies. Some Japanese said they had been told by the police that they could cancel their applications when they wanted to.

A major focus of the committee was the Japanese nationals, people who had entered Canada legally and many had lived up to forty years in Canada. They were now to be booted out. It pointed out many had tried to become naturalized but red tape had snarled them up repeatedly.

It meant nothing to the government. Plans were made to ship 900 Japanese to Japan in December from Vancouver, even though the government knew that Japan was war-torn and millions of people could possibly starve to death that winter. The government virtually nailed the coffin lid shut on December 17 when the Prime Minister tabled three orders-in-council and these provided for the deportation of five classes of Japanese. These orders were passed under the War Measures Act, which was to expire on January 1, 1946, just about two weeks away. This caused an uproar across the country.

The only action possible at such late date was legal action and Andrew Brewin, who was a Toronto lawyer, stepped in as senior legal counsel for the committee. They had to stop the loading of those 900 Japanese on that boat in Vancouver harbour January 6. So, on December 27 Mr. Brewin went to Osgoode Hall in Toronto and filed two writs claiming that the orders-in-council, which by the way were numbers 7355, 7356, and 7357, were invalid and illegal and beyond the government's powers. That stopped that because the Minister of Justice agreed then that the orders-in-council would be referred to the Supreme Court of Canada. The Co-operative Committee on Japanese Canadians was now operating in a pretty heady atmosphere.

You can't go up before the Supreme Court on a shoestring budget and it was felt that 7,000 dollars was needed, but voluntary contributions from all segments of society, including money from Japanese Canadians across Canada, quickly brought in more than 10,000 dollars. So the plans went ahead. Public meetings were called across Canada and on January 24 the case was heard. Mr. Brewin and a constitutional expert J. R. Cartright for the committee, supported by the province of Saskatchewan, which you must remember was CCF [Socialist] at the time. The attorney general of B.C. was against the appeal, along with the federal government, of course. Two days of hearings.

On February 20 the decision came down. Defeat. Or partial defeat, but bad enough that the committee unanimously decided that an appeal would have to be made to the Privy Council in London. In essence, the Supreme Court said that parts of the orders-in-council on deportation were invalid but that they were, in turn, considered to be legal because they had been issued under the War Measures Act—even though the War Measures Act was no longer in force. However, despite all that, a majority of the judges said the wives and children should not be deported and two judges said the whole deal was invalid where it applied to Canadian-born or naturalized citizens. So partial victory, but defeat. The War Measures Act conquered all.

The committee said in a statement that surely the government would not persist in a program, a policy of inhumanity as far as its Japanese were concerned—but yes, it would. No plans were changed. So, the Privy Council—and you don't go to the Privy Council on a shoestring budget either. While the committee was raising a hoped-for 10,500 dollars, another campaign was launched to acquaint the Canadian people with the facts, and pointed out that no other country had pursued such a policy of exile for a couple of hundred years. Fifty thousand copies of a new pamphlet were distributed, citing ten points why the orders-in-council should be set aside. Every Canadian was urged to write or wire the Prime Minister's office.

And so in early July Mr. Brewin went before the Privy Council in London. In early December, 1946, the decision was handed down. Its ruling was simple. The orders-in-council were valid because under the War Measures Act the government could do anything it considered necessary for the safety of the country. The Privy Council decision said it did not have to consider the wisdom or propriety of the policy because determination of that policy is exclusively a matter for the Parliament of Canada and the Cabinet.

The committee pointed out that, in effect, that meant that the final question of the orders-in-council rested with the people of Canada because they elected the Parliament. The committee also asked again for the government to abandon its policy of forcible deportation, stating that there was no war emergency existing and that the Japanese had been dispersed to many parts of Canada. It meant, of course, that if the government had once considered the Japanese a threat, it no longer could do so.

Then, suddenly, on January 24, 1947, the Prime Minister announced that the orders-in-council had been repealed. Just like that. Victory. No real advance warning. Just a simple statement. Somebody signed a document and it was all over.

The committee did all the right things, issuing a statement thanking the government for repealing the orders-in-council, and stated that this continuing cause for shame on Canada had now been erased. The long campaign of this citizens' committee was over—but it was not full victory. While the arguments and appeals had been going on, the government had been shipping Japanese Canadians back to Japan, a total of 3,700. These were volunteers. Half of those 3,700 were people born in Canada, true Canadian citizens. That was something that could not be erased. It should be pointed out, though, that these people had gone voluntarily, but the committee pointed out that the fact that they would choose to go to a war-devastated and starving country was a severe indictment of the way thay had been treated in Canada. Treated as enemies, herded into camps simply because of their racial origin. Years of work destroyed overnight through no fault of their own. The committee pointed out that many of these people felt they just did not have the resources or strength to start all over again in Canada in the face of continuing hostility and unreasoning prejudice. These people, the committee pointed out, had found no justice in Canada.

The government's decision on January 24, 1947, did not end the committee's work. Still much to be done. The property issue. Getting a fair price for the fishing boats, the land, the homes, the businesses, the possessions that the government had seized, confiscated, sold, lost, what have you. The committee and its lawyers worked on that for many months, and while few Japanese Canadians were satisfied with the settlements given, at least most received some additional compensation.

The claims were mainly settled by 1950 but there were a few tag ends to clean up, but to all intents and purposes the work of the Co-operative Committee was over. In the fall of 1951 it officially dissolved. During those six or seven years of its life, it accomplished a great deal. A lot of people, in most parts of the country, worked very hard. Some put in hundreds of hours and some must have put in thousands. They actually worked unheralded, for today how many Canadians in a thousand would know what the Co-operative Committee on Japanese Canadians stood for, or did? They might be able to make a kind of guess, that it had something to do with the treatment of the Japanese Canadians in the last war, but even that thing, the war, has faded away. People don't talk about those things. But there were lawyers, church people from all churches, welfare workers, social workers, just ordinary men and women, university students by the hundreds, as well as Japanese Canadians, a lot in the Toronto area. It is a little-known part of a very large picture and one that should be remembered, if people only knew.

13 *You Can't Go Home Again*

Home. What did it mean to the Japanese Canadians?

Home was not where it had been before Pearl Harbor—the fishing village of Steveston on the Strait of Georgia, the islands up the coast of B.C., Little Tokyo on the Vancouver waterfront, or the hundreds of farms of the lush Fraser Valley.

In 1949, when the last of the bans on Japanese Canadians was lifted, home was Alberta for 3,900. Saskatchewan was home for 450; Manitoba for 1,300 more. In Ontario, with the largest concentration in Toronto, there were 7,800. In Quebec, 1,300. Even the ten Japanese Canadians in the Maritimes or the forty in the Yukon considered those areas to be home for the time being at least.

In all of B.C., where once there were 22,000, there were 7,000.

Dispersal, painful and embittering and prolonged, had finally been achieved to a degree that must have satisfied the politicans—or maybe they were just as worn out by the struggle as the Japanese were.

Some did go back to B.C. Men with fishermen's blood in their veins. Some with farmer's blood went back to the land, a small patch in the Fraser Valley. Some went into business, small businesses. Some retired, to walk along the beach. There was still some hostility—that sidelong glance, that questioning look. But they had endured worse, a thousand times worse, so these small things they could take.

334

Others made the long trip by car or rail and visited Steveston and saw nobody they knew, for it was now a white man's town. They realized that Little Tokyo would never be the same again. That part of their lives was gone. They visited old neighbourhoods, looked up old friends, assessed the situation, and made their decision. They pointed their cars eastward or got back on the train and went back to their homes—right across Canada.

No Government Help

There was no government help at all when we came back. None at all. Not even our railway fares paid. Nothing.

They had packed us up, some of us in the night, and they'd sent us away to the mountains, to the beet fields. They sent us to road camps and bush camps and to tomato fields and onion fields in southern Ontario. They took away our possessions and we never got any of them back and what money we got if they were sold, why, it was so little that it didn't really count.

And then we had to come back, and we had no money.

No one got any help from the government but I will say this, that the fishing companies, to their credit, backed up the Japanese based on their previous performance. We had a reputation for fishing and somehow or other it is not the Japanese nature to run away from our debts and we had a good credit rating. So when the Japanese fishermen were allowed back on the coast, well, the companies said, "We'll take a chance on these fellows. We'll back them." So some of our people got established again as fishermen, but there were so many others who didn't have hardly any money at all. A man of sixty with a family could start off as poor as he had when he left his father's farm forty years before to work for a neighbour. Most people had nothing.

Everything they had earned when they were East of the Rockies had gone on food and shelter and clothing and little things. Life has to go on, you know. Even if you are in exile.

They got no help at all from the government.

I remember one man telling me he'd come back in 1950 and taken the B.C. Electric Railway up the Fraser Valley. Yes, to the place, the station where he'd had twelve acres of land. He and his family had planted strawberries and raspberries and put in drainage until they had a nice farm, about nine acres cultivated. It had taken years. When he saw that farm it was not the way he had left it. It had gone back to bush. The willows were higher than the fir trees and the small orchard he had planted. He said he cried. The waste of it all. And when he tried to borrow money to buy it back, the bank or whoever it was laughed in his face. They said they didn't want any more Japs around that district. That went on all the time.

You know, the native people now, the immigrants, are very fortunate now. Everything is done for them. If immigrants want to come to B.C. they get a plane ride or at least a train fare. An Indian wants to go work somewhere, there is an agency somewhere that puts him on a plane and gives him a few dollars to spend.

But here we were. Born in Canada. Canadians. Why, my father was born in Japan, but he still had the Union Jack flying at our front gate when I was a kid and he loved that flag. Us kids at school used to sing "God Save the King" just like the other kids did. But when we came back, nothing. Not even a kind word from a lot of people. We had to find houses, find jobs, start from scratch. Even find out what living in B.C., Vancouver, was like again. That had even changed a lot. The war.

We were people going into a foreign country where the government didn't like us, the people didn't like us, and no money. Just a few clothes in suitcases, a few pictures of our relatives and so forth in our possession and really, not much else. That's the way it was like for an awful lot of us and I'll never forget it.

Return to Powell Street

The family went to Tashme. I spent a year there but all I could get was a job at 25 cents an hour stuffing sawdust into bags and God but it was cold. So I said I was going to Toronto. Mr. Best, the teacher, said that was a good thing and so I went to Toronto and then to Burlington, and after the war I came back to visit my folks. They were at Greenwood then. This was about 1949 and Japanese could go back to the coast.

I asked my dad if he was going back. He still had his dry-cleaning equipment stored with a neighbour, a white guy on Fraser Street, and it was safe. My old man said no and I guess I was a little surprised. He said he had this house, and it was a good house. Small but good, but you don't need a big place to be happy. A small, warm place will do. He worked in a box factory that had started out. He belonged to the union and got the union rate. I think it was $1.15. Damn good money for those times. He said my mom was happy, the two girls were happy. My sisters. They had lots of friends. In fact, they even had all got together and built a swimming pool. That was a progressive town. They thought right about the people that came in. I think it was because of the mayor they had. Dad said the girls would marry boys from the district. Both did. One from Kelowna, another from the old Slocan camp. He said he and Momma were happy. Plenty of rice. Plenty of *miso*. Plenty of beer. They liked the town and Momma had flowers in the house all through winter. What else?

He said Vancouver, my dad said the Vancouver we knew was gone. There was nothing for us there. I asked him if they'd pulled down all the houses and stores and he said no, nothing like that. He just kept saying there is nothing left, nothing like the old days. He couldn't quite say it, so I went anyway—I wanted to see for myself.

I went first to Powell Street, right from the train. I saw a few people around but I didn't know them. They weren't from Powell of the old days. Then I saw the Arai kid I'd known in Tashme and he was still shooting off pictures with his camera, telephone poles and anything he saw. Ernie's was gone. The noodle parlor was still there but nobody was in it. A few Chinese but no Japanese kids jiving. I saw Nishikawa, who'd been a good athlete at the camp, and we talked a bit and he said nothing was there. But he said to give it time, people would come back. All the shoe stores and the jewellery shops and all the other stores were gone. Some were other stores now.

I went down to Woodward's and got funny looks from some of the clerks. Remember how we'd go down to Stanley Park? Oh yeah, you weren't there. But we'd go down to the park and see the Japanese [World War One] memorial and it was there. It could have stood a good washing. I phoned out to Steveston to the billiard parlour but they said nobody was there. I walked around some more. Had a meal at Scott's Café just like we used to do after the show before the evacuation and it was still the same. Real comfortable and friendly, lots of food. I did some more walking and saw a couple more guys I recognized. Even that guy who was always climbing the mountains at Tashme, but we didn't have much to say. He said he was working in a restaurant. He said he thinks or thought they thought he was Chinese.

Finally I said to hell with it and got on the train and went right through to Toronto. I stopped in Winnipeg to see friends and we had a good time and I told them and they said yes, they'd been there and then a gal named Sumiko said, "There's no . . . no . . . no . . . " and I could see she was looking around for a Japanese word to say what she felt, but she couldn't find it. Finally she said, "The war took all the good times away." I guess that said it for all of us. That's what my dad meant when he said there was nothing there.

How the Fishermen Came Back

All before Pearl Harbor and then after it, the unions had been very much against the Japanese. It was a fact you couldn't deny. We had lost a lot of our fishing licences before the war, even as far back as the early '30s, and damn few Japanese were coming into this country who were fishermen. Then the war came along and we lost everything, and our places like Steveston and other villages were all white now. White and Indian.

But when I came back I had an old friend named Homer Stevens who was a top man in the United Fishermen and Allied Workers Union on the coast, and I can remember him telling me, he said, "So you're going back fishing, eh, Buck? Well, if you go back fishing now"—and this was not long after I came back to the coast—"the old law is going to come in saying that fishing will only be allowed to those Japanese who served in His Majesty's Armed Forces and by you fishing right now, you'll just be perpetuating the discrimination that is bound to come, and that you were used to before the war. Why don't you wait awhile? Wait awhile!"

So I said I'd wait and he said that he was sure there was going to be a change on the part of the white membership about Japanese coming back on the fishing. And he said that when that change comes, we'd be able to get those precious licences that we needed.

So, gradually as time went by, Homer would talk to the boys when he got some together, when he met with a few, and he'd lecture them on fair play and everything else, being an extreme leftish person but being very fair. Finally, toward the last convention, enough of the membership saw they had better be fair when the Japanese came back again. You know, open the gates as far as membership of the union which would allow them to participate in the fishing again.

Not the kind of fishing that the Japanese fishermen were used to before the war, where they were restricted to one-line fishing or one area as before, but they could fish wherever the white man fished.

So, then people think it was the canneries that brought in the first Japanese after the war. Well, listen to this.

When the War Measures Act was lifted, a bunch of Japs who had been fishermen before the war got fishing licences from the federal government and they came out here with their licences in their back pockets and they went to the big canneries and they asked for boats and gear to fish off the canneries. A lot of people think the canneries gave them boats and gear right away. No. Nobody would go and take them.

Other fishermen fishing for the canneries said, "You bring those Japs in here, we quit. We'll go and picket your place." In various ways they threatened the canneries and the canneries never went beyond that.

Then myself and my cousin, we were both war veterans, we came up the river and first man who would talk to a Jap was Dugald Bartlett of Glenrose Cannery, a small outfit, and I said, I asked him if there was any chance of us fishing for him. And I also told him I needed financial help. All of us did.

Mr. Bartlett asked if we had a place to stay and we said no, so he said for us to look along the river and see if we could find a place to stay and a suitable boat and if you can, he said, "We'll back you."

I thought that this man was sure sticking his neck out for me when every other outfit on the coast was saying no Japs. Hurting himself. Well, I found a house, a little shack, and a boat, all for about 2,000 dollars. Somebody who wanted to go back to the prairies, I think. So I got backing and I bought the place and the boat and I was the first to come back into the fishing industry.

Then J. H. Todd Fisheries took two other Japs but the big ones didn't touch us.

The canneries held the line on us and a lot of the white fishermen didn't change their attitude, although a lot did. I remember one incident when a whole gang of them, about thirty, jumped on two of our boys out in the river and threatened to sink them, beat them up, chased them out and said don't show their faces around Steveston again. They left because they couldn't fight 'em all.

I told them not to worry but stay in our part of the river and fish and things would be okay. But I thought, "What the hell am I going to do? Those guys expect a lot of me and if I don't do something now, it's going to happen to every other Jap as they come along. They'll all get run off the river even though they got as much right to fish there as these white guys."

So I phoned Vancouver, told Homer Stevens what had happened, and he said to leave it to him. He went right out to Steveston and talked to the local out there and gave it to them real good. He said that if any Japanese fishermen wanted to fish out of there, they would be protected and not harmed. The membership of the local passed it because Homer had laid the law down to them. The local would see to it that any person of Japanese origin on the river would be protected from those other fishermen. That's the way it happened.

Well, darn it, as soon as the local said that, B.C. Packers made a grab for all those guys with licences in their back pockets and they gave them boats and gear too. So did Nelson Brothers. Canadian Fishing started a recruiting drive in the rest of Canada.

So that's the way it happened. It wasn't the big companies who brought back the Japanese fishermen. It was the union guaranteeing the safety of the Japanese on the coast. That is why the Japanese fishermen are so close to the union. They understand.

The whole Pacific coast fishing industry owes that guy [Homer Stevens] an awful lot. They can swear at him, they can do what they like, but he did an awful lot for everybody.

There were still incidents, of course. Human nature. It took some time for the hatred, the animosity, to die down. Rammings at night. Guys cutting Japanese nets. White guys putting down the nets just upstream of Japanese fishermen to catch all the fish. Now you just don't do that. That's an unwritten law. People being shot at. At Campbell River. The guy still has a bullet in his head.

Yes, this continued for a while but every time there was an incident Homer and the executive squelched it.

And that's how the Japanese fishermen came back to the coast. First, because of the union.

Getting the Vote

We didn't have the vote. They didn't want to give us the vote. People could give money until they were blue, money to committees to go down to Ottawa and ask for the vote. What happened? Nothing. People there probably said, "Well, if they haven't got the vote I guess the government doesn't trust them. Then they're not good people." In those days I'll bet you not one person in five knew that Japanese had the vote in every province but B.C.

Then it all happened in a funny way. After the war.

In January, 1948—no, in June, 1948, the House of Commons passed a bill that gave the Japanese the federal vote. What I mean is, they deleted an amendment which I think was passed during the war which deprived all Japanese in Canada, nationals, home-grown, or otherwise, of the vote. So now they had the federal vote.

But this still didn't give the Japanese in B.C. the provincial vote. That was what they wanted. That was what they'd been paying out good money for for years, to lawyers, to get some say down in Ottawa, and of course in Victoria for that matter.

But things were moving right along. You didn't need a telescope to see how it was all going to turn out. First, in 1947 the province, the MLA's passed this bill which gave the Chinese and East Indians the right to vote. But they thought B.C. wasn't ready for the Japanese. All those years. All those politicians.

Those posters about Zap the Jap. All those speeches and those filthy pamphlets. Stones through windows. Dirty remarks. That union, the fishermen's union with its campaigns and those Indian leaders saying they wanted the Japs off the coast forever so they could catch all the fish that was going.

In 1948 the deal for the Japanese vote came up in a committee meeting of the legislature and we were turned down. A lot of people were surprised at that. But the government knew which way the wind was now blowing. I guess there was a lot of quiet talking, the Japanese leaders and the CCF and the United Church and Anglican and Catholic people going around and finally they decided that—well, I guess they decided what the hell. Everybody knew a lot of Japanese would be coming back to B.C. soon and why beat the old drums. It just meant keeping hatreds alive and you know, with the United Nations and a new world and people looking at things differently, the old ways were going.

Vancouver was the first to lead off with it and they okayed giving the vote to everybody, and that meant Japanese and Indians. And when that passed it was like a door swinging open. As I recall it went through the legislature without one person voting against it. And just think, five years before—enemy alien. The Yellow Peril. All those kids growing up in damn near ignorance in the evacuation camps and the hatred and the problems and everything. But now, no war. No nothing. So why not?

I can't remember how we took it. Headlines in *The New Canadian*, I suppose. But after all those years, well, it just seemed like you'd been fighting a monster and suddenly the monster was lying there dead. I can't remember how it was treated in Toronto. That's where we were. Something in the *Star*, the *Globe* but just what. But it wasn't a big thing to most people not Japanese.

But as we saw it, Japanese could now become lawyers. Druggists. Did you know that included serving on juries? Working on government work projects? A whole lot of things. For the Japanese who were moving back into B.C. it meant a whole range of new jobs. It meant the old-age pension.

What it actually meant for the Japanese in B.C. or going back home was a whole new deal. Just when they needed it. It made, I think, a lot of younger people, and older people too, go back to B.C. when otherwise they might have stayed in Ontario or Manitoba or Alberta.

But when victory was won, I mean it didn't come with—like skyrockets going off in the night. It was a quiet thing, I think, as if everybody looked around at each other and said, "Why didn't we do this sooner?"

Teddy's Story

I had this friend called Teddy. Actually I think his name was Tadoshi, if there is such a Japanese word. I'd worked with him in Hamilton and when I moved out to the coast after the war he stayed at the plant in Hamilton because Japanese were still not allowed to move to the coast. That didn't come until 1949 when everything was opened up. They got the vote and could move around. But he always said he spent eight years in exile.

His wife had died in Hamilton and he had a young Japanese girl looking after his two kids and often I'd meet with him in the beer parlour and he'd talk about the evacuation. There were other Japanese who wouldn't talk about it but Teddy would. I can't say he was bitter but I can't say he was happy about the thing either. He'd often talk about how he and his family had been kicked off his farm and the land given to the Veterans' Land Settlement Board and how that land was reserved for soldiers coming back from overseas after the war.

Now I didn't know this. That hundreds of these little Japanese vegetable and berry farms had just been scooped up and they were for the soldiers. He said they got very low prices. I think he said he got something like 700 dollars for his seven acres, but that included a house and tools and he'd cleared the land and planted the vines or whatever it was that raspberries and strawberries grow on, and he'd dug all these ditches. Put fences around. All the things you do to a farm. He said why couldn't they just let him rent it out to a neighbour like he wanted to do? But no, they had to grab the thing and then the assessor came around and in a couple of years he got his money. Of course, what he was saying was that the 700 dollars wasn't enough. I thought, well, 100 dollars an acre seems like a fair amount but he said not when you've spent hundreds of dollars and hundreds of hours clearing it. The picture he showed me one day was of a nice little farm with a house and a couple of sheds. It wasn't much but like you say, it was home and it was all he had and it made him a living. He was doing all right. Until Pearl Harbor.

In about 1950 he came back to the coast. I actually thought he woud stay but he came out with his two kids. Not with the Japanese girl though. I thought sure as shooting he would have married her, but I guess she was looking around for somebody who didn't have two kids.

I had a house on Prince Edward Street at that time and he phoned me and I said to come over and so Teddy came over. He didn't have much money but he had found a place for his kids with somebody at Steveston and he was looking for work. I said I could probably get him in at the Bay. Warehousing, that was all. I don't think the people of Vancouver were ready for the Japs for anything else yet. Warehousing. Swamping. No, he had a line up on a job and all he wanted to know was if I had a car. Well, it so happened I had. A '37 Chev. All I could afford because cars were still scarce, but it got you there and back. Would I take him out to Matsqui? Sure. That Sunday? Sure. I knew what he wanted. He wanted to see his farm. That's natural, Why not? But I think he wanted to know how it was being treated, like who was on it.

Going out, he said, "You know, I don't think these soldiers really want farms. A guy from Saskatchewan he wants about a section of land and that's what a farmer is." Then he laughed and said, "Who the hell can make money on seven acres of land other than a Jap?" I had to laugh with him.

We went out the highway to Chilliwack, took our time. It was a nice day. At Abbotsford we turned off and headed down to the river and he showed me where to turn and finally he said to stop. He said to go down this side road and then stop. He just looked and I asked him if that was his farm. He said yes. That was it. Except it wasn't a farm anymore. I mean there was the land. It was always there. You couldn't take that away. But the house, which had been a small place anyways, that was in ruins. There was no sign of anybody living on it. No equipment. Everywhere there was bush growing up. Some quite good size poplars and firs and that. Well, I'll put it this way. It wasn't a farm anymore. It was a slum of a farm.

Teddy and I walked around and he said, "Watch out, there's a well right here," and sure enough there was but it was caved in. Everything was gone and it looked like the neighbourhood kids had played cops and robbers in the house. Part of one wall was burned away. The two sheds where he kept his stuff were down and he said he had had three rows of ornamental trees over on one side. I couldn't even see a stick.

Teddy got in the car and he said it was no more than he expected. He asked me if I'd ever been to Japan. Of course I hadn't. Well, he had as a kid. A lot of Japanese Canadians kids were sent to Japan for part of their education. It was a common thing, he told me. It wasn't disloyal or anything, I guess, but it did strike me as funny. Anyway, he said, "In Japan, they take soil from the valley and they carry it up into the hills and the mountains and where they find a flat spot they put it and then they carry up some more and soon they've got a little field, maybe the size of a dining room table. Then they plant something there. Tea or something. That's the way the Japanese farm. That's the way I was farming. Seven acres."

He asked me to drive him over to his neighbour who'd promised to look after the farm during the time Teddy and his family were away. I think his name was Matthews. A good stick, I thought. He told Teddy what had happened. The farm had just lain there for a couple of years while everything rotted and kids messed up the house. It was a real lover's lane. Then when a buyer did show up, this soldier or sailor or airman, whoever it was, things were in such a mess that nothing could be done. The guy apparently tried for a year but it was a losing proposition.

Like Teddy said, I guess, only a Japanese could make land produce that well. He said, "We treat every vine and root and plant with real care, as if it is the most important thing there is. That's the only way."

I asked him if he was going back to farming and he said no. His kids liked town and if he'd gone back to a farm it would mean starting all over. I know what he means now because I know another family that started up again in Surrey, in greenhouses, and they make a good living now but it took more time and work than any white man would have been willing to put into it.

I met him downtown about two years later and he said he'd put in for more money for his land, more than it had been sold for, and then later he told me he'd got another sock of money for it. This judge had given a lot of them more money because they obviously had been gypped by the Canadian government.

He was no dumbbell. We used to meet the odd time for a beer and he told me that television was going to be big. Real big. He could see it and he was going someplace down in the States and take a course. We didn't have television then but they did in Montreal and I guess in Toronto. The last I heard of him he was in television down East. I used to get a Christmas card from him and it always said, "Doing well. Business good. Teddy."

And Still Discrimination

I know how a Negro feels. I know how an Indian feels. No jobs. Nowhere.

You'll remember it was in 1949 that the federal government said it was okay, fine, you Japs can go back to the coast and carry on as before. Carry on what? My father was in a nursing home outside of Toronto, my sister was living with my mother, but damn it all, I'd go back. I had high school and one year working at John Inglis and I figured I could get a job. Vancouver was where I wanted to go. I'd been born on Triumph Street. Well, damn it all, to put it short, Vancouver was my home. All that had been before, from '41 to '49, had just been a bad dream for the Japanese.

So I told my father what I was going to do and he said that was fine with him. He didn't ask if I would send for him when I got established, but I damn well planned to do it. Vancouver was his home, too, even though he'd been born in some little Japanese village. I'd send for him and my mother and my sister.

Vancouver was just the same. Except Powell Street wasn't there any more. No place to go and just hang around. Another thing. There were hardly any Japs and none that I recognized. Where the hell had they all gone? And then I remembered Toronto and how many had gone there.

This is where the Negro part comes in. Looking for a place to stay. Well, I must admit I found a place fairly quickly. After all, I could pay a month in advance and that's all that seemed to matter. It was a place at Cambie and Beatty. Right downtown, close in.

I hung around a few days just getting the feel of things again. Went out to the house on Triumph and thought, "Oh my God, did they really sell that house for 1,600 dollars?" It was worth 4,000 dollars if it was worth a nickel. That and a lot of other things went on in my mind. I went out to Dog Island and there were a couple of Japanese there. A couple at Steveston. Two or three families brought back by the fishing company. But then I had to go to work. My 300 dollars was going downhill.

First I tried the walking-around bit, going downtown and starting at one end of the street and knocking on doors. Just asking, "Any work?" Most of the places they'd have a girl at the switchboard and she'd just look at you and shake her head. They say, and I think it is true, that a lot of white people can't tell a Japanese from a Chinese, but those little girls at the switchboard sure could. Once in awhile I'd be given an application form, but only like they were just passing them out and not as if they really meant it. I'd fill them in anyway. Day after day. Up and down. I worked the whole of the downtown area and there were lots of jobs I could have done. I was the first one in line when the Vancouver *Province* came out about noon and then I'd rush across the street to buy the *Sun* too, and I'd be first in line at such and such a place and somebody else got it. Always. It never failed. Somebody else would get that stinking job, even if it meant shoving rotten vegetables into barrels at Slade and Stewart or shovelling pig shit down on Mitchell Island.

I knew I was facing discrimination. You never saw it in the paper. Nobody talked about it on the radio. But it was there. I even thought I'd go and see that famous columnist on the Vancouver *Sun*, Jack Scott, but I gave that up. One of my friends said it would be hopeless. You could always get a job in Toronto but in Vancouver—in the city where I was born, went to high school, where my father paid taxes for twenty-five years—I couldn't get a job and yet I was smart, strong as an ox, and I'd do anything. I was down to about one meal a day now. There was just no money coming in. This was in late June, I'd say, and there I was hoping there would be the biggest goddamned snowfall in Vancouver's history so I could get a few days shovelling snow.

I felt like getting a soap box and standing up in Victory Square on Saturday afternoon and telling all the bums my problem. Look, here I am. Hiroko Oye. A Canadian citizen. I can even vote in British Columbia now. Be a doctor, a lawyer, do anything I want. Except find a lousy stinking job.

But I didn't. I just got a lot of nickels and went the telephone route. Sure, come over, a voice would say. It's husky work but it's here. In our warehouse. See Mr. White or Mr. Green or somebody. Bring the paper with you. So I'd go, first over. Sorry. You'd see the look come into his eyes, or rather, it was no look at all. Everything went out of them. He'd say sorry. At least Mr. White or Mr. Green would say sorry. Some of them seemed to mean it. In fact, there was one fellow at Mc and Mc who told me, he said, "Look, isn't there anybody fishing you can go with or up the valley, some of your family before the war who will give you something?" I told him there were no Japs that I knew of who had fishing licences. And as far as going up to Pitt Meadows or down to Surrey, I'd starve before I'd do women's work. Stoop labour. He said he understood but then he said, "You know, most firms frown on hiring Japanese workers." What was the point in telling him that I didn't start that war in the Pacific, that I was a Canadian citizen, and that I had as much right to work as the next guy? You can't get mad at a guy who thinks he's giving you some kind advice. Now can you? Can you?

He didn't say that all the big firms had got together in a big meeting and decided they wouldn't hire Japs who came back. He just said that the companies frowned on doing it. What the hell in goddamn Jesus Christ, man, does the word "frown" mean if it doesn't mean that they've got a sort of agreement about it?

Anyway, there was discrimination. It happened to me twenty or thirty times. Oh, I lost count. Maybe forty times. By this time the berries were getting ripe out in the valley, so you could see how long I'd lasted on my 300 dollars. I don't think I could have done it if my room hadn't been in the basement of this house and cost me only 4 bucks and I took out the garbage. So I went out in the valley and picked and they were glad to see me, saying, "Oh ho, here's a Jap. A good picker." Rubbing their hands. But I wasn't any good. To me it was a pile of shit. I lasted less than a week and then I grabbed the bus and came back into town. The first place I stopped from the bus depot was a restaurant on Robson where I used to eat a lot and the guy had got to know me. I was eating away and he came over and asked how it was going and I said I guess I'd better try and get back to Toronto because I knew I'd find work there. Then he said he'd give me a job. Hell, man, I just about jumped into his arms. It wasn't much and the pay wasn't much, eight a week and meals for being janitor and flunky and night watchman in his restaurant. This Greek was okay. I'll say that for him. He wasn't paying me much money, but what Greek ever did? But he was giving me a start and he didn't mind when I fixed up a little bedroom in one of the little rooms down in the basement—in fact he liked it because his night watchman would be on the job all night then and that suited him fine. I had a cot and there was a washroom down there and that was fine.

This went on for a time and it wasn't too bad. I was meeting more guys who were coming back. Then one day I was on Powell Street and I thought I'd go into the drugstore. I forget the name of it but the man who ran it was named Shaw. For some reason he remembered me and we shook hands and he asked how it was going and so on. I said fine, or, well, okay I guess, and we went across the street for coffee and I told him my troubles. He thought a bit and then he said, "You come back and see me in a few days." So in a few days I went back to see him and he said he had a job for me. He said, "Would you like to go swamping on a sawdust truck for a raghead?" and I guess he could read my expression because he laughed like hell and slapped my shoulder. It was just his little joke. No, he'd found a job for me in a warehouse on Homer Street and he gave me the name of the man to see and even phoned ahead. So I went down and the man wasn't all that friendly. Well, let's say he was half and half. All he asked me was if I was willing to work. You're damned right I was willing to work. Work like hell. I worked. I got a raise and by this time I'd moved back into my old room on Cambie, although I could have stayed at the restaurant. The Greek wanted me to but I wanted to be alone and things like that. So that's how I got my first real job.

I mean I didn't get it going door to door. I didn't get it by reading the Vancouver paper ads when the paper came out in the morning and I didn't get it by putting nickels in the phone booth and asking. Somebody got it for me, helped me get it. Of course, when I had it, keeping it was my problem, but that was no problem. I guess Japs are born to work. I know I was. That's the way it all started. It went good after that. I could finally bring my family out here, except my sister, who was married by then. But how I got that job was knowing someone, a guy who had remembered me from before the evacuation. I remember often thinking that I was glad I'd never pinched anything out of his store like some other guys did. Like a bunch would go in and when he was serving two or three, another guy or so would be up at the front putting things in their pockets. I never did anything like that. I wouldn't have felt right if I had done that and then he got me a job.

14. *Could It Happen Again?*

The story is over. The issues so bitterly fought over are things of the past. All the savage rhetoric and millions of newspaper words have been forgotten. Almost.

I recall that statement the Right Honourable John Diefen-baker made in the House of Commons in 1960: "One finds it difficult to forget the wrongs committed in freedom's name but a few years ago."

But was it in freedom's name? Were the Japanese Canadians threats to Canada's peace and security? Or was it racial? Was it economic, this mass 'arrest' of thousands of people? I don't know and I don't know anybody who does know, positively, absolutely.

It seems appropriate to end this book with a few statements by Japanese Canadians and Occidentals on the period described in this book—thoughts about where the Japanese Canadians have been and where they are now and where they are going.

Also, thoughts about the future of some other ethnic group in Canada, whichever one it might be. There are fears expressed that the same thing could happen again, as if there is something deep within the Canadian psyche that generates these fearful events. I don't think so. A few hoodlums prowling in the night, maybe, but not a government. Canada is a different country than it was in 1941. We are a different people.

I believe so. But I cannot guarantee it.

One Man's Philosophy

You ask if there was any bitterness? Here?

This is one man's musings about all that time. Take it as you wish. Yes, there is still bitterness. Among older people there is quite a bit of bitterness at the whole thing.

But when it was all over I think there was this vast sigh of relief that they had lived through this period. Even though they no longer had their land, their stores, their boats, their homes, their money, even that, they figured, "Well, it is a sort of relief. We endured."

Over the long period during and since, I have developed a sort of a philosophy. Hmmmmm. Well, our people were not given the privilege of wearing a uniform. Their sons weren't. But if they did, if a family had five kids at least two in that war would have been killed or injured. You know. That was for the privilege of serving your country.

If you had a choice at the beginning, the average good-sized family, if you could control your family, would you go through the hatred and the harassment, the evacuation and the hardship, for the right to save the lives of maybe two of your children? The answer would be yes.

In your case it was forced on you. You were almost God's chosen children. You and your family were chosen to fight a war. And lose people in death.

And I think maybe we did contribute a bit toward the conscience of the Canadian people themselves. That they are not so God-like—even though they go to church—as they thought they were or as they think they are. They know now that they are capable of doing what any other human being is capable of doing. Racism! Right! And in knowing this it gives them a moment of pause, to say, "God, maybe next time I won't do it as harsh or maybe I won't do it again."

As a matter of fact this generation of younger [Japanese

Canadian] people can't understand their parents. They say, "Dad, don't tell me you took part in this thing, that you didn't lift a voice at that time." Our young people don't seem to understand what their parents—what the circumstances were that forced their parents to do what they did, and why they did it.

And don't think that the Japanese Canadians just because they were persecuted were so flawless. They must have had some of the most irritating faults so far as their approach toward Canadian society. They must have been most aggravating. But they meant well. They didn't mean to do anything deliberate. They just didn't understand Canadian society and that caused so much of the trouble in all those years leading up to the war and the expulsion. But having said that, they must have been irritating.

And what would we, the Japanese, have done if the shoe had been on the other foot? We would have been just as human. As a matter of fact I would like to think that the Canadians and Americans maybe were a shade, if anything, kinder than people of Japanese origin would have been.

That is an old man's thoughts on the whole matter.

A Lawyer's Observations

You ask me to flash my mind back to 1948 when I was dealing with the Japanese on their compensation claims and you ask if I found much bitterness and I say, "Very little."

You have to understand something about the Japanese and I refer you to a book called *The Chrysanthemum and the Sword* by Ruth Benedict. She is an anthropologist and she talks about the—it's an interesting book—she's talking about the Japanese culture and the Japanese training and the fact that training in the Japanese culture was always to accept the discipline of the orders from above. If the emperor and his people made a decision then that was acceptable and that was right, and to her that was the sword in the title. The sword means they followed blindly the instructions from their superiors.

When I was studying Japanese and preparing for intelligence work, we were told to never worry about getting information from a Japanese prisoner because he had been taught that he would never lose the war, and because he would never lose he was never told how to prepare himself for it. He must always be prepared to die for his emperor.

The result is that they were taught to follow discipline and the whole patriarchal structure of the Japanese family was the same thing. The father gave the orders and the adult sons put them into practice, and she talks about that as being the reason why they would use the sword and be cruel in the prison camps to Allied prisoners of war, because their order was that it had to be this way.

But the chrysanthemum represents the beauty of the Japanese culture, the costumes, the flower arranging, the dancing, the traditional arts. That author was showing how two things that seemed a contradiction could co-exist.

So, I was not surprised to learn that when the Japanese Canadians received orders they followed them and accepted them. They resented them, but those who rebelled were very few. They couldn't get a mass movement going in B.C. or in Canada protesting about what had been done to them by the Canadian government. The administrators discovered that in the camps, and it must have surprised them, that there was no rebellion.

There was a movie shown lately, recently, "Farewell to Manzanar," which was about how the United States removed all their Japanese, and it showed life in this camp and how a few tried to rebel against what was happening to them, against the conditions, and they couldn't get anybody to go along with them.

That was my experience with dealing with the Japanese Canadians. After the war, I'd talk to these people who had been kicked out of B.C., or were put in the ghost town camps, and I would say, "I could never stand for that! How could you?" They would shrug their shoulders. They wouldn't have an answer. They couldn't say, "Because of your training." All they knew was that it was not in their nature to rebel, to fight back against this action which was taken against them, a whole people just shoved out of their homes on a few hours', a few days', a few weeks' notice. They had been taught since childhood that orders from on high, from superiors, were obeyed. They couldn't question those orders. They didn't know how.

But know the glorious thing that arose out of this terrible thing we did to the Japanese people was to make the younger people feel that they were no longer bound by this tradition.

When I met the Japanese in Winnipeg after the war it was the second generation that was beginning to spread its wings, to feel they had a right to fight back. I'm quite sure it is true, it's not just theory. Because I have seen it. They were rejecting the old ways, the training they had received all their lives. They were trying to make their way into the Canadian culture.

So the Nisei, the younger ones but still fairly old, they were starting to take over from their fathers, to speak for them, to take over the job of getting matters settled. That transition from the first-generation power to the second-generation power was clearly evident among the Japanese, and this was clearly the result of getting out of the ghettoes they had lived in in British Columbia before the war. It put the Japanese out into the marketplace, where they had to move into the Canadian culture to survive.

A Blessing in Disguise?

Some say that the Japanese evacuation might have been a blessing in disguise. Oh! That makes me so indignant. Because I think that if we had remained in Vancouver we would have used all the opportunities that were available, you know, because of the shortage of labour to have found a place for ourselves.

We have made a contribution in all these communities that we have settled in, which is pretty good, but we could have made an equal contribution in British Columbia and British Columbia would have been the better for it.

When I see how colourful and flourishing the Chinese community is in Vancouver and how much it has added to the atmosphere, I say to myself that we could have had an equally flourishing and interesting Japanese community in Vancouver. It is a pretty pathetic Japanese community in Vancouver now. They're afraid to be conspicuous. They're still afraid. They say we want to intermarry, we want to assimilate, we want to forget our Japaneseness. We don't want to call attention to ourselves. We are afraid of any political activity. We are not what we were before and we will never be again.

Why could they not have left us alone? If there were some who were considered subversive, then put them in the camp. Like they did with some Germans, some Italians. To move out a whole people, thousands, most of them naturalized or born in Canada, dreadful. Just dreadful. What kind of men were they and what were they thinking when they were moving us out by the trainloads? Were we cattle?

"Let Us Do It Ourselves"

Like they said, it was the best thing that ever happened to us. Getting us out of Vancouver and into good jobs in Ontario. If they had let us do it ourselves that would have been fine.

That made a lot of people bitter. We don't talk about it much now although there is always some agitation for something. And remember they're talking about things that happened thirty years, thirty-five years ago, but some of the old, old people still think they'll be getting a better deal for the bad deal they got. Like when Pearson came along some people said things would be changed and Diefenbaker and then Trudeau. A lot of people thought Trudeau would be for us. I told them, I said, "Look, fools." I can talk to them that way. I'd tell them that the war is over, Japan lost, Canada won. It is all over. But still they think and there is always some old poppa trudging off to see his lawyer when he gets a bright idea about something. I tell them, forget it. I tell them Toronto is a good city, like it, make lots of money. They say Toronto has no mountains and no sea. I point to the lake and tell them what the hell is that. The sea at Vancouver never freezes, one old man told me. I guess he shut me up.

Mackenzie King, his boys just said, "You're enemy aliens." So we were. I don't know if there were spies in our own bunch, but I never met a Japanese fellow once on the coast that I'd say was disloyal to Canada. I mean that. Oh, a lot were giving money to send to the Japanese and things like that but people always do that. There's an earthquake in Greece and every Greek in the country shells out 50 dollars. That's the way it was. Japan, after all, was our historical land. Where the old folks had come from in 1900, 1907, in around those times. We weren't the enemy.

I'm not making sense maybe, but what I'm saying is that they should have talked to us. If we knew of somebody who was really disloyal, going around spreading a lot of crap, we'd have told on him. But let the rest of the people alone. They wouldn't have hurt the war effort. They'd have helped. Look at Hawaii. They left the Japanese alone and things were okay. We were no different. But those politicians. That Neill from Vancouver Island. Wilson, the Vancouver alderman. Oh, we remember those fellows. They just would not let us alone.

I think the time was coming when we'd have—a lot of us would have moved out to Toronto and London and St. Catharines and other places on our own. I could see the time coming. You could see it and hear it. But then the war had to come along, Pearl Harbor Day and all those battleships, and that was the end of it. Another few years and we'd have been all over

Canada, just like Germans and Italians and Hungarians and Chinese guys and everybody. But time just seemed to run out on us and it was too bad. Some people still haven't got over it, and they never will. Just listen to them talk among themselves.

The Spy-Ring Theory

If you ask me, the Japanese had spies in Canada, especially on the west coast. Vancouver. Victoria. Other places. I think it came out at the war crimes trials that MacArthur staged in Japan after the war.

The Americans knew there were spies. That's one reason they went ahead with the relocation of the Japanese from California. And if Roosevelt said there were spies in the States, it just stood to reason there would be in British Columbia. After all, B.C. was nothing but the northern flank of the North American battlefront, if it had ever come to that. The Americans couldn't afford to have their flank unprotected and that is why the Canadian Japanese were moved out, no matter what reasons were given out, like protecting the Canadian Japanese against violence from the Canadians. Racial hatred and all that. Clean out all the Japanese and you clean out their spies.

There's an author named Bergamini who writes in a book called *Japan's Imperial Conspiracy* that Japan had spies in every major city in North and South America. Could be. That would include Vancouver. Victoria, too, because the Esquimalt naval base was there.

He says that when the Japanese took the Philippines, ordinary Japanese labourers like plastermen and carpenters took over top-level jobs for the Japanese government. You see, lying low. Just waiting. Why not in Canada? It didn't have to be done through the Japanese consul. In fact, it probably wasn't. That would be too obvious.

If you ask me, there are Japanese still living in Canada that can tell you a few things.

And if you really want to know, I'll bet there are secret files down in Ottawa, files that we'll never get a chance to see. You know, those Mounties are a tight-mouthed bunch and anything labelled TOP SECRET or CONFIDENTIAL, well, I'll bet it stays that way. But I think they could do a thing or two to set the record of history right. Why did they swoop down the day of Pearl Harbor and arrest a whole gang of them, schoolteachers, union officials, ordinary guys, and everybody was saying, "Why throw those guys in the clink? What did they do?" I think those files would tell you a thing or two.

If they said at the war crimes that—at the trials—that there was a world-wide system of Japanese spying, then I think there was. I'd say some of the people who testified were people who were spies themselves, counterspies, espionage experts, counter-intelligence, and anything else you want to call them.

So Japan had them in Canada, and I think a few, not many but some, maybe ten or fifteen Japanese here were spies. It just bloody well stands to reason, doesn't it? No, I don't have proof. But you ask some of those Mounties . . .

That's where the U.S. and Canada outfoxed Japan. They threw out every Japanese from the west coast. Put them into the mountains, into the deserts, as far away as North Dakota and Alberta. Then there could be no more secret reports going out. No more fishboats meeting Japanese submarines ten miles off Point No Point at midnight. If that happened. I'm not saying it did, but why not? And those radios. Short-wave goes a long way. If the Japanese in B.C. could get Radio Tokyo, well, it would work the other way. Why, I've picked up the control tower at Haneda Airport in Tokyo on an atmosphere bounce. So it could work.

I'd say the Japanese knew every gun, every barracks, every airfield on the coast and every vital bridge, every ammunition plant, if we had them. From Alaska to the Panama Canal. It just stands to reason. Makes common sense. A Japanese spy or twenty can pass off among about 25,000 Japanese in B.C. easily, or he could be born here.

You can't blame the Japanese for doing it, if they did it, and I believe they did do it. Why not? It was war. The only thing, they hadn't declared it yet but everybody knew it was coming. The Japanese knew it best though because they were the ones who had Pearl Harbor all planned, signed, sealed, and delivered.

Not One Act of Sabotage

Well, remember that in those days everything moved from the East to the West, troops, guns, food, supplies, everything, by rail. By the Canadian Pacific Railways through Calgary and Banff and by the Canadian National through Edmonton and Jasper and through the Coquihalla. There were no roads as we know them today. The Trans-Canada Highway was a joke and there were no airplanes as we know them today. I think a big airliner was one that carried twelve passengers. So rails were everything. So what did they do? What they did do was put all of the West Coast Japanese into the Interior where they had close access to these important rail lines, and at any time, whether on the CPR or the CNR, there were bridges and trestles that they could have burned down in a single night, which would have effectively cut off the West Coast from the rest of Canada for months. They could have burned them down or blown them up.

A lot of these Japanese had been farmers in the Fraser Valley and they knew how to use stumping powder and if they could use that, then they could use dynamite. Others who worked in logging camps worked with dynamite in building roads and they could have used their knowledge. And there always was dynamite around in magazines at all these road camps the Japanese were working at or they could have stolen it. I don't think dynamite was a problem.

So what happens? The B.C. Security Commission locates one of the biggest camps in B.C. at the old Trites Ranch. The

Fourteen-Mile Ranch. That's what was called Tashme just fourteen miles east of Hope and Hope is exactly or amost 100 miles from the coast. It would have been as easy as batting an eye for half a dozen of these men to swipe dynamite and be gone from that camp for three or four days, because there were less than half a dozen Mounties in the camp and no bed checks or daily roll calls or anything like that.

And what lay before them? Well, everything lay before them.

They could have walked away from that camp and down that fourteen miles into Hope at night and worked their way up the railways a couple of miles, five miles, and found bridges and blown them to hell and gone. Same with the highway. They could have easily knocked out the highway bridge over the Fraser at Hope. That would have been simple.

Or if they really had wanted to get ambitious and do the right job, they could have hiked—and it would have taken a few days, I guess—but they could have hiked up to Lytton at the top end of the Fraser Canyon and blown both the CNR and CPR main bridges at the same time because they both crisscross the river at the same place there. Mind you, that would have taken a real dynamite expert and a lot of sticks, and I think they had guards on those bridges too, but if some gang was desperate . . .

You know the Fraser Canyon. About sixty miles long. Well, it is the key to the West Coast and any place along there, dozens of places, bridges, trestles, slide areas, a group of saboteurs could have done a terrific job of gumming up the whole damned thing.

Then there was Trail. Consolidated Mining's big smelter. Biggest in the world, and they were making heavy water there too. Now *that* was really guarded. That I've heard. Bells ringing, lights flashing when the slightest thing went wrong. The Allies needed the products of Cominco as much as they needed anything from Canada. But a bunch of determined men could still have loused things up forever and a day by knocking out the trestles and bridges on the Kettle Valley Railway. It would have been simple. As simple as knocking them out where it came down through the Coquihalla Pass into Hope.

As one writer put it, if the Japanese had wanted to, and if

they had been organized, with communication, and if they had had the means like dynamite and fire, in one short hour on any given day they could have effectively cut off the West Coast from the rest of Canada. Then the whole of the coast would have been wide open to enemy attack. And they would have rolled right on in. Nothing to stop them. A few guns. Old boats. A few men.

But the most important thing is this. Nothing ever happened. There was never a bridge burned, blown up, a railway switch broken causing a derailment, a highway dynamited, an irrigation or power damn blown up. None of these terrible things. Not once. Not one single instance.

You know why? Because they were loyal. The Japanese people were loyal.

It's the Young People Now

People have pretty well forgotten it now. You know, they've got good jobs or they've got farms or boats or they've managed to start up in the old business again and they find that people don't hate them anymore. Not like before the war. I know what these Pakistanis are going through right now. A rock through the window at night. No, nobody ever threw a rock through my windows, but I've looked at guys, been in New Westminster at the market, things like that, and I've seen guys who were thinking about rocks through windows.

But I think the beefs are gone now. The old guys—you know one who came over before 1910, he has to be over eighty now—they don't talk about it. Now and again you see one or somebody throws a birthday party for somebody who is ninety but the way it goes, those who lost the most, the Issei, you know, they're dead or keeping pretty quiet.

It's all the young people now. Even the Nisei, me, we're old-fashioned now. Now it's our kids, all going to U.B.C. or

Simon Fraser and getting high marks and winning all the prizes for mathematics and science and Russian. Very competitive, you might say. And you know who they're competing against for these prizes, those A's? The Chinese kids, that's who. The Chinese. So you can see how things have turned around and run the other way. It's a tide. Can't be stopped. These kids don't ask much about the old days, the war and what the English did to us. Sometimes one will and I'll tell them and they might say, "How could you let them do that to you? What was the matter with you?" Not much use you telling them how it was. One kid said to me, "Would you have been rich today if the evacuation hadn't happened, if there had been no Pearl Harbor?" I said to him that no matter what I wished or thought or did, or every Jap in Canada wished or thought or did, there would still have been a Pearl Harbor. Nothing would change that. But I did say that yes, I probably would have been rich. I would have had a lot of land, vegetables, berries. Yes, I guess I would have been pretty well off.

But that's the way it was. We went to the station with our bundles and boxes and trunks and suitcases. All clearly marked. The police said everything had to be clearly marked. Name, destination. As if we wouldn't recognize them. All our life was in those few boxes, suitcases. We'd know them.

I thought it would only be a few months, half a year, and we'd be back on the farm and going into Westminster with our stuff to sell. I didn't know it would be eight, nine years and that our stuff would rot, be sold, and the farm sold and I'd be starting all over again. That didn't enter my bean. How could it? We thought, oh just a few months. A few years, more like it.

Security Is So Important

You know in Toronto and in and around it I know many Nisei families and I only know one family that does not own their own home. It is the same practically wherever you go in Canada. They all own their own homes. The homes may not be mansions but the roof they are under, they own it. And I think it is because of the circumstances.

Like before the war, a lot of people owned their own homes if they lived on berry and vegetable farms. Those homes might not have been much but they were their own. But there was a lot of people, like fishermen and sawmill workers and people living in Vancouver where the wages were so low that they could never hope to own their homes. And then the years in the camps or in the beet fields, and for those who came to Toronto and southern Ontario, too, nobody could hope to own their own homes. They were lucky to live in a rooming house or stay in a shed that the family they were living with had fixed up for them. So there was this strong feeling that to be secure, away from all that dirty business of the evacuation and the camps, one had to own his own home. That is why. That is one thing the war did. It got us out of British Columbia. Well, the truth is, we were practically forced out, but when we got out and got a little money together with everybody in the family helping, then we bought homes. Homes, of course, were cheap then. Mostly we couldn't afford new homes then, the ones they were building, so we took these old red brick ones and they were good for us.

I think to us, after all that, that security is so important to us.

A Good Thing or a Bad?

Where are the Japanese Canadians going? Ah no, we're not holding together. When you realize that today 90 percent of us are marrying non-Japanese. Ninety percent! Yeah. Well, we are damn good providers, we bring home our money and I know hundreds of Japanese males and I don't know one who is an alcoholic. That's a pretty low average, eh? And I only know one who is a homosexual. But on to your question.

Sometimes I really don't understand what the Japanese Canadian is because he is totally different from the Caucasian and he is totally different from the people in Japan. I guess we're some kind of bastard. You know, people come from Japan and they live it up and they drink, but we don't drink. I don't touch a drop, I hate the stuff. You never see a Japanese Canadian get drunk. You'll see them drunk in Tokyo.

I think it is all because we feel we have to project a certain kind of image to the Caucasian—and I think the average Japanese, whether he was born in Japan or here, feels that the Caucasian is still the superior person.

Not the Chinese. The Chinese are different. The Chinese are a lot more proud. Their culture. You see Chinese walking around the streets talking to themselves at the top of their voices. You never see a Japanese do that. They just whisper to themselves. Because we're much more inhibited. Is it because we're ashamed? I don't think so. I don't think we're ashamed of ourselves. But we hold back. We're more reticent. Amongst the whites we sort of retire within ourselves.

If we keep up this business of our sons and daughters marrying Caucasians we're going to be wiped out. The only possibility is that we get more immigration from Japan. But they are more quickly adjusting to the Canadian way, these people who come in from Japan, than we ever did ourselves. When I say "we," I mean the Nisei. I think one of the things today is television. A newcomer to this country is just immersed in English. We didn't have to cope with that situation when we were kids.

Is it a good thing or a bad thing? Well, I'll tell you this much. The average Nisei do not really like their kids to marry non-Japanese. My wife doesn't like it at all, but what can you do? This is a condition that we live in today. I think that somehow the Caucasian finds the Japanese very attractive. I was saying this the other day. If you had a family of four kids, the chances of all those four kids marrying Caucasians are very good, but the chances of all those four marrying Japanese, you got more chances with the million-dollar draw.

"We Have a Role to Play"

I think from the standpoint of the 25,000 Japanese still in this country we have a role to play. We have already failed that first test in 1970 when Trudeau proclaimed the War Measures Act in Quebec—and I see our existence now as not cultural but political. We are the major group against whom the War Measures Act was invoked, and as a group that was clearly wronged under conditions of panic, we the Japanese have a special responsibility to remind people whenever that happens and it is directed against anybody else. I feel that when the War Measures Act was applied in 1970 every goddamned Japanese in the country should have been up in arms and on to Trudeau's back—and nobody did.

When that Tom Campbell [former Vancouver mayor] was hassling hippies, every Japanese in this city should have been on that guy's neck, for he could say "hippie" today and "Jap" tomorrow. It is the same thing.

I think this is the ultimate tragedy of the Japanese evacuation in 1942. It has made us so terrified of standing out, of running the risk of being incarcerated again. We've become bigots like everybody else.

The Story Must Be Retold

I think the value—I agree that there is a need to flesh out our story, that there is a need to tell this so people should be aware of it, but also the greater relevance of the story to me is that nothing has really changed.

The particular racial group may be different but the factors that contributed to our incarceration could just be as quickly turned against the Pakistanis or the Chinese, or the native Indians. The bigots are still here, so the story must be told and retold and retold because we have to inform people that it is very easy to give in to this kind of latent racism and fear and panic and this sort of thing.

"How Far We've Come"

This goes a long way back but when we were writing the constitution of the Japanese Canadian Citizens' League in 1930 we only had the faintest of dreams of equality in Canada. We had never known anything but the second-class citizenship we had.

But we knew what it could be.

But insofar as achievement of those dreams were concerned, it was in some long unforeseeable future, but we wanted those dreams, equality. We wanted it for ourselves and if we couldn't achieve it in our generation, we wanted it for the next generation.

Teachers and others who were liberal had expressed the democratic approach, the democratic philosophy, so we knew it was workable—and yet at that time we knew that the others had it but it was outside of our reach. We wanted part of it.

We wanted to be able to serve our country, Canada. We weren't even given the chance to serve. No opportunity to serve the country, the people, or our own community. And we wanted it.

We have that now. The doctors, the lawyers, the architects, the farmers who made contributions on the prairies, those who own businesses in Ontario, those who are in government, and you sit back and say, "My God, how far we've come."

It Could Happen Again

You ask if it could happen again?

I'd like to say no but I don't believe it. I don't think human nature changes that much. There is still hysteria, still racial prejudice, still economic pressure, and I would say that today we have more selfishness than we've ever had in our past history, individual as well as collective selfishness.

I'm okay, to hell with you—that sort of thing.

You find it, whether you go into the trade union movement or big business or any pocket in a city or in the country, it is there. And I think it is worse than it ever has been.

So I am afraid it all could happen again.

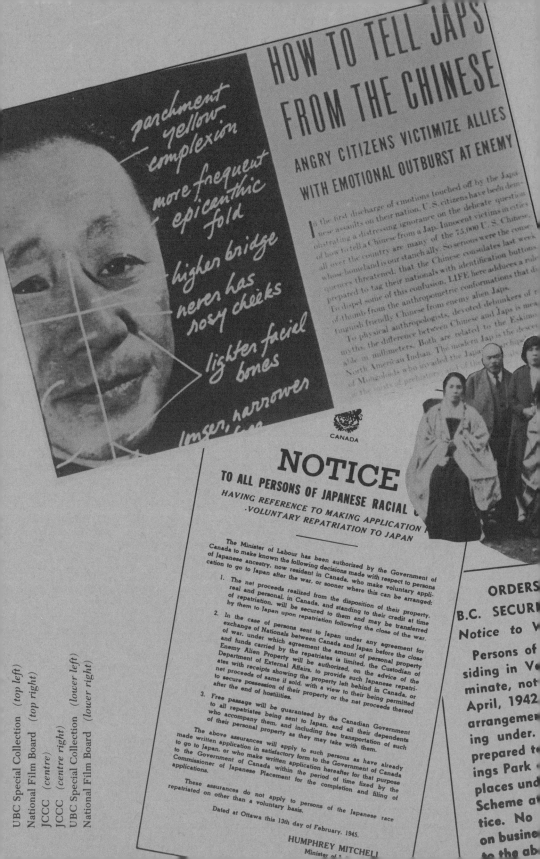

HOW TO TELL JAPS FROM THE CHINESE

ANGRY CITIZENS VICTIMIZE ALLIES WITH EMOTIONAL OUTBURST AT ENEMY

parchment yellow complexion

more frequent epicanthic fold

higher bridge

never has rosy cheeks

lighter facial bones

longer, narrower face

CANADA

NOTICE

TO ALL PERSONS OF JAPANESE RACIAL ORIGIN

HAVING REFERENCE TO MAKING APPLICATION FOR VOLUNTARY REPATRIATION TO JAPAN

The Minister of Labour has been authorized by the Government of Canada to make known the following decisions made with respect to persons of Japanese ancestry, now resident in Canada, who make voluntary application to go to Japan after the war, or sooner where this can be arranged:

1. The net proceeds realized from the disposition of their property, real and personal, in Canada, and standing to their credit at time of repatriation, will be secured to them and may be transferred by them to Japan upon repatriation following the close of the war.

2. In the case of persons sent to Japan under any agreement for exchange of Nationals between Canada and Japan before the close of war, under which agreement the amount of personal property and funds carried by the repatriates is limited, the Custodian of Enemy Alien Property will be authorized, on the advice of the Department of External Affairs, to provide such Japanese repatriates with receipts showing the property left behind in Canada, or the net proceeds of same if sold, with a view to their being permitted to secure possession of their property or the net proceeds thereof after the end of hostilities.

3. Free passage will be guaranteed by the Canadian Government to all repatriates being sent to Japan, and all their dependents who accompany them, and including free transportation of such of their personal property as they may take with them.

The above assurances will apply to such persons as have already made written application in satisfactory form to the Government of Canada to go to Japan, or who make written application hereafter for that purpose to the Government of Canada within the period of time fixed by the Commissioner of Japanese Placement for the completion and filing of applications.

These assurances do not apply to persons of the Japanese race repatriated on other than a voluntary basis.

Dated at Ottawa this 13th day of February, 1945.

HUMPHREY MITCHELL
Minister of Labour

ORDERS

B.C. SECURITY

Notice to V

Persons of
siding in Ve
minate, not
April, 1942
arrangeme
ing under.
prepared t
ings Park
places und
Scheme at
tice. No
on busine
to the ab

UBC Special Collection (top left)
National Film Board (top right)
JCCC (centre)
JCCC (centre right)
UBC Special Collection (lower left)
National Film Board (lower right)